The
Son of a
Boilermaker

by Tom Twyford

ISBN: 1-4392-5786-8

Trade paperback

©Copyright 2009 Tom Twyford

All Rights Reserved

Requests for Information should be addressed to:

info@www.tomtwyford.com

www.tomtwyford.com

All design and layout by Diol Productions

Printed in the U.S.A.

Acknowledgements

Andrea Scarpino, who taught me what editing was all about and how to say more with fewer words.

Danette Gallagher, who without her assistance, encouragement, and belief in me, this book would not have become a reality.

Michael and Danni Elena Diol, whose expertise I could not have done without.

Robert I. "Bones" Medley (1935-2007) my boyhood friend and companion who helped jog my memory of details I thought were long forgotten.

Marge Bedortha, my sister, who set me straight on the sequence of family history and where to put a comma.

The People of Steubenville, Ohio, both past and present, who were so much a part of my youth and responsible for much of the spice and flavor of this memoir.

Dorothy (Parks) Twyford, my wife and high school sweetheart, who understood the importance of this endeavor and gave me the time and space to do my thing.

DEDICATION

I dedicate this memoir to the memory of my mother,
Frances Alma (Woods) Twyford (1902 – 1955),
who was part of the unsung ranks of cherished
mothers everywhere whose lives were never accorded
the recognition and acclaim they so rightly deserved.

"Every reader substitutes his visions in place of
the author's. The latter gives to him black and white,
and he rubs on them this imagination"
        —Anatole France (1844 - 1924)

Table of Contents

VIII   The Son of a Boilermaker

Introduction

I began writing this story of my early life with the idea that it would be a legacy for my two grandsons. Well, it still is, but once I began the process it occurred to me that this accumulation of personal reflections of the mid-twentieth century might have a wider appeal.

As I wrote the words, it seemed as if the past became more tangible and perhaps my narration would have significance for others. My memoir is an authentic account of the times, in which I have emphasized the humorous side of the maturing experience.

In one sense, it is ordinary, if not unremarkable, but, at the same time, it is complicated and uncommon as all personal history tends to be. Trying to fit my life into some perspective of time and history is actually shocking to me when I put it down on paper.

I was born only 17 years after the end of World War I. My mother and father were born less than 30 years after Custer's Last Stand and the Wright brothers had not yet gotten that first airplane off the ground. Being born between the two great wars of the 20th Century and during the Great Depression shaped my view of the world and my interpretation of the events that influenced my life. I was witness to the changing of our nation from a society in repose to a country whose people were constantly on the move.

The affordability of automobiles and the construction of interstate highways enabled our citizens to venture outside their hometowns and, in the process, changed the face of America. This also sparked the move to the suburbs, which altered the character and makeup of Steubenville, Ohio, my hometown, as well as small towns across the nation. The implications of these changes were far-reaching in the sense that the portion of my life that I describe in this memoir encompassed a time of transition that marked the end of innocence for me, as well as the nation.

Best Wishes, Tom Twyford (2009)

Chapter 1

Youngest of the Clan
(1935–1941)

First steps with the "Old Man" for balance

"Why should I have him circumcised?" my mother asked the doctor an hour after my birth on September 5, 1935 at Ohio Valley Hospital in Steubenville, Ohio.

"Well, it's what we are recommending for all male newborns at this time," Dr. Bevins answered.

"How much more will it cost?" my mother asked. Dr. Bevins started to explain all the medical and hygienic reasons that this procedure should be done, when my mother interrupted him by repeating the critical question: "How much?"

"This can be done at a nominal charge of five dollars," he said. Without a moment's hesitation, my mother, who was still groggy from childbirth, but ever mindful of the state of her family's finances, told the doctor, "Let's just skip it for now."

When I appeared upon the scene, another mouth to feed was the last thing my parents needed. It was the midst of the Depression and at eight and one-half pounds, I didn't eat much. However, there were other more compelling reasons I was a burden to this established family unit.

As soon as I was able to understand the meaning of body language, plus a few key words and phrases, like "shut up," "hurry up and go," "get out," and "No, No, NO," my place in the family hierarchy was defined. Things didn't really change a whole hell of a lot as years went by, but not to worry. I learned to cope.

I was the youngest of four children. My sister, Virginia, was ten, sister Marjorie was five, and brother George (Billy) was eight at the time I was born. It is a certainty that I was not a planned addition to this brood. Accident or not, I'm kinda glad it happened.

My Mom was born Frances Alma Woods on May 8, 1902 in Steubenville, Ohio. She had brown eyes and thin brown hair that lacked any curl. Her nose was a tad too long but complimented the soft curves of her full cheeks. Each night at bedtime, she slathered her face with Pond's cold cream and put rubber curlers in her hair. The nightly grooming gave her white skin a flawless complexion and her hair the body it lacked. Her face was unlined and her hair had never a trace of gray. At a slim five-feet-six, she was considered tall for a woman of her time. Overall, her appearance was that of a most attractive woman.

My old man was a short man, standing no more than five-feet-six in his steel-toed work boots. He was slightly built, never weighing more than one hundred forty pounds. His hair was a dirty blond,which he parted in the middle. The sides were trimmed well above the ears, leaving too much bare space, the net result being a haircut that was unstylish and old fashioned. I'd say his facial features were balanced and pretty regular, although his nose was slightly bulbous with large pores and there were deep craggy lines on each side of his mouth. There was no way he would ever be mistaken for a patrician. He looked just like what he was: a mill worker who answered to the nickname of "Runt."

My parents were married in Steubenville on December 29, 1923, while dad was in the Navy and stationed in Rhode Island. If ever there were two people who were unsuited for each other in every way, it was my parents. Where my mother had a reserved and refined quality, my father was what people referred to as a "rounder" and "one of the boys." Drinking, gambling and sometimes fighting crowded out family responsibilities.

Whereas my Mom was a regular churchgoer, my dad referred to the men who attended church as hypocrites. Before I was born, dad was an intricate part of the family unit. However, by the time I came along, he was not much more than an infrequent visitor.

My dad worked in the paper mill. His pay was twenty-five dollars per week. Safety conditions in the paper mill were not any better than the wages. I can remember Dad telling us about helping remove men from the "rollers" after their bodies were completely mangled and flattened. It so happened that he got his left hand caught in a chopping device and had three fingers amputated at the second joint. He never missed a day of work after this injury and was compensated the grand sum of five hundred dollars by the company. Upon receiving this money, he lost it all the same day in a poker game.

Shortly after the war began, the old man quit the paper mill after fifteen years and went to work as a union boilermaker out of the Pittsburgh local. As a boilermaker, his work took him where the jobs were. He worked in steel mills and power plants all through Pennsylvania, New York, Ohio and as far away as California. He tried to get as much work as possible in the areas close to home, and was sometimes able to be home on weekends. These jobs would last anywhere from a month to a year. So, for the most part, my father was absent from home when I was growing up. As a result, I can only recall one occasion when he and I did anything or went anywhere together. This happened to be a very big deal. We saw Jersey Joe Walcott knock out Ezzard Charles at Forbes Field in Pittsburgh to win the heavyweight championship. The old man won a hundred bucks betting on Jersey Joe. He collected his winnings at a bar near the stadium, where he drank several boilermakers while treating me to a fish sandwich and a Coke in a frosty beer mug.

One of my earliest recollections, likely based upon hearsay and bits and pieces of visual images retrieved from a seldom-used recess of my mind, was the whole family walking to Grandma Woods' house on a chilly night. This was prompted by our family's reaction to War of the Worlds the famous radio hoax created by Orson Wells and the Mercury Players. This was a Sunday evening radio broadcast that vividly dramatized a Martian invasion of the East coast of the United States. More than half the people in the country were convinced that this outer space intrusion by hostile beings was actually happening.

The announcer on the radio was trying to keep a calm reassuring voice, but the fear could not be disguised. He was explaining the numerous sightings of Martian spacecrafts, when all of the sudden there was a break in his speech followed by total silence. The next thing that could be heard was "They're Here," "They're Here" then "No-No-No, -Ah-Ah Ah," and silence again. After a minute or two, some other guy came on the air in a frantic voice shouting that they were evacuating the building. Then he too screamed and was cut off by a"buzz-buzz-buzz" sound and that was all. The last thing I remember was the voice of the Chief of the New Jersey Highway Patrol advising all citizens to flee to the countryside. It was just a matter of time until the spacemen got to Steubenville. So, my mother decided that we should all die together and we walked to Grandma Woods' house to await our fate. My sister, Marge, recounts that they were making fudge at the time they received this shocking news. My brother was quoted as saying, "This will be our last pot of fudge."

When I was about five or six years old, we were living in the south end and rented off a man named Mr. Cocomelli, who owned a bar and restaurant around the corner. When it came time to pay the rent each month, Mom would send me to the bar with the rent money. Now here I was, a skinny, watery-eyed little urchin clutching a twenty-dollar bill with instructions to turn it over only to Mr. Cocomelli. When I handed him the twenty and said, "Twyford rent," he'd give me a sorrowful look and say, "Wait a minute, kid." Then he'd go back to the kitchen and momentarily appear with a pot of steaming spaghetti and meatballs. He'd say, "Here take this home to your mom before it gets cold and bring back the pot." "Thank you, sir," I'd say, knowing there would be good eats that night. After awhile, we began to depend upon the generosity of the landlord, and I'd show up with a twenty in one hand and our own pot in the other. Now, Mom wasn't dumb. It was me who delivered the rent each month.

I attended kindergarten at Lincoln Grade School when we lived at a place called "out the run." Not far from where we lived was a creek that ran alongside Lincoln Avenue. There was a slaughter house located by the creek where they killed big animals. I'm not sure if they were pigs or cows, but I remember seeing guts and entrails of these creatures lying along the creek bank. Sometimes, when I crossed Lincoln Avenue to wade in the creek, I noticed the water had a red color. This was, of course, venturing outside the boundaries designated by my Mom. It was around this time that I got the mumps, but it's doubtful that they were connected in any way to the red water of the creek that ran "out the run."

At age five, I devised my first entrepreneurial enterprise. I charged a penny toll for every kid who passed on the sidewalk in front of my house on their way to the candy store. Outraged mothers complained to my Mom about my Gestapo tactics of extorting pennies from their snot-nosed darlings. Occasionally, with some of the boys, I had to resort to violence or some other form of intimidation. The girls were more compliant and just bawled as they handed over their penny. If I caught them on their way back from the store, I demanded a share of their candy in lieu of the toll. I was smart enough to waive the charge for big kids who were not likely prospects for my shake-down operation. Finally, the complaints became so numerous that I was put out of business when my innocent denials were no longer believed.

My mother and Grandma Woods had always attended the Fifth Street Methodist Church. The church was located in the north end at the corner of Fifth Street and North Street. It was only a couple of blocks from downtown but was attended by both downtowners and people who lived on the hill. I believe it was one of the oldest congregations in Steubenville. Anyway, when we lived "out the run" it was just too far to walk to church. So, at the expense of the church, the preacher sent a taxi cab to pick up the Twyford family (minus my dad) and transport us to church, Sunday school and back. I remember waiting for the taxi at curb side all dressed up in my church clothes. Mom would spit on a handkerchief and roughly rub my face if she saw a speck of dirt. Since I was not accustomed to riding in a car, I usually got car sick. The taxi ride to church was no more than two miles, but that was far enough to trigger my up-chucking mechanism, much to my mother's embarrassment and aggravation. I really never gave anythought to why the church would send a taxi cab to transport the Twyford family to Sunday services. As far as I knew, we were the only members of the congregation accorded this service. One thing for sure, it wasn't because we all had such good singing voices, or because we were likely to drop a big chunk of dough in the collection plate. Maybe it was just a nice thing to do.

We lived on South Fourth Street when I attended the first grade at Grant School. I had the same teacher that both my sisters and brother had when they were in the first grade. It was inevitable that comparisons would be made. They were all very cute, bright and adept at impressing adults. I did not possess these same attributes, so when comparisons were made, I didn't fare too well. "Tommy, why aren't you more like Billy, Virginia or Marjorie?" was a question that was put to me quite often over the years.

There were times when Dad came home after a long absence and things would be great for a day or so. I even observed some open displays of affection between my parents. I'd anticipate his arrival and on occasion he'd bring home some gift for me. Once, he brought me a double-barreled pirate cap pistol, which temporarily made me the envy of my playmates. Unfortunately, these periods of normalcy and good feelings in the home were short-lived. The old man always screwed things up by "going out for an hour" and returning at two or three o'clock in the morning, drunk, having lost the rent money in a crap game. At these times, I'd lie in bed, listening to the fighting and arguing, and cry myself to sleep.

After this scenario had been repeated more times than I care to remember, my father left home for good. I was eleven years old. His final departure didn't really change things. At some point, he obtained a divorce from my Mom. One thing for sure, there was no custody battle over who would get me. Mom got this prize by default. They both shared equally in the property settlement. The terms were clearly spelled out. They each got nothing. I do believe that there was some agreement which provided that he pay Mom a specific sum on a regular basis as child support and maintenance. Quite predictably, however, this proved to be nothing she could come to depend upon.

The average family income in 1935 was $1,632 a year. My dad made twenty-five bucks a week, which put our family about 25 percent below the average. I think it would be safe to say that we always lagged behind the average when it came to income. However, my sisters,Virginia and Marjorie, along with my brother, Billy, were anything but average. Mom made sure of that. The Twyford kids were clean, well dressed, well behaved, smart and very talented. If there ever was a bright spot in Mom's life, it was my sisters and brother. She basked in the spotlight of their many achievements and compliments that came her way because of those remarkable children of hers. They were always the stars of the dramatic and musical productions at Grant School and their report cards were rarely less than a perfect 100 percent. Then I came along as a surprise addition to this brood of geniuses and had the same consistent level of success as the family income maintained: about twenty-five percent below average.

The relationship that I had with my Mom is difficult to define. I never felt it was emotionally safe for me to confide my innermost thoughts with her or anyone else. She rarely had any words of love or touched me in an affectionate way, but I don't believe it was because she was a cold person. It seemed to me that she had been so emotionally victimized herself that by the time I needed the nurturing all children require, she was spent and had nothing left to give. Still, there was a bright side to this sad situation and I found it.

It might be assumed that my position in the family pecking order would brand me with some sort of weird complex, but it didn't. What it did do, however, was give me an attitude, a rebellious and defiant one. I knew that whatever I did, I wouldn't measure up to my sisters and brother in Mom's eyes. Of course, my behavior didn't encourage a lot of warm fuzzy feelings to flow my way. So, as much as anyone else within the family circle, I did my share to reinforce my crappy image.

Believe it or not, I got a certain self-satisfaction or comfort level in being different. It was like playing a role that pitted me against everybody else, which was a much more powerful motivator than looking at somebody else's old report cards. Rather than making me feel inadequate about all the praise heaped on my siblings, it had the opposite effect upon me. I was energized with a strong determination to prove the nay-sayers wrong.

8   The Son of a Boilermaker

Chapter 2

My Hometown–
Steubenville, Ohio

Market Street, looking east toward the river

The Allegheny and Monongahela Rivers come together at the city of Pittsburgh to form the Ohio River. Forty miles to the west on the Ohio is the town of Steubenville. It is situated at the site of Fort Steuben, which was an outpost for surveyors assigned to map the Old Northwest Territory. The fort and the town were named after Baron Von Steuben, a Prussian general who aided General Washington in the training of troops during the American Revolutionary War.

The recognized date of the founding of the town was 1797, which makes it the second-oldest town in Ohio. As was customary and quite logical, the town was designed with the river being the eastern boundary and the streets, avenues and boulevards running in an east-west, north-south grid. From the very beginning, Steubenville was an industrial and commercial center for this region of the upper Ohio Valley. It soon became known for the fine pottery and glass manufactured there. Mining of coal became a major endeavor, which led to the establishment of steel mills. In time, Steubenville and the surrounding area manufactured a large percentage of the country's high-quality steel and played a major role in ushering the United States into the industrial age.

People in Steubenville and other towns up and down the river just called it "The Valley." The Ohio River cut through the hills and formed the valley with Ohio on the western bank and West Virginia on the eastern side. All up and down both sides of the river were manufacturing plants, hydroelectric plants and steel mills.

The manufacturing of steel was the life blood of Steubenville and "The Valley," as well as the economic foundation of the community. In one way or another, everyone's financial welfare was dependent upon the smoke, fire and pollutants that billowed from the stacks and furnaces that lined the river banks and gave a perpetual red glow to the night sky.

None of the fathers of the kids I knew wore a suit and tie or carried a briefcase when going to work. They wore work clothes with their mill badge and number clearly displayed that gave them their identity. Their tan or blue shirts and trousers were made of a sturdy cotton canvas or denim material bought on the cheap at the Army Surplus Store or Sears and Roebuck. These garments usually showed some evidence of repair where tears were mended and holes covered with patches. Headgear could be anything from a cloth cap to a well-worn fedora. These would often be replaced with a hard hat once the men entered the mill. Steelworkers wore ankle-high, thick-soled, steel-toed boots. Bad things could happen to a man's head or feet if he wasn't careful while making steel.

A black lunch bucket gripped in a calloused hand contained the sustenance needed to finish an eight-hour shift. It was a rare thing to see a steelworker going to the mill in dirty work clothes. Some even had neat creases ironed in their freshly laundered work trousers. However, at the end of an eight hour turn, they left the mill sweaty and grimy thinking about that first beer at home or in the neighborhood tavern. Steubenville was a blue-collar town. This was the Steubenville that I remember as a kid.

It pissed me off to no end when some "would-be comedian" thought he'd come up with an original one-liner and refer to Steubenville as "Stupidville." My unspoken comeback for this low-brow comment was, "What the hell's so special about where you come from?" Of course, I'd just force an insincere laugh and give them credit for being the dumb shits they were.

The town was first populated by people of English, Scottish/Irish and German descent. Then southern blacks followed in search of a better life. As industrialization took a firmer hold, immigrants from Eastern Europe began to arrive to fill the new jobs. They were Poles, Serbs, Slovaks and Greeks. However, by far the largest group of immigrants to make their homes in Steubenville was Italians, who came mostly from Southern Italy and Sicily. It was the Italian immigrants and their descendants who became most closely identified with Steubenville. This may be the reason I love, capacole, locatelli, roasted peppers, ripe olives and all things Italian. Somewhere on my unexplored family tree there must be a Paesano hiding somewhere.

One Paesano who became a show-business superstar was Steubenville's own Dino Crocetti (Dean Martin), who was born in my hometown in June 1917. This man was the ultimate entertainer. He captivated audiences with his dark good looks and smooth confident style of delivering a ballad. His crazy impromptu antics as a comedian and his serious acting abilities took movie critics by surprise. There was always a debate about who was the best singer, Dean or Frank, but in my mind there was no doubt. When Dean was serious, he had it all over Sinatra, hands down.

In spite of the fame and recognition he achieved, Dean never forgot his roots. He often made reference to Steubenville on his television show and in his Las Vegas performances. When anyone from Steubenville was in the audience during a performance in Vegas, he saw to it that they were moved up front with drinks on Dino. He was a benefactor of Saint John Hospital and a generous patron of The College of Steubenville. A major north-south route through the city was named Dean Martin Boulevard, and a larger-than-life mural of Dean graces a wall at the shopping center. The city honors his life every June with a Dean Martin celebration hosted by one or more of his family members. For a tough Italian kid from Steubenville, Dino didn't do too badly.

While I was growing up in Steubenville, my perception was that it was a pretty big place. For one thing, there was a certain hustle and bustle on the streets of downtown with people always coming and going day or night. It was impossible to go downtown and not see people you knew by name, along with familiar faces who were a constant part of the scene. The sidewalks were wide enough to accommodate two-way pedestrian traffic, except when two or more "Micks" from St. Peter's would refuse to yield and give me a sharp elbow as I passed. If I was alone, I'd ignore the challenge. But, if accompanied by some of my pals, there was usually an exchange of insults, "Yeah, and your mother wears muddy combat boots with a short skirt."

The stores, businesses, theaters and offices were located within the parameters of a two-block area north and south, with Washington Street and Adams Street as the north and south boundary and 6th Street and 3rd Street as the east and west boundary. The neighborhoods had grocery stores, confectioneries, cigar stores and bars, but everything else was situated in the downtown area. That's where the action was.

Automobile ownership wasn't a given for every family and it was rare for one household to have more than one car. Therefore, much of the townsfolk depended upon the public transportation system of Ohio Valley Transit Company. The buses were a must for the people who lived on the hill and an option for people who lived in the north or south end. I never lived any place that wasn't within easy walking distance of downtown.

The Pennsylvania Railroad Station was downtown on Sixth Street and was one of the busiest places in town. Steubenville was on a mainline for passenger trains moving east and west across country. A train was either in the station, just leaving or almost due and whole families would congregate at the station to greet or bid farewell to passengers. During the war years, train travel was probably at its height as servicemen from all over the country were on the move. The U.S.O. had a permanent canteen set up at the station that provided free coffee and donuts to men in uniform. If I happened to be close by, I'd sometimes take a detour and just walk along the platform to look at the trains and the people who were coming and going from some place I'd never been.

Steubenville had three Five & Dime stores, five movie theaters, three department stores, four banks, eight drug stores, fifty cigar stores and at least fifty whorehouses. The town had a population of forty thousand people. It seems reasonable that we needed the Five

& Dimestores, department stores, drug stores, banks and theaters. But why did we need so many cigar stores and whorehouses? The only thing I could figure out was that maybe Steubenville was overpopulated with horny smokers.

Ever since the prohibition era of the 1920s, vice was a major business in Steubenville. Many of our leading citizens acquired their wealth selling bootleg whiskey. When the sale of alcohol was again made legal by the repeal of the 18th Amendment, gambling and sex were the logical enterprises to replace bootlegging. There was a period during the 1930s that Steubenville was known as "Little Chicago." People came from all over Ohio, Pennsylvania, West Virginia and parts unknown to gamble and get their ashes hauled.

Most of the cigar stores were fronts for one type of gambling operation or another. Just about everyone in town played the numbers. It worked much like the state lottery, only you could bet anything from a penny on up, and it was operated by some guy named "Vinnie" or Cosmo" or some name like that. Many times when I ran errands for neighbors, I'd be given a nickel or a dime and instructed to stop at the cigar store and place a bet on some number that was connected to a dream, birthday or some other event. Playing the numbers was a perfectly legal and normal activity as far as I knew.

My introduction to the serious gambling industry came as a high school freshman. I met my dad, on one of his infrequent visits, at the Venetian Café. After we left, we stopped at the Rex Cigar Store. This was nothing more than a hole in the wall where they sold tobacco and chewing gum, but, it had a back door that opened into a spacious room where about two hundred guys were playing slots, black jack, chucka-luck and roulette. Once inside, we were greeted by this gorilla-type guy named Carmine who seemed to be a good friend of the old man's. I just walked around the place, taking it all in, while dad played blackjack and drank shots of Corby's whiskey. To me, there was nothing unusual about any of this; it was just an opportunity to visit with my dad. After an hour or so, we said goodbye on the street outside the Rex and he slipped me a couple of bucks. I wouldn't see him again for another year.

The houses of prostitution were located in a three or four-block area of High Street and Water Street near the Market Street Bridge. This red light district had one whorehouse after another right down the line. A trip there was appropriately referred to as "going down the line." On a Friday or Saturday night, the place looked like the midway at a carnival. Groups of guys were crowding the sidewalks going in and out of the houses all along the street. Cars with Pennsylvania license plates were parked on both sides of High Street, Water Street and under the bridge. Men were laughing and shouting their recommendations of one house or another. Overall, it was a scene of coarse behavior, which my teenage buddies and I would sometimes be a part of when we were looking to add a little spice to our lives.

We never went down the line unless there were four or five of us. One guy walked up on the porch and knocked on the door. The others followed a little behind. It took only one knock and the door opened about six inches and a fat black woman peeked out and said in a loud whisper, "Come on in, boys."

Once inside, we were greeted by the Madam and invited to have a seat in the living room. Some of the houses had jukeboxes so we could play records and look at magazines with pictures of naked women. Before long, a couple of the girls would show up, sometimes in a bathrobe or just panties and a bra. Mostly, they were older, probably twenty-five. They'd joke around and seemed to enjoy just bullshitting with us. However, one thing that really got them pissed off was if one of the guys got too personal and asked, "How did a nice girl like you ever get started in this business?" It never failed; the answer was always the same: "None of your fucking business." Then the Madam asked us if we had any money. When we told her we were broke, she'd tell us to leave and laugh and say she was going to call our mothers. It didn't happen exactly like this every time, but this was pretty much the routine.

Once I happened to notice a small sheet posted on the wall in the entry hall that had a list of prices: straight $5.00; half and half-$7.00; around the world $10.00. I assumed that this was in some way associated with card games. When I mentioned to one of the girls that I knew quite a bit about playing cards, she cracked up in a hysterical fit of laughter as she shared my boast with the other girls and customers sitting around the room. I didn't see what was so funny about it, but I didn't say anything. It wasn't until we got outside that one of the guys explained, in graphic language, what the sign meant. I told the boys, while wearing a weak smile, that "I was only kidding." "Yeah, Twyford, we know" was all they had to say.

All of this funny business was going on right under the noses of the cops and city officials. Police cruisers patrolled the area, driving real slow up and down the street, but rarely stopped to ask questions or make arrests. The only time they raided a house was when the grand jury was in session. Then the Madams were all forewarned and "the organization" moved all the prostitutes to Wheeling or Canton until the heat was off. Once in a great while, token raids were made or houses were raided because they had not made their pay-offs on time. When this happened, the names of the men who had been arrested were printed in the newspaper along with their addresses and the charge, which was "loitering." Loitering may sound like rather harmless conduct, but everyone knew exactly what it meant.

I don't want to give the impression that this was a frequent activity of mine. I suppose my number of visits "down the line" wouldn't total more than four times, which was four times too many. However, my very last visit "down the line" was a memorable one. We hadn't been in this house more than two minutes when the Madam locked the door and told us to turn out all the lights because she got word there might be a raid.

Holy shit! All I could think of was the headlines in the Herald Star: "Tommy Twyford charged with Loitering." Mom would kill me; she'd never be able to return to the Fifth Street Methodist Church, and I'd be kicked out of the Methodist Youth Fellowship. I had to get the hell out of there and fast.

One of my friends must have had the same thought. He helped me force open a second-floor window and out we went, dropping about ten feet to the alley below. Neither of us were athletes, but we both could have qualified for the Olympics that night. We didn't stop running for six blocks and I wasn't even out of breath, but my heart was pounding out of my chest.

In all truthfulness, we were all cowards and too chicken to spill our newfound manhood upon the thighs of these faceless harlots. It was strictly a form of adolescent entertainment Steubenville style. Of course it was stupid, foolhardy and dangerous, but that's what we did.

I don't mean to imply that Steubenville was all that bad. There was alot that was good separate and apart from any vice or corruption. We had good schools, parks, tree-lined streets, many fine homes, beautiful churches and jobs were plentiful. Steubenville of the 1940s and 1950s was a gem. With few exceptions, you could walk anywhere in town and not be concerned for your safety. Steubenville was a great place to grow up.

An oasis of natural beauty in contrast to the stark grittiness of the steel town that surrounded it was Union Cemetery. Most people have the idea that cemeteries are foreboding, spooky places filled with dark images and depressing thoughts. To me, Union Cemetery seemed more like a park than a bone yard. Old-growth hardwoods and gigantic rhododendrons, along with ornate grave markers, dominated the hilly landscape. Stone bridges arched across the creek, separating the old section from the new. A large granite monument marks the final stop for "The Fighting McCooks" of Civil War fame. Not far up a series of steep banks lined with less-impressive markers are the graves of the not so famous Grandma Woods and my Mom.

I knew everyone on both sides of the street on my block of North Fifth Street. Most of the houses had front porches with swings, gliders and wicker-type chairs on them and people actually used their porches. On summer nights up and down the block, the adults sat out playing the radio, listening to soft music or Pirates baseball. As kids, we played ball or other games under the street lights. Without television or air conditioning, there was no reason to spend the evening indoors when you could catch the summer breeze on the front porch. On occasion, I'd be sent to the corner confectionery for a treat, which sometimes was a pint of hand-packed ice cream or a large bottle of orange or root beer Par-T-Pack. It wasn't unusual to stay out until eleven o'clock or even midnight in order to delay retiring to a hot bedroom. Since people got out of their houses, everyone knew their neighbors. As a consequence, friendships were formed and people had a sense of community that enriched our lives.

Making new friends was something that came easily for me. I was able to strike a common chord with any stranger, whether it was another kid or adult. It was a special treat for me to engage adults in conversation. I'd listen spellbound to the stories from their childhoods and have them tell me how it was "back when." Considering that I was just a kid myself, and not "dry behind the ears," I had quite a few friends who were probably past forty or fifty years old. Mom would ask me, "Tommy, how in the world do you know so and so?" and I'd tell her and she'd silently shake her head from side to side as she rolled her eyes in amazement.

I think that most of my older friends just wanted to have someone to listen to them and appreciate what they had to say. It didn't take me long to perfect the art of being a good listener. I knew when to nod my head at just the right time while making the one-word exclamation of "really." When it seemed like the story they were telling was starting to wind down, I'd encourage them to tell me more, or promise to continue our discussion another day.

The mature network of friends and acquaintances I had came from anywhere and everywhere. Some were neighbors, some were customers on my paper route, and others were people I just struck up conversations with wherever I happened to be. There was also a certain kind of person that attracted my attention as I seemed to be drawn to the most weird and peculiar types.

Down along the river banks, squatter shacks were scattered here and there. These were occupied by old black guys who mostly just fished in the river. The only fish in those polluted waters were carp and yellow bellied catfish, which I'd never think of eating. I recall a flood when the waters quickly receded, and fish were trapped in shallow pools. A quick-witted ten-year-old could scoop them up and put them in a burlap bag. I had so many I could barely carry the sack of still kicking fish.

I managed to drag and carry this prize catch up to one of the squatter shacks and was warmly greeted by the occupant, who was an old, bent-over guy with white, kinky hair that looked like a Brillo pad. He was astounded that I was making a gift to him of this fresh carp and catfish. Well, this was the beginning of a friendship between the old black man and me. Whenever I could sneak away and go down by the river, I'd stop by to see him. His name was Zeek and he was from somewhere in the south. He told me about working on a farm when he was about my age, many years before he had come to Steubenville to work in the pottery. When he got hurt and could no longer work, he took up residence by the river. Whenever I paid him a visit, he always greeted me with a loud hello and a wide toothless grin. I don't think my Mom would have liked my friend, so I just kept this to myself.

Maybe the strangest person I got to know was this guy who was a familiar sight on the downtown streets of Steubenville. His face looked like it was put together with spare parts, with wide set eyes, a small, right-angled nose, thin mustache and lips and no chin, whatsoever. He dressed in clothing that looked like some kind of theatrical costume. His head cover was a black beret and he wore a swallow tailed suit coat with puffy, silk, Baghdad trousers. But the adornment that stood out the most was a brightly colored ascot tied around his neck, which he had in every color imaginable. Now, his way of dressing was really weird, but the most bizarre thing about him was that he barked. Yes, he barked and yapped just like he was trying to communicate with Lassie or some other canine friend. With my sometimes sick sense of humor, I loved it.

When I was about thirteen years old, I was having a cherry phosphate at the soda fountain in Belle and Steele's drug store, and who should come in and sit down next to me but the "barker boy." What a stroke of luck for me! I immediately struck up a conversation with him. To my surprise, he talked just like any normal person, and even bought me another phosphate. I kept waiting for him to let out a bark, but nothing doing. Finally, he got up to leave and said he enjoyed talking with me. Just as he got to the door, he turned around and looked at me and gave out with a "Woof-Woof " Without thinking, I barked back at him as loud as I could. From then on, whenever I saw him on the street, he and I would exchange a friendly bark.

Then there were these two elderly brothers named Beehee. They operated a Sunday-morning-only bakery out of their garage in the alley behind Sherman Avenue. The only pastry they made were cinnamon sweet rolls and boy, were they delicious. The Beehee brothers had an emaciated look about them. Their faces and arms were covered with flour and they had the appearance of the living dead. I got to know the brothers pretty well, and I explained to them that I couldn't get to the bakery until after Sunday school. By that time, they were sold out, but they'd set aside a roll for me, which I'd pick up before noon. One of the brothers would reheat it for me and put some extra icing on the hot pastry. The roll cost three cents, which I tried to hold out of my church collection money. If I didn't have the full amount, I still got my warm sweet roll. One Sunday, I showed up only to be told by one of the brothers that the other one had died. I'll never forget him telling me in a most dramatic fashion, "Tommy, the Beehee brothers will never bake again."

From time to time, I'd wander down under the railroad bridge and shoot the shit with the hobos who camped there. They were from all over the place and all had some sad story to tell. It never failed that one of these guys would try to put the bite on me like I was some kind of Daddy Warbucks. Of course, I made it very clear that I was temporarily financially embarrassed, but otherwise I would have been more than willing to stake them to two bits.

Another familiar sight on the downtown streets of Steubenville was a couple of notorious painted ladies known as the Rarey sisters. These old broads were in semi-retirement from the world's oldest profession. I say semi-retirement only because it was rumored that as a special accommodation to old customers, they would still turn a trick now and then for "Auld Lang Syne.'

The Rarey girls wore multiple layers of face makeup and were dressed to the nines with wide, flowered hats and garish-colored dresses. They'd smile in unison and say a sweet hello to any man who looked their way. The old man told me he remembered them walking the streets when he was a boy, but no amount of makeup could disguise the seven-decades of well used flesh encased inside their girdles.

There were certain establishments in every part of Steubenville that added character and class these were the neighborhood bars. I was most familiar with the north end bars of Bill & Fay's, The Field Club and The Shamrock. Each of these places had its regular clientele with seldom any cross-over. All of them were crowded six days a week (closed on Sundays), with every bar stool filled. The taverns displayed a sign which read, "Booths for Ladies." It was a serious breach of etiquette for a lady to sit on a bar stool.

On Fridays, the bars cashed payroll checks from the steel mills with the hope that a good chunk of the man's weekly earnings would be spent before he got home. It was a common sight on a Friday or Saturday night to see men, still in their work clothes, with the wife and a couple of grubby kids sitting in a booth having beer, soda pop, fish sandwiches, and pickled eggs. The women showed up to make sure the old man got home with the rent money. They'd drag the snot-nosed kids along, as it was unheard of to have a babysitter. The haze from unfiltered Camels and Lucky Strikes penetrated every corner of the bar as the jukebox blared out tunes from "Your Hit Parade." A Friday night at Bill and Fay's was just about as good as it got for a family night out in the neighborhood.

All of the bars fielded a fast-pitch softball team that was part of a city-wide league. The men on the team were not necessarily patrons of the bar but were recruited for their talent, as this was a very competitive league. Good pitchers were highly sought after and in short supply. The sponsor bars had their respective teams decked out in bright-colored uniforms, which was expected since they played under the lights before crowds of a thousand or more fans at North End Field. The bleachers were always filled, so I usually sat up on the bank next to the railroad tracks along with hundreds of others to watch the game. After the games, the teams and their fans retired to the sponsoring tavern for some serious libations.
Of course, being a kid, I never got to participate in any of these after-game celebrations. However, standing out on the street looking in at the warm congeniality, fun and laughter seemed to pull at me like a magnet.

Most of the houses in the north end were situated directly on the street with very little in the way of a front yard. But between the sidewalk and the curb was a grassy strip of mature trees. Their roots had, over time, caused heaves in the sidewalks, making them uneven in many places, which caused us to exercise caution while roller skating The trees were poplars, elms, sycamores and maples with an occasional oak thrown in. By the 1940s and 50s, these trees were quite old and their presence provided shade to the porches they faced, as well as a certain grace and dignity to the neighborhood.

It was common practice for people to sweep the sidewalks in front of their houses every day. Some would go so far as to wash it with a broom dipped in a soapy bucket. Sweeping the porch and sidewalk became a routine chore for me. In the fall I swept and raked fallen leaves into large piles in the street next to the curb. I took a special delight in setting fire to the leaves and watching the flames. The smell of burning leaves meant it was October. Yet, that pungent aroma still transports me to the springtime of my life.

A notable exception to the absence of front yards were the expansive lawns on LaBelle Avenue, where old mansions faced eastward toward the river and the lawns sloped down toward the street. In winter, we'd appropriate the use of these natural slopes for sledding until some chauffeur, butler, or rich owner came charging out and spoiled our fun.

Near the top of this hilly expanse of lawns grew dozens of stately buckeye trees whose branches spread out to touch one another and form a canopy of green. By October, the leaves were yellow and the ground was covered with thorny green pods that contained the brown and russet buckeyes. These were highly treasured by any kid smart enough to recognize that buckeyes were something special. We spent hours collecting and opening the pods to inspect the uniqueness of each buckeye. Even though these nuts looked good enough to eat, they were poisonous.

However, we were ingenious lads and used our pen knives and ice picks to carve and drill holes in the buckeyes, transforming them into necklaces, bracelets and rings, which looked as good as a lot of stuff in the window of Shanton's jewelry store. There was never an autumn during my grade school years that I failed to make a hand-carved buckeye necklace for my Mom. The only trouble was that after a few weeks, the buckeyes would begin to wither and the once-beautiful necklace would lose its luster and be nothing more than shriveled nuts on a string.

I spent a lot of time in Steubenville's five movie theaters. The Capitol, Paramount and Grand were considered to be respectable theaters. Uniformed ushers escorted theater-goers to their seats with a flashlight and quelled any loud talking, cheering or other disruptive behavior. On the other hand, the Rex and Olympic had no ushers, just a ticket taker, and were patronized by some of the lesser elements of the town. Naturally, my friends and I gravitated toward the Olympic and the Rex. For one thing, you could get in for a dime and see a double feature plus a serial if it was a Saturday afternoon.

A serial was a week-to-week cliffhanger where each episode ended with the hero in a hopeless situation and about to meet a tragic end. This ensured our return the next Saturday to see, if by some miracle, the hero survived. During the course of the movies, the audience yelled, cheered, booed, and banged on the backs of the sticky wooden seats. Most of these seats were partially held together by wads of chewing gum stuck to the bottom and the arms.

The Rex was known to have rats that supposedly ran across people's feet and grew fat upon discarded food that littered the aisles. Whole families attended these double features with brown paper bags full of peanut butter and jelly sandwiches. The place smelled of garlic and urine, but that didn't seem to interfere with our enjoyment. Often we sat through an entire double feature twice.

Many of the shows were action features starring cowboys like Johnny Mack Brown, Lash LaRue, Cisco Kid, and Gene Autry. Detectives like Charlie Chan and Boston Blackie were also favorites of all the guys. One feature I never missed was Leo Gorsey and the Bowery Boys, also known as the Dead End Kids. This bunch of tough, wiseguy kids from New York were in constant trouble but redeemed themselves by the end of the movie by bringing the crooks to justice.

We never thought it peculiar to get in at the middle of a movie. There was no specific starting time. The show just started whenever we got there and quite often I saw the ending before the beginning. Most of the movies at the Rex and Olympic were low-budget, Class-B movies. The movies with the big stars played at the other theaters. When Lon Chaney, Jr. and Bela Lugosi were playing their monster roles in Frankenstein, Dracula and Wolfman , I'd see them in the luxury of the Grand or the Paramount.

Quite often, on a Friday, the Rex would have amateur night, which always drew a crowd. The acts were varied but mostly the performers were singers, dancers and instrument players. The most common instrument was the accordion. It never failed that some "squeeze box" player performed "Lady of Spain"—shaking his head and rolling his eyes to emphasize the more difficult and dramatic parts of the piece.

We tried to get there early so we could get a front-row seat. It was our logic that from that place in the theater our clapping and cheering would have the most influence on the judges. From where they sat they could easily hear and see whether we approved or disapproved of a particular act. For some perverse reason, we saved our cheering and applause for the very worst acts. The most talented performers would get boos and the old raspberry from the front row. That is, unless we happened to know them. Then we would yell and cheer our lungs out, just like we did for the acts that stunk.

I can't forget this short, fat Italian kid from the neighborhood who came on stage wearing a black suit that was way too small and a purple bow tie. His dark hair was oiled up and plastered across his forehead. Since we all knew this kid, we put up this wild cheering and whistling when he was introduced by the master of ceremonies. Young Anthony Corrochie made a low bow and commenced to sing a song called "Lavender Blue" in a deep, operatic voice. The audience was stunned that this sound was coming out of that body. He employed exaggerated facial and arm gestures as he got into the chorus of "Lavender Blue-Dilly-Dilly, Lavender Green-I'll be your king-Dilly-Dilly, You'll be my queen." Well, we just howled with laughter and applauded till our hands hurt. Based in large part on our enthusiastic approval, Anthony was awarded the third place prize of two free tickets to the Rex and a tube of imported Italian salami.

Chapter 3

Garfield School
(1942–1947)

Fifth Grade Class at Garfield School (1945)

Garfield School was an imposing two-story red brick structure that occupied the corner of North Fifth Street and Madison Avenue. Built in 1884, it was named after our martyred twentieth President of The United States, James A. Garfield. It was dedicated to the education of generations of children who would go out into the world and accomplish great things. The prospect of my being one of them as I entered second grade in 1942 was indeed quite slim.

Beyond the heavy wooden front door was a wide entry hall with classrooms off to each side. An expansive staircase at the rear of the hall ascended to the second floor and more classrooms. The floors, stairwell and hallways were covered with oiled pine. There were tall windows that looked out at Fifth and Madison Avenue and a brick school yard on both sides of the building. At recess, the boys played on one side of the building and the girls on the other.

The segregation of the sexes on the playground at recess was something I didn't question. Along with everybody else, this was accepted as a rule to be obeyed. We were taught to form lines and march from place to place without speaking, touching, or shoving one another. Not all of these rules were scrupulously followed by all the pupils, especially me. My big mouth wouldn't let me.

Chewing gum was viewed as an impediment to thinking and learning. All of the teachers were under the mistaken impression that a stick of Juicy Fruit, Spearmint, or Black Jack would turn a would-be genius into a moron. I tried to perfect a way of chewing that curtailed any detectable movement of my lower jaw. Actually, I almost mastered the technique, but what tripped me up were the rare occasions when I got so engrossed in thinking about a subject and started chewing like crazy. That's when I got caught and punished for doing what I was supposed to do in school—learn. No wonder I sometimes felt persecuted.

Each classroom was equipped with thirty wooden desks bolted to the floor. The tops of the desks lifted up so books and school supplies could be kept inside. Every desk had an ink well where we dipped our pen for writing. Each kid in the class was assigned his own desk. This would remain your place for the entire school year, unless the teacher moved you for disciplinary reasons. During my years at Garfield, I got moved around quite a bit.

The curriculum was heavily weighted toward teaching the three Rs with some history and geography thrown in. The wooden teacher's desk was at the front of the room, facing the students. Centered on the top of the desk was a metal name plate. This was a constant reminder of who the teacher was, in case one of the slower kids forgot.

The teacher made maximum use of the blackboard situated behind her desk, which covered most of the width of the classroom. It had a metal gutter attached at the bottom to hold the chalk and felt erasers. A large, retractable colored map of the world hung on hooks from the top of the blackboard. With the use of a long wooden pointer that resembled a pool cue, the teacher called our attention to something on the blackboard or map she wished to emphasize. Also, the pointer came in handy to crack the knuckles or poke someone who wasn't paying attention.

In most respects, these years represented a simpler time. World War II signaled a change. Although at the time we didn't realize it, the war permanently impacted the lives of us all. This conflict would forever shape our view of the world as well as our personal attitudes and beliefs.

Without notice, we'd have periodic air raid drills at school. On occasion, there were city-wide alerts where sirens sounded all over town. If this happened during school hours, the children were sent directly home and told to stay off the streets until the "all clear" sounded. The drills were monitored by adult air raid wardens who wore white plastic hats with a red triangle on the front and were in charge of a two-or three-block area. They made sure everyone was in their homes and off the street. If the mock raid took place at night, a strict "lights-out" policy was enforced and black blinds covered all the windows. Now, the chance of Steubenville, Ohio ever being attacked by German or Japanese bombers was rather remote, but the wardens visually scanned the skies just in case an enemy bomber slipped through our defenses. This was all considered serious business and not to be taken lightly.

The other type of drill involved only the school, so no city wide sirens were sounded. We did, however, have our own warning siren that triggered the evacuation of all the classrooms, but not before designated students helped teachers cover the windows with black cloth.

During these drills, the teachers herded us all to the wide wooden stairway between the first-floor hall and upstairs classrooms. We sat tightly crammed together on the steps that were worn and wavy from generations of children's feet stomping and running on the treads. Once all were assembled, the music teacher led us in song. We mostly sang "The Marine Corps Hymn" ("From the halls of Montezuma to the shores of Tripoli..."), "Anchor's Away," as a tribute to our sailors, "The Caisson Song" or 'Army Field Artillery Song," ("Over hill over dale we will hit the dusty trail..."). But my absolute favorite song was "The Army Air Corps Song." It was the action words in the lyrics that a patriotic schoolboy could really relate to:

"Off we go into the wild blue yonder, flying high into the sun. Here they come zooming to meet our thunder- Atta boy give um the gun."

At the point in the song where it said, "give um the gun," all the boys let out with a deafening imitation of machine gun fire: "Ratta Tat Tat-Ratta Tat Tat-Ratta Tat Tat." The song went onto say, "We live in fame or go down in flame; nothing can stop the Army Air Corps." After the final verse of that song, I was ready to join up. I'd show those Germans not to mess with the Americans; I wasn't the least bit afraid.

During the war years (1941 to 1945) we were subjected to war propaganda that made us hate the Japs and, to a lesser extent, the Germans. Along with my fellow grade schoolers, I adopted an almost fanatical hatred of the Japanese. They were depicted in comic books, newspapers and movies as blood thirsty, buck-toothed killers. We spent countless hours playing army and fighting pretend wars. We took turns in being good guys, Americans, or bad guys, Japs. Often we acted out war movies where the good guys always won. I must have killed hundreds, if not thousands of Japs during my years of playing army.

Garfield School was fully behind the war effort. Competitions were held between the classes to see which one could collect the most newspapers and magazines. We roamed all over the north end of town on these paper drives soliciting for the war effort. When our wagons were full, we'd empty them at school and return to the streets in search of more newsprint. We were given access to people's basements, which were often stacked to the ceiling with old newspapers and magazines. I never figured out why so many people in Steubenville hoarded old newspapers, but they sure did.

A war stamp booth was set up in the downstairs hallway of the school. It was decorated with red, white and blue bunting and covered with patriotic messages. Certain days of the week were designated stamp day, when each student had the opportunity to buy war stamps, which cost 10 cents each. These stamps were pasted into a book. When the book was full, there were enough to buy a twenty-five dollar war bond. I was issued a stamp book along with all the others, but I never had more than four or five stamps pasted in my book. If the outcome of the war was dependent upon the financial support of people like me, we'd all have been eating rice and fish heads.

The children who went to school with me at Garfield came largely from low-income, working-class families. There was a wide ethnic mix of kids who lived in the north end of town. This part of town was in the fifth ward which had been settled early on by Irish immigrants who were called "Fifth Ward Irish." The Italians joined the Irish a little later in the immigration process, to be followed by English, German and people of African origin. Many of the children at school were first and second-generation Americans. However, more than half the Irish and Italian kids were Catholics, so they attended St. Peters parochial school.

I don't remember that going to school with black kids ever presented a problem. Although most of the parents of the white kids were prejudiced against Negroes, this didn't surface at school. Certainly, discrimination in many forms was all around us, but it was not something I thought about as a child.

Two black kids who were in my class at Garfield stand out in my mind. One was Clarence "Sugar Doll" Lawson. He was by far the biggest kid in school. "Sugar Doll" was two heads taller than any of the rest of us, and most likely several years older. He had the beginnings of a stubble of whiskers on his chin and a faint black mustache on his upper lip. Whatever Sugar Doll lacked in intellectual curiosity, he more than made up for on the basketball court. Naturally, he was the star player on our team.

The other was Joe Jackson who lived up near North End Field. Joe was an excellent student, an accomplished athlete and a good friend. His skill at baseball landed him a starting position on the high school team and a college scholarship to Mount Union College, where he went on to graduate.

No reference to my Garfield friends and classmates would be complete without making mention of Lu Ann Myers. She was my first girlfriend. I guess you could call it a classic case of puppy-love. Lu Ann was a beautiful little girl with brown hair and bangs. She was the object of my affection throughout grade school. When I think of Lu Ann, I see her wearing a red plaid jumper with a white blouse underneath.

Lu Ann lived up on Riverview Avenue, which was quite a distance from me, and in an area which had much nicer homes than where

I lived. When Lu Ann had a birthday party, I was always invited. We played games such as "post office" and "spin the bottle," which involved some dispassionate kissing. If I was lucky enough to get to kiss Lu Ann, this made the party a most special occasion.

Each year at Valentine's Day, every classroom had a large cardboard box decorated with hearts. For a week or so before Valentine's Day, the kids dropped their Valentines in the box. When the day came, the cards were drawn from the box one by one and each person was called forward by the teacher to accept their Valentine. It turned out to be a popularity contest of sorts, where the most popular kids got the most Valentines. I felt sorry for the ones who sometimes only received two or three cards. I always made it a point of sending a Valentine to the least likable kids. Ralph Dunn, who smelled bad and was a habitual booger-eater, always got a card from Tommy Twyford. Poor Ralph didn't die from eating boogers, but was killed at age 17 while a soldier in Korea.

About once a month, the school nurse would pay a visit to Garfield. She made it a point to see children with chronic problems and acute infections. At times, she'd administer inoculations and dispense medications. It was a good thing I got to see the school nurse because we had no family doctor. There was not a single occasion where my Mom took me to a doctor. Before Mom would ever consider calling a doctor, my condition would have had to deteriorate to the point where I was ready for last rites. After all, doctors charged as much as three bucks for a house call and there was no sense in being too hasty about seeking their help. Whatever ailed me would no doubt improve with a generous application of Vicks to my throat. Many times I'd go to school with an old sock tied around my neck that had gobs of Vicks smeared on it. That was Mom's treatment of choice for head colds, flu, cough and sore throats.

All medical consults came from a book of home remedies Mom got from Grandma Woods. A cure for small breasts that came from this book suggested that the breast be massaged with cold water twice a day in a counter-clockwise motion. There was a word of caution, stressing the importance of massaging each breast equally, to avoid one boob becoming larger than the other and creating a lop-sided effect. While obviously not applicable to me, this gives you some idea of the quality of medical care I received as a child.

If I could stand up and was halfway lucid, I went to school. Even though I was a puny-looking child, I must have been fairly healthy because I survived these years and always had excellent school attendance. However, when I think about it, it should have been obvious that I needed glasses many years before I ever got them. My eyes were frequently red and watery. On winter mornings I sometimes awoke with matter caked to my eye lashes. When I finally got my "specks" the world became a bigger place.

Not all kids came to school clean. I was able to distinguish new dirt from old dirt. Any dirt I had was new and certainly not left over from a day or two before. It was pretty easy to spot a permanent ring of grime around some kid's neck. For sure, I never went to school with old dirt, at least not any exposed to public view.

Several times each year when the school nurse made a visit she examined the hair and scalp of each child. Moving up and down rows of desks, she stood behind us probing our heads with a wooden tongue depressor. The search was for head lice, otherwise known as "cooties." Sometimes she'd hit pay dirt and find a head crawling with these nasty critters. When this happened, no attempt was made to hide the discovery from the rest of the class The nurse announced in a loud voice to the teacher, "Here's one who's got 'em," and the kid or kids with bugs were asked to leave with the nurse once all the examinations were completed. The next day, the children who had the infestations showed up with a buzz cut and white powder sprinkled on top of their heads. This telltale evidence was enough to start a chant on the playground "Charlie's got cooties." I kept my distance from these kids because I was told that a cootie could jump at least fifteen feet from one head to another.

As well as cooties, there were a fair number of kids at Garfield that got impetigo and what we called "wing worm." These were highly contagious skin ailments that were generally considered to be associated with a lack of proper hygiene. Naturally, no such germs would dare consider making the skin of a Twyford their home, so I was safe.

During the winter months, the teaching process was routinely interrupted by the coughing and hacking of kids in the classroom. Very few boys ever came to school with a handkerchief. Snotty runny noses were tended to, if at all, by a long swipe of the nose with the back of a shirt sleeve. Some of the boys wore the same shirt to school every day of the week, so by Thursday or Friday at least one arm of their shirts had a mighty slick sleeve. As a result of this practice, myself and others would sometimes call a kid "slick." Knowing this would likely cause a fight, it didn't deter me in the least.

To make sure all the kids at Garfield got a daily dose of Vitamin D, the school had a milk program. Each day before we went outside for recess, a one-half pint bottle of milk was distributed to each child. The cost was five cents for those who could pay and free to the rest of us. The teacher had to keep track of the payers and the non-payers. On occasion, if the money wasn't collected ahead of time, we were instructed to form two lines as the milk was handed out. "Ok, you poor kids line up over here." Well, I was in the poor kids' line and was glad to get the milk.

As well as assuming some concern for the state of our health, student safety was high on the list of responsibilities the school took seriously. All the children who attended Garfield lived within walking distance, so potential traffic hazards existed for kids who had to cross the streets. To protect the kids from getting smashed by a car, we had a school-boy patrol that manned gates on the four corners of Fifth Street and Madison Avenue. You had to be in the fifth or sixth grade in order to be a patrol boy. This was a position of real authority and evidenced by a wide white belt that was worn around the waist and crossed diagonally across the chest. On the part of the web belt that crossed the chest was pinned a silver badge, which had a number on it as well as lettering that spelled SCHOOL PATROL. For four years I had aspired to be a patrol boy, and I assumed my duties two days a week when I reached fifth grade.

I had to report to school early on my duty days so we could get the crossings set up. We carried out the wooden gates that looked like a smaller version of the gates at railroad crossings. The gates had a metal swivel that fit on a four foot metal pole located on each of the four corners outside the school. My corner was the southwest corner of Fifth Street and Madison Avenue, only three houses north of a small cottage on Fifth Street where my Mom was born.

We manned our posts each morning, at lunch time and after school. The patrol had a captain and several lieutenants. One of them stood at the corner and blew his whistle to indicate when our gates would turn to stop traffic or let kids go by. On rainy days, black oil cloth slickers and hats were distributed to the patrol boys. All of them were several sizes too big for me. The hats were shaped like those worn by Glouster saltwater fishermen. The front of the brim slipped over my eyes, while the back funneled cold rainwater down my neck.

Aside from the foolish-looking proportions of my patrol boy rain gear, I was very particular and self-conscious about my appearance. In the sixth grade, I inherited a blue pullover sweater my brother Bill had worn. It was in pretty good shape considering he had worn it for five straight winters. Holes were worn in the elbow of each sleeve, but Mom bought one of those patch kits at the five-and-dime store and stitched black patches on each elbow to cover the holes. I really liked that sweater, but thought it looked better with a shirt collar turned out over the crew neck.

I liked the sweater so much that I continued to wear it well into spring when the weather had turned warmer. One very warm spring afternoon, Ms. Neeley, our sixth grade teacher, spied me with this heavy wool sweater and asked me to take it off and hang it in the cloak room. This presented an awkward situation for me and I just sat at my desk pretending I didn't hear her. After the third time, she said, "Tommy, I want you to take that sweater off right now." All eyes in the room turned to me as I stood up but still made no effort to pull the sweater over my head. I was far from being the most obedient kid in the class, but no one ever openly defied a direct order delivered in that way by a teacher. Everyone could see the crisp white collar that was turned out over the neck of the sweater. As I reluctantly complied with Ms. Neeley's order and pulled the sweater over my head, all I had on from the waist up was a white collar called a "dickey" that I had appropriated from my sister. I knew that only girls wore them, but I never dreamt my secret would be exposed. Well, there I stood with this white collar hanging around my neck with nothing else to cover my scrawny physique. All the guys in the class let out a howl of laughter while I saw tears in the eyes of a couple of the girls. "That will do," Ms. Neeley said, "and Tommy, you may put your sweater back on." Miss Neeley was really a nice teacher and I guess she felt worse about the "dickey incident" than I did. One thing is for certain I'd never go to school without wearing jockey shorts, because you can never tell what's liable to happen.

The children of Garfield School put up decorations to commemorate holidays. Out of all the holidays, Christmas was the best. The two weeks prior to our annual Christmas vacation was an exciting time at school. Each classroom tried to outdo the others in decorating its room for Christmas. But the most elaborate display of all was the Christmas tree and manger scene in the first floor hall at the foot of the staircase. It was just the fifth and sixth graders who took part in setting up the most prominent of the school's tributes to the Christmas season. All of the children in my class were Christians to some degree or another, save for Ieda Bernstein, who was Jewish. However, this was never perceived to be a problem or even a matter for discussion. At that time and place, any effort to have the manger scene or Christmas tree removed from the school would have been considered outrageous and downright un-American.

Ieda and I were particularly good friends. She was the smartest kid in the class and often let me look at her papers, which never failed to have the right answers. Sometimes she'd get impatient with me for my apparent ignorance and give me a scolding and threaten never to help me again, but she always did. At Christmas she'd invite me to stop by her house on Bridgeview Avenue and her mother gave me a fruit jar filled with homemade Jewish wine to take home to my Mom.

Besides the singing of Christmas carols and reading Christmas stories, the climax of the celebration at school was the gift exchange, which took place the last day of school before vacation began. The name of each person in the class was put in a box and each of us drew a name. The name was the kid for whom you were to buy a gift. This name was kept an absolute secret until the day of the exchange, when the gifts were opened. No gift was to cost more than fifty cents. Believe it or not, you could get some pretty nice stuff for half a buck. For some odd reason, I always seemed to draw a girl's name. So I'd consult with my Mom about what to buy. She'd ponder the question and give it a great deal of thought, but her answer was always the same "A hanky would be nice." I'd go to McCroy's Five and Ten Cent Store and pick out a white hanky with flowers on it. After all the care I took in selecting this gift, it really bothered me to think the girl who got it would just fill it with snot.

We had a big party on the last day of school in June, 1947. This marked the end of my grade school years at Garfield. Pop, hot dogs and ice cream were served out on the playground to the sixth grade graduating class. This was one of the few times that the boys and girls co-mingled on the playground. Individual kids and groups provided entertainment and we all applauded and whistled our approval. Ieda Bernstein played a classical piece on her violin that, for obvious reasons, was not as well received as she had hoped. Donald Shively, George Bailey, Bobby Medley and I formed a quartet that lacked any trace of harmony. We sang a popular ballad of the time"I'm Forever Blowing Bubbles." "Pretty bubbles in the air, they fly so high they nearly reach the sky, then like my dreams they fade and die. Fortunes always hiding, I've looked everywhere; I'm forever blowing bubbles, pretty bubbles in the air."

Grade school had ended and I looked forward to a long summer vacation. Come September, I would be twelve years old and in the seventh grade at Grant Junior High School. Being full of confidence and acting like a big shot, I knew my bubble wouldn't burst, as good fortune was sure to be found at my new school.

36   The Son of a Boilermaker

Chapter 4

Boyhood Days I

Catwalk

Panhandle R.R. Bridge
and two not-so-smart ideas!

You're So Smart to Smoke Parliaments

"Anything for a smoke."

One winter day when I was seven years old and hanging around the north-end field not doing much of anything, I spotted this dog running loose, trailing a length of clothesline from her neck. She was a rather large dog of mixed breed, brown and white with a black muzzle. Her appearance was similar to that of a collie/ shepherd mix. Right away, she came up to me, wagging her tail and licking my hand. So I grabbed the clothesline around her neck and we beat it out of that neighborhood as fast as we could. As soon as I thought we were a safe distance away from where anyone might claim her, I paused long enough to make up a story to tell Mom.

First, I got rid of the clothesline because it might cause suspicion that she had escaped from her owner. Then I thought it would be good to tell Mom that I made several inquiries of people in the area as to whether they knew to whom she belonged. Of course, nobody did, and I had no other choice but to bring her home, since she wouldn't quit following me. Mom bought the lie and said I could keep her only until we found her owner. In the meantime, this dog needed a bath and in the tub she went. What a transformation!

Her color lightened to a beautiful reddish brown and her white chest gleamed. This was one great-looking dog with a disposition to match. I think Mom fell for her as much as I did. For about a week I made half-hearted efforts to locate her owner, which really meant I did nothing. I named her Boogie and she was mine. As it turned out, Boogie became my closest boyhood friend and companion.

There were really only four of us at home the whole time I was growing up: Mom, Virginia, Marge and me. My brother Bill (who now went by his first name George) graduated from high school and left for the Army at age seventeen. He and I were not close, so his departure from home had little effect upon me. With my Dad absent, and George gone, that left me at home surrounded by three women. I made this situation work to my advantage.

The usual restraints of adult supervision didn't apply much to me. Of course, my Mom tried as best she could to keep track of my comings and goings but she wasn't all that successful. After she went to work when I was a little older, (eleven or twelve) I think she gave up trying to control me. I got yelled at a lot but it went in one ear and out the other. I was a free spirit and did pretty much as I pleased. The only way I was able to pull this off was that I found ways to earn money, which was my ticket to independence. To the extent I could, I tried to avoid asking for anything.

I ran errands for neighbors, collected scrap iron to sell at the junk yard and performed chores for anyone willing to pay a skinny kid two bits. With some of my friends whose circumstances weren't much better than mine, we celebrated any snowfall during the winter. This meant really big bucks shoveling sidewalks and driveways. A good five or six-inch snowfall easily put ten to twelve bucks in my pocket. I never charged more than seventy five cents for any job, and most often less. In order to earn ten or more dollars, it was an all-day job. During particularly snowy winters, I developed a regular clientele for my services.

Lots of kids set up lemonade stands as a way to make money during the summer. The lemonade usually sold for three cents a glass. This was o.k., but I had a way to do them one better. My brother had an ice shaver that I appropriated when he no longer had a use for it. This was something like a wood planer, only the blade was designed to shave ice off a block and it accumulated the thin shavings inside the housing. This was perfect for making ice balls, which were put in small paper cups and flavored with cherry, lemon or root beer syrup and sold for five cents each. I owned the only ice ball shaver in the north end, which meant I controlled all the ice ball operations north of Market Street. Flushed with this newfound power, I was able to negotiate half the profits for the use of my shaver. The kids who operated the stand had to supply the ice, syrups, cups and wooden spoons. All I had to do was shave the ice and collect my money.

For over a year, I had a regular job watching an old man so his wife could go shopping and get a break from him. He must have had Alzheimer's, but they just called it hardening of the arteries. Mom had known Lizzie Leaper for many years from the Methodist church and insisted, over my objections, that I take the job. I really felt sorry for her and hated to take money just to sit there and do nothing, so I'd insist she take back a quarter if she gave me fifty cents. She was as poor as I was.

Without a doubt, my freedom gave me plenty of opportunities to find mischief wherever it might be. On many occasions, I was the ringleader who led other boys down the path to trouble. On the opposite side of the Ohio River is Weirton, West Virginia. The two states were connected by two bridges for vehicular traffic, one being the Market Street Bridge, which was downtown, and the Fort Steuben Bridge, located in the north end. Alongside the Fort Steuben Bridge was a railroad bridge to accommodate train traffic. At the point where the railroad bridge crossed the river, the river was probably five hundred yards wide. The bridge itself was an old iron structure with two sets of tracks, one for eastbound trains and the other for trains going west. The tracks were more than one hundred feet above the surface of the water. Rising above the tracks was the superstructure of the bridge, which, at its highest point, was another hundred and fifty feet high looming about two hundred-fifty feet above the Ohio River. Along the top of the superstructure was a catwalk about four feet wide with iron rails on each side. For reasons unknown, this cat-walk presented a challenge I couldn't resist.

One summer day when I was about eleven years old, I was just hanging around with three of my friends from Garfield School: Bobby Medley, George Bailey and Donald Shively. George asked if we could guess what he had in his pocket. When we couldn't, he produced a pack of Parliament cigarettes he had swiped from his mother's purse. Acting like the big shots we all thought we were, what else could we do but smoke them? One thing for sure, we didn't want to get caught. That's when I came up with the idea of climbing up on the catwalk of the train bridge to have a nice, quiet and undetected smoke.

It was a long, steep climb, but finally we reached the top. The view from this vantage point, up and down the river, was spectacular. We could see for miles into both Ohio and West Virginia and watch boats and barges full of coal ply their way to the mills and power plants in the Ohio Valley. But we weren't there for the view; we were there to light up.

The wind kept blowing out our matches and, with only a few left, we finally got our cigarettes lit. We made attempts to draw deep breaths of the smoke into our lungs. George, Bobby and I commenced choking and coughing, but Donald Shively was having no such difficulty. He breathed in the smoke smoothly and let it drift out his nostrils. He was in the process of giving us a demonstration as he leaned back against the railing of the catwalk and took a big drag. Just then, the rusty and corroded railing gave way and Donald was on his way to a watery grave. It all happened in a split second, but the moment when he was tottering on the edge seemed to freeze in time. Bobby and I reached out simultaneously and each caught hold of his shirt. I was immediately relieved to know that I wouldn't be called upon to explain to Donald's mom why he wouldn't be home for supper.

Without saying a word, we all knew it was time to get the hell off that bridge. We hadn't taken more than a few steps when we heard a train coming. As the freight train started across the bridge, the catwalk started shaking and rattling like a roller coaster. The vibration felt like the whole thing was ready to give way. I tried to picture just how I would position my body in mid-air to minimize the impact of the water 250 feet below. I'd hold myself stiff' and straight with my arms glued to my sides and try to enter the water like a bullet. The noise was deafening and we dared not cling to the railing that had almost caused Donald to go into the drink. All we could do was crouch there, holding onto one another, until the longest train ever to pass from Ohio to West Virginia finally crossed the bridge. I can't remember whatever became of the Parliaments, but that was my last visit to the train bridge.

Lighting a cigarette on top a train bridge wasn't easy, but neither was getting a lump of coal to burn. From the time I was in the fourth grade, we lived at 600 North Fifth Street. Located in the dirt floor cellar was a furnace that needed to burn coal if we expected to have any heat. During the 1940s just about every home in town was heated with coal. In the hills of eastern Ohio, coal was plentiful. It was common to see miners going to and from work at the "High Shaft" coal mine wearing hard hats with lights attached to the front to enable them to see while deep below the earth's surface. You could easily identify a coal miner, as he looked like a raccoon with his black face and white rings around his eyes.

There was a "coal chute" located on the side of the house. This was merely an opening which had a metal sliding board leading to the "coalbin" in the cellar. When the coal was delivered, the coal company generally put the load in the chute so the bin would fill. But if they dumped it on the street and the customer shoveled it into the chute themselves, there was a discount on the price. Naturally, our loads were dumped on the street so I could get some exercise and save Mom some money.

* * *

I had a natural curiosity about many things that were none of my business. Somehow, I had the knack of drawing information out of people by asking questions that were downright intrusive. The surprising thing was, I rarely offended anyone. My areas of inquiry extended to anything I perceived to be mysterious or had an element of secrecy.

The top right-hand drawer of my Morn's dresser was designed for handkerchiefs or hosiery, but that's not what it held. This drawer belonged to my dad, and this is where he kept his stuff. Anything in this dresser was off limits to me, but especially the contents of the top right-hand drawer. Because of the way we lived and my dad was

frequently gone, I was home alone much of the time.
The temptation of the forbidden drawer was more than I
could resist, so whenever I got the chance I'd make a complete
inventory of the contents.

The old man had all kinds of neat and exotic stuff crammed in
the drawer. I got familiar with just where in the drawer each item
was located, and was careful to replace it in just the exact spot I
found it. Much of what I discovered were items of memorabilia
from my dad's navy days. There was an envelope with pictures of
black people standing beside grass-covered huts with a jungle in
the background. Some of the people held spears and the tits of all
the women were sagging and uncovered. These photographs were
taken in Capetown, South Africa. In the same envelope were a
couple of pictures of my dad in his navy uniform posing with other
sailors. There was a picture of a naked woman lying on a Roman
couch. She was not any relative I recognized. There was a black
leather change purse that was full of foreign coins from countries
around the world. Some of the coins had square or triangle holes in
the middle with Chinese characters on them. There was a switch-
blade knife, a set of brass knuckles, a cigarette lighter shaped like
a derringer, and a metal dog crouched in a pooping stance. A small
wooden box with carved and painted designs had an exotic odor
of what I imagined a foreign land would smell like. I visualized
this box came from some strange bazaar in a place where palm
trees grew and swarthy people wore turbans on their heads. I was
completely fascinated with all of this treasure and would get it out
to handle it at every opportunity. I told myself that some day I'd
travel and have my own collection of stuff from far away places.

My old man had seen a lot of the world. Even his job kept him
on the go from place to place. It must have been a carry-over from
his navy days, to pick up odds and ends as a reminder of where
he'd been. I can't recall us eating off a matched set of dishes or
tableware. We had parts of sets and miscellaneous bowls, cups,
saucers, plates and utensils. The old man brought home odds and
ends of this kitchen stuff. I never asked where he got it, but I knew
when he was out of town he ate at diners and lunch counters, and
most of our dishes had a certain sturdy commercial quality to them.
If I had to guess, I believe we ate off of "hot" tableware and used

mostly "hot" utensils. However, when towels and washcloths with hotel names imprinted on them began to show up in the bathroom, this pretty much confirmed my suspicions that the old man had some larcenous tendencies.

I never really looked upon this minor form of pilfering as a crime. What the heck, the old man wasn't mixed up with the Mob or outlaws or anything like what I listened to on the radio. Our radio was a floor model that looked like a piece of furniture. Even though the sound carried throughout the house, it was my practice to lie on the floor with my ear glued to the instrument for fear I would miss something. The cowboy programs were my favorites. "Tom Mix" and "The Lone Ranger" were two shows I tried not to miss. The excitement, action and vivid descriptions, coupled with my own imagination, provided a picture of the wild west that has stayed with me to the present day. These programs had ongoing story lines so you always had to tune in for the next installment. One consistent thing about the programs was that the good guys always won out in the end and truth and justice always triumphed. I probably learned more valuable moral lessons by listening to "The Lone Ranger" than I ever learned at Sunday school.

Kids' programs were generally sponsored by some breakfast food company and lasted fifteen to thirty minutes. Wheaties, Shredded Wheat and Kix always had some kind of promotion going on where you could send in a box top from the product plus ten or fifteen cents and receive a valuable something or other used by the hero of the show. Once I sent for a special ring worn by the famous detective Dick Tracy. This ring had a slot in it that contained a mirror. By holding the ring up to eye level, you could look in the mirror while walking down the street to see if you were being followed by an enemy agent. This ring stayed on my finger night and day for months. Finally I had to take it off when my whole finger turned green and Mom said I was developing a paranoid personality by thinking I was constantly being followed by a bad guy.

During the evening hours, there were many quality radio programs such as dramas, music and comedy. In the 1940s, these programs were a staple in every home in America. Just about everyone listened to "Edgar Bergen and Charlie McCarthy,"

"Fibber McGee and Molly," "The Jack Benny Show," "The Fred Allen Show," "Burns and Allen," and "Your Hit Parade," which featured the top ten songs in the country for that week and was brought to you by your favorite cigarette, "Lucky Strikes."

I was a fidgety kid, never content to sit still or be quiet. I always had to be doing something. An expression I heard over and over again from my Mom was "Tommy, you're making me a nervous wreck" or "You're going to drive me to Massillon," which was where the state insane asylum was located.

One notable exception where I was content to sit quietly and do nothing was when my favorite radio programs were on the air. In my mind's eye, I had a picture of what each of the radio characters looked like, down to the smallest detail of their dress and physical appearance. This addiction to the radio gave me a vivid imagination which enabled me to conjure up stories about anything and everything, which I did with regularity. Starting when I was very young, I'd make up preposterous stories to tell Virginia and Marge. I got a big kick out of putting them on while using a serious and innocent expression as I detailed my numerous fabrications.

Once, when Marge was in high school and looking for a summer job, I told her of a job I knew about at Quimby's Bakery and that she should put in her application right away. This got her all excited and she asked if I had any information about the particulars of the job. I told her I didn't know too much, but I knew that one of the job requirements was that you had to have very good eye sight. Marge became a little concerned because she wore glasses, but I assured her it would be all right. She wanted to know why her vision would be so important to work at a bakery. I told her that a big part of the job involved "picking fly shit out of pepper." I must have had a real knack of convincing people of the absurd, because Marge actually went to Quimby's to apply for work. Need I say that she was seriously pissed off at her little brother when Quimby's failed to hire her.

Did I view making up elaborate stories as lies? Heck no. It was all part of the enjoyment I got out of being a practical jokester. Lying had to do with avoiding responsibility or cheating, and I didn't like that idea. I'd always "fess up" unless it involved squealing on one of my pals, then I'd lie my ass off, and I must say, I was convincing as hell. I got the reputation of being a good alibi which kept me in the good graces of the stronger troublemakers who recognized me as a loyal guy. As a consequence, nobody gave Tommy T any shit, so I became a survivor in a sometimes hostile environment.

With a natural curiosity about people, places and things, I always wanted to be where the action was. When it came to sports, I was a reluctant spectator, wishing from the sidelines I could be a player and part of the game. Whenever I saw a ship, plane or train, I'd pretend I was a passenger. I'd make believe I was leaving the drabness of Steubenville behind, and headed for some beautiful spot in a far corner of the world. I was not content to live my life through the fictional exploits of my movie and radio heroes. I was determined that some day I would experience all these adventures first hand.

Transportation was never a problem for me because I walked everywhere I went. There were perfectly good sidewalks in Steubenville, but all of my buddies and I preferred to walk in the alleys that ran behind the streets. I didn't think about why we chose the alley routes. Maybe it was because we could kick a tin can as we walked along or jump a fence and steal some grapes from an Italian guy's yard where they grew to be made into wine. In late summer, tomatoes were also targeted for our thievery and we would throw them at one another in messy tomato combat. We never really considered this sort of conduct stealing.

Walking in the alleys also presented a great opportunity for two or more guys to engage in one of our favorite pastimes, whizzing contests. We would line up side by side about six feet or so from a wooden fence or garage door. On the count of three, all the participants would let go with a forceful stream of urine. The object was to see who could make the highest wet spot on the target fence or door. I was of the opinion that the guys who were circumcised had a definite advantage. Unlike some of us, their moms had been willing to spring for the extra five bucks which made them better whizzers. Six decades later, I would look back and consider what we were all able to accomplish as nothing short of miraculous, circumcised or not.

Walking everywhere had its limitations. For one thing, there were certain parts of town that were further than I cared to hike. One exception was walking to the swimming pool, which was located up on the hill at LaBelle Park. To get there we had to walk up the hill to the top of Franklin Avenue. This was over a mile from home and seemed a long way. About halfway up the hill, there was a natural spring where water bubbled out of a pipe in the hillside and we'd stop to drink.

Many of my summer days were spent at the pool doing dives, flips and cannonballs off the high and low boards. I had no fear in this regard and had the reputation of a daredevil diver by the regular crowd. However, my form left a lot to be desired. After hours at the pool, I'd trudge down the hill at the end of the day tired, sunburned and hungry. LaBelle Pool was not integrated, so the black kids had their own pool on Adams Street hill. We all called it "The Ink Well."

Summer seemed to last forever, and to a boy who was free to roam where he pleased, there were infinite possibilities of how to spend the day. Aside from swimming and baseball, I liked searching for places to explore among the wooded trails and creek bottoms leading from Beatty Park up to Union Cemetery. This journey of three or four miles could last all day as we turned large flat rocks in the creek looking for snakes, crawdads and salamanders. Often, I had trouble finding other kids to accompany me on these adventures because most guys had to get the O.K. from their moms and didn't have the degree of freedom I enjoyed. However, I was usually successful in convincing their moms that I knew what I was doing and wouldn't get anybody lost. This sometimes worked out quite well because once permission was granted, the concerned mother would insist we take a lunch. A bologna sandwich and a piece of devil's food cake was just the ticket after a few hours of exploring.

About four miles north of Steubenville on Route 7, which ran along the Ohio River, was Stanton Park. By the time I was a boy, this place had long since seen its day. My Mom told me that when she was a girl, it was a popular amusement park with a host of rides, including a wooden framed roller coaster. There was a pavilion where concerts and dancing to the music of a live orchestra was a nightly summer activity for the people of Steubenville and the surrounding valley. It was the primary location for family picnics and the Fourth of July fireworks display.

By the time Bobby Medley, brothers Charlie and Bill Adams, and I chose Stanton Park as a place to explore, the only thing remaining was a spring-fed swimming pool with clear, cold green water that turned our lips and bodies blue within a matter of minutes. The sides of the concrete pool were crumbling from age and neglect. At a depth of twenty feet, the deep end challenged our lungs to the point of bursting as we made a game of swimming to the bottom to retrieve rocks. What was really fun was that we had this place all to ourselves except for the occasional snake or turtle. The hike up Route 7 to get there was long and dangerous as coal trucks and semis buzzed by, but, the four mile trek was worth it once our naked bodies pierced the surface of the cold spring water.

True to her pessimistic outlook, Mom always said that summer was as good as over after the Fourth of July, but I never believed a word of it. "Just you wait," she would say, "when you're my age, you'll see how short the summers are."

Mom rode the city buses and at times would buy a weekly pass good for unlimited rides. The pass was good from Monday through Sunday, so it ran out on Sunday night. Sometimes on a Sunday afternoon she'd use the pass to take me on a bus ride. There was no specific destination. We just rode the bus for the entire route and be dropped off where we started. Sometimes, to prolong the enjoyment, we'd go around twice if I wasn't getting bus sick. Mom wanted to make sure she was getting her money's worth. This form of family entertainment was likely unique to the Twyfords.

My Mom had a knack for coming up with ingenious forms of cheap entertainment. One of her close friends was Mabel Mayhew. She was older than Mom, and had a dumpy figure and frizzy hair. Mrs. Mayhew had a much-deserved reputation as a gossip who had the low down on everybody and everything. Much of this knowledge was acquired by being a regular visitor at all the funeral homes in town. Going to funeral parlors two or three evenings a week was part of her routine. She'd read the obituaries in the Herald Star and somehow decide which corpse held the most promise for an interesting and informative visit. She'd call Mom and ask if she saw who was "laid out" at such and such mortuary. Before long, my mother got hooked on this gruesome form of entertainment. Mind you, these people were generally strangers they didn't know from a load of coal. One good thing about it was that there was no charge for admission. Once at the funeral home, Mrs. Mayhew and Mom would saddle up to the bereaved family members and try to illicit as many of the lurid details as possible. Upon leaving, they always conducted a critique on how good, bad, or life-like the deceased appeared in the casket.

Mom often spoke of a trip she made to Columbus, Ohio to visit with my Uncle Tom and Aunt Marie. Since you could count on one hand the times she ventured beyond the Steubenville city limits, this was an important milestone in her life. The highlight of this visit and what she talked about the most was a tour she took of the Ohio State Penitentiary. This was in the year 1940, and regularly scheduled tours were conducted so law-abiding citizens could go behind the walls to gawk at the less fortunate souls who resided there. It must have been on the order of a visit to the Pittsburgh Zoo to look at the caged animals behind bars. There was a walk down the hall of the cell block called death row that housed the condemned prisoners. However, the most popular attraction was the death house, which contained the electric chair. Each visitor on the tour was allowed to sit in the upright oak chair, which had straps and wires dangling from it.

As I grew older, I tried to reconcile the idea of my Mom finding entertainment value by sitting in an electric chair and visiting funeral homes, ideas that somehow seemed at odds with her Methodist values. At the very least, it seemed a bit peculiar. The only conclusion I could reach was that this was just the dark side of a complex person.

Without a family automobile, certain places and things were beyond our reach. Every once in a while some thoughtful neighbor offered to take us a ride in what Mom referred to as their "machine." I know she really enjoyed these outings but always kept her fingers crossed in hopes I wouldn't get car sick and puke all over the seats of our friend's machine. It was a special treat at Christmas to be driven up on the hill and out Sunset Boulevard to see the Christmas lights and decorations on what Mom called all the "big ten thousand dollar homes." For several years in the 1940s, blue and silver colored outdoor lights were all the rage. It was my hope that someday I'd be rich enough to afford blue lights on a white flocked Christmas tree. This would be definite proof that I had become a man of means.

While I attended Garfield grade school, we lived at two different locations in the north end of town. We lived in the second floor garage apartment at 930 North Fifth Street for two years. Then when I was in fourth grade, we moved to 600 North Fifth Street, just three and a half blocks away. The house was a two-story frame double, which sat directly on the street with a front porch, no front yard, and only a small patch of grass in the back.

I quickly made friends with everyone on the new block. The move didn't require much in the way of an adjustment for me, since I was still able to maintain all my contacts from the old neighborhood. One of my new friends who lived on the block was Chuck Lafferty. Chuck was two years younger than I and went to St. Peters Catholic School. Despite the age difference, we seemed to hit it off quite well. Naturally, with me being older, I was the leader and made most of the decisions of what, how and when we would engage in any activity. Chuck was an only child. His father was the president of the union at Weirton Steel, and Chuck was only eight years old when his father had a fatal heart attack. Chuck's mother, Ethel Lafferty, was a handsome, prematurely silver-haired woman in her forties when Mr. Lafferty died. I think Mr. Lafferty left her rather well off, as she spoiled Chuck and sometimes me in the process.

Mrs. Lafferty's gray hair was the silver kind that had a purple tint to it. Maybe it was for this reason that she was partial to any color with a hint of lavender or violet. All of her hats, shoes, handbags, coats and dresses were some shade of purple. That's the only color she ever wore, except on Saint Patrick's Day when, to pay homage to her Irish heritage, she took to "the wearin' of the green." She must have known every Irish ballad ever written, and often played records of the famous Irish tenor, John McCormick. My favorite songs were "Rose of Tralee" and "Danny Boy," which she would willingly play for me whenever I asked.

Without a doubt, nobody ever treated me any better than Mrs. Lafferty. Anything she did for her son she also included me. If Chuckie wanted to go to the movies, she would give me the money for both of us, along with popcorn money, too. Often times, if she bought something for Chuckie, like a cap gun, she made sure I got one as well. Anytime I was at their house, she made sure I was fed and provided me with treats I never got at home. Had it not been for the kindness and generosity of Mrs. Lafferty, the quality of my young life would have been substantially diminished. All in all, Mrs. Lafferty was a surrogate mother to me for many of my formative years.

Chapter 5

Boyhood Days II

Mom with Boogie and me

For a person who lacked size, strength, coordination and speed, I was an unlikely prospect to ever achieve success in the world of sports. If only I could have possessed two of these attributes of athleticism, I might have excelled in some sport. As it was, I was lacking all of the characteristics that endowed a sports star, save one: desire. So, with an unrealistic optimism, I threw myself into the arena with a degree of enthusiasm unmatched by my talented friends.

Most of my participation in sports consisted of pick-up games of sand-lot football or baseball played with other neighborhood boys. Each neighborhood had a gang of cohorts who comprised football or baseball teams. These rag-tag groups often would issue challenges to meet on the field of play, with boasts of beating the shit out of each other. For days preceding any contest, that's all we seemed to talk about. Although I wasn't one of the best players, I was a natural when it came to talking.

These games were played in the streets, alleys or vacant lots. We played football at Flat Iron Park, which was not much more than an undersized field full of rocks that bordered the Ohio River. I recall that some of these games were quite rough and I often came away bruised and sporting a fat lip. Nonetheless, I loved it. Due to my size and skill level, I was generally the last guy picked when we chose sides.

The six grade schools in Steubenville formed a basketball league. I was a member of Garfield's team. Our games were played on half court at the high school gym on Saturday mornings. Being a team member didn't necessarily mean you got to play in the game, at least not when it came to me, but I did manage to get into a few games during the course of the season. This meant that my name would be included in the box scores that were published in the newspaper.

Usually it would indicate something like "Twyford: Shots-2 Field Goals-0 Points-0." On one occasion, I did manage to make a basket, and a foul shot. When my name appeared in the newspaper with "Field Goals-1 Foul Shots-1 Points-3," I cut it out and carried it in my Indian-stitched Lone Ranger wallet for more than a year.

When it came to baseball, my skill was also wanting. The Pittsburgh Pirates and the Cleveland Indians were my teams. The radio announcers, Rosey Roswell for the Pirates and Jimmy Dudley for the Indians, made these teams a staple of my life for many summers. I made it my business to memorize the batting averages, hits, home runs and runs batted in of every player in the starting line-up for the Pirates and the Indians. I was a walking encyclopedia of baseball trivia and didn't mind showing off this knowledge to whomever I could get to listen. Each day, I would read the sports page of the Herald Star absorbing all the information I could about the world of sports. I didn't care if the article was about baseball, football, basketball or boxing. I read it, and could discuss sports with anyone on an adult level.

Beside the sports page, I never missed reading the funnies. I had many favorites, including Dick Tracy, Terry and the Pirates, Snuffy Smith and Mark Trail. However, one comic strip character whose heroic sports exploits I followed every day was Osark Ike. Osark was portrayed as a three-sport super jock in baseball, football and basketball as the comic strip kept pace with each evolving season. Ike could always be counted on to hit the winning home run, score the winning touchdown or hit the last second shot at the buzzer. That was the fantasy I harbored for Tommy Twyford, picturing myself as another Osark Ike.

One summer when I was around ten or eleven, I began saving every penny I could get to buy a new first baseman's mitt at the M & M Hardware Store. Even though I didn't consider myself a first baseman, I still wanted that glove. Well, the day finally came when I had the ten bucks. When I got to the hardware store, I needed another fifty cents for tax, but the man said, "forget it," and even threw in a can of special glove conditioner for free. He told me I needed to grease the pocket and keep slapping a baseball into the glove to get it broken in. For weeks thereafter, I was never without that glove, day or night. I was constantly banging an old baseball held together with friction tape into the pocket of that glove until Mom made me quit, as she said it was driving her crazy.

My big break came when the guys I played pick-up ball with formed a regular team and joined the city A league. For some reason, they asked me to be on the team. While I couldn't hit worth a darn, I was actually pretty good with a glove. They stuck me in right field where they figured I'd do the least amount of harm. The next thing I knew, we had a sponsor for our team. Our benefactor was the Doris Embroidery Shop, and we were to get uniforms with our name embroidered on the front of the jersey. Finally, the big day came and they were beautiful. The hats and jerseys were green with yellow embroidered lettering that said "Doris Embroidery Shop" on the back and "Tommy Twyford" in smaller letters on the front. Well, I only took that jersey off long enough for my mother to wash it. Otherwise, I wore it every day, game or no game.

I didn't have a stellar season for Doris Embroidery, but I do recall one game in particular where I was called upon to perform far beyond my capabilities. We played seven-inning games and it was the bottom of the seventh and I had already struck out twice. We were behind by two runs and there were two outs and bases loaded and it was my turn to bat. There was nobody available to pinch hit for me, so the game rested on the powerful bat of Tommy Twyford.

Mind you, I don't think I had more than five hits all season. The opposing pitcher promptly got two strikes on me and the guys started packing up the equipment. On the third pitch, I swung late on a fast ball and drilled the ball by the third baseman down the left field line. The ball rolled all the way to the fence. Running the bases was just a blur and everyone was yelling out my name. I wound up on third with a stand-up triple. The game was over, we had won. It was the first and last time I was ever the hero of any game, but I'll never forget it.

I reported for football tryouts when I was in the seventh grade at Grant Junior High School. The coach was Milan Zori, a man of gigantic proportions at about six feet six, and he was strictly business. I knew I was in over my head from the get-go. All of the biggest and meanest guys in the school were on the field that day. Mr. Zori put us through a series of drills to test our strength, speed and endurance. After the two-hour session was over, I was still gasping to regain my breath when Mr. Zori took me aside and with his huge hand on my shoulder said, "Son, I don't think football is your game, but thanks for trying out." Mr. Zori was one very smart coach.

During the winter months, the YMCA was my home away from home. I spent hours on end at the Y, where my friends and I played ping-pong, shot pool and participated in organized activities supervised by a staff member. For the most part, it was a safe place where a lot of poor kids could hang out. It was at the Y that I was introduced to boxing and competitive swimming.

There was a cop by the name of Officer Peronne who organized a boxing team at the Y. The members of the team were known as "Peronne's Tigers" and I was a flyweight Tiger. At this time, I was eleven years old, and we were given instructions on how to defend ourselves as well as how to throw a jab, cross and hook. All of the boys on the team were veteran "scrappers" who were schooled in fighting in the neighborhood or on the playgrounds. But, as one of "Peronne's Tigers" we had to learn boxing by the rules with sixteen-ounce gloves. Using sixteen ounce gloves pretty much ruled out the possibility of anyone getting seriously injured.

There was a series of elimination bouts conducted in each weight division. I was classified as a flyweight, which meant that I entered the ring at about eighty-five pounds. Most of the boys in this weight division were younger than I, and I was able to kick some serious butt in my first few fights. Flushed with success, I became quite cocky and swaggered with an air of invincibility. This winning streak carried on through my first five fights.

My next fight was a black kid who was fighting out of the Wheeling, West Virginia YMCA. When I entered the ring and saw this guy, I knew my winning streak was about to end. Although he was skinny, all of his muscles were well defined as he confidently shadow-boxed in his corner. After round one, my worst fears were confirmed. He knocked me all over the ring. We fought three two-minute rounds. By some miracle, I went the distance and with blood running from my nose, heard the judges declare a unanimous decision for my opponent. I was gracious in defeat, with little of my former bravado surviving. I found out after the fight that this kid was considered a real hot-shot fighter in Wheeling. All of my fighting stable mates said I fought a good fight, considering the top caliber of my opposition. Despite their encouragement, I decided to retire with a respectable five wins, one loss record. So much for Peronne's flyweight Tiger.

For all of my daredevil lifestyle, I reached adolescence relatively free of any serious injury. The most trauma I suffered was at the hands of my teammates on the YMCA swim team.

I was the smallest guy on the team and decidedly the least talented swimmer. I was thrilled to accompany the team on an overnight stay in Canton and get to swim in a meet against their YMCA team. They had a great facility with a six-lane pool. My race was the one-hundred yard freestyle and I was in the sixth lane. I can recall my teammates, Bobby Medley and Charlie Adams, walking along the side of the pool yelling encouragement to me as I struggled to finish the race while all the other participants were out of the pool, well on their way to becoming completely dry.

Our YMCA pool was only twenty-five yards long and just wide enough to accommodate four lanes. The ceiling in the pool area was no more than ten feet high and a dense steamy fog hung over the pool.

After we completed practice, it was goof-off time, an event in which I did excel. It became somewhat of a ritual for four of the guys to grab my ankles and wrists and swing me back and forth to see how far they could throw me into the water. They had done this often enough to get quite good, but on one occasion, their timing was off, not all of them releasing my extremities at the same time. I went straight up and hit the ceiling and landed on the side of the pool, half in and half out of the water.

I took it right under the chin, harder than I had ever been hit by any uppercut in a boxing match. There was a sizable gash under my chin that was pumping a lot of blood. My side hurt even more as they dragged me up on the deck. I stood up on wobbly legs as they put a towel around me and held one to my chin. The Y director led me to his car and I was taken to Ohio Valley Hospital, where I got five stitches and was told I probably had some cracked ribs.

My Mom was called, but she had no way to get to the hospital, so after I got stitched up, I was taken home. I recovered without incident, but I bore the small scar under my chin with the same pride as if it were a medal I won in a race.

My puny physique was partially a result of genetics, but diet was likely a contributing factor. Mealtime at our house was something short of a gourmet's delight. Mom was not much of a cook. Since our daily menu was mostly dictated by the affordability of food and my Mom's lack of ingenuity insofar as preparation was concerned, we generally ate a simple inadequate diet. Through the week, our meals consisted of bean soup and a dish called "slumgullion," which was basically a poor man's chili, minus any meat. Even the word "slumgullion" had a very unappetizing sound. It reminded me of something that a farmer might feed to pigs.

We also dined on liver and onions on a regular basis. During the 1940s, beef liver was cheap, so cheap the butcher almost gave it away, so naturally this became a family staple. Sometimes we would have Jello for dessert with a can of fruit cocktail dumped in it. If the Jello had shredded carrots or cabbage in it, then it was a salad.

During the summer months, the entree for the supper meal was often corn on the cob with sliced tomatoes or string beans, which simmered on the stove for hours until they got nice and mushy and every nutrient was cooked out of them. A bright spot in the regular fare was the dessert, since my Mom was partial to sweets. The main course was usually lacking in many of the nutritional essentials, but the coconut cream pie, devil's food cake and brownies made up for any deficiencies in the main course.

Steubenville is a long way from the ocean, so we had very little fish in our diet that is, until Mom discovered Mrs. Paul's frozen fish sticks. The package they came in didn't specify what kind of fish were in the sticks, but they were cheap and didn't require much effort to prepare. After Mom went to work, I'd sometimes get supper started so that it would be ready for her when she got home. While I was in high school, we seldom all sat down to have supper at the same time, so a bowl of cornflakes or a fried egg sandwich would suffice as the perfect meal for a man on the run.

There was a supermarket of sorts called the Thoroughfare on Washington Street where I often accompanied Mom to buy food. It was a source of embarrassment for me when Mom paid for the groceries at the cash register. When the cashier told her the cost of our purchases, she'd take a deep breath and let out a loud sigh and shake her head from side to side as she fumbled through her purse for the money. After carefully counting out what she came up with, she'd sometimes pick up an item or two and look at me and say, "Here Tommy, go put these back on the shelf." All the while, the cashier shot us an impatient, dirty look. I didn't like the idea that anyone would think we didn't have enough money to pay, so I tried to avoid going to the Thoroughfare whenever I could.

Although the standard fare at mealtime left a lot to be desired, I made sure old Boogie wasn't neglected when it came to chow. She ate "Rival" or "Red Heart" canned dog food. It cost ten cents a can and was the cheapest dog food on the market. Sometimes I'd spot an eyeball, snout or other miscellaneous animal part in the food. Fortunately I had made good friends with Mr. Berringer, the butcher, at the Mar-Kay Market. If I went right before closing time to the back door, I could get scraps and bones for Boogie, which I'd boil up or fry so she had as fine a diet as any dog in town.

* * *

Of course, holidays have a special place in my boyhood memories and one particular Christmas, I had my heart set on getting a basketball.

We had basketball nets and back boards on the playground at Garfield School. After school and on weekends, there were games going on or guys just shooting around. By the time I was a sixth grader, I was actually getting pretty accurate with my two-hand set shot. If I only had my own basketball, I could go to the playground anytime I wanted and practice my shooting skills. So, I let it be known in no uncertain terms that I wanted a basketball for Christmas Just to make sure there was no hinting around on my part, I just flat came out and said it. I figured that a good regulation outdoor basketball with a tough rubber surface would cost about ten bucks. This sum would probably be at the outer limits of what Mom could spend on my Christmas present, but I really needed that basketball if I was ever going to be the star player I knew I could be.

On Christmas morning, I was up very early. Mom, Virginia and Marge were already up and in the living room. They looked at me and were all smiles. I could tell they were anxious for me to look under the tree. Sure enough, there it was, a perfectly square box just the right size to contain the regulation basketball I wanted. I took one look at that box under the Christmas tree and knew exactly what I would be doing that afternoon. It was sunny and cold, but there was no snow on the ground, so it would be a perfect day for dribbling and shooting hoops at the school yard. Beside that, it was Christmas and I'd have the whole place to myself. Just in case the ball didn't have enough air in it, I could borrow Chuck Switzer's pump and maybe he and I could play a game of H-O-R-S-E. Mom proudly urged me to open the box. I tore open the carefully wrapped package and there it was a leather-covered volleyball. It was all I could do to conceal my disappointment, but I managed a weak smile and thanked all three of them for getting me this great "basketball." I just didn't have the heart to tell them that it was a volleyball. Their knowledge of sports was so limited that they didn't know the difference. Since my "basketball" was much smaller than a real basketball and had a leather cover, I couldn't use it on the rough playground surface or in the alley. So that's probably the reason I never perfected my two-hand set shot.

In addition to the Christmas festivities at school, every year I was part of the Christmas program at the Fifth Street Methodist Church. The primary department of the Sunday school always had a short Christmas play or a reenactment of the nativity. Sometimes, children would recite Christmas poems as part of the program. I recall being a shepherd one year. My costume was an old, ratty-looking bath robe that had belonged to one of my sisters. I put up quite a fit with my Mom about wearing this feminine garb, but she said shepherds always wore bathrobes. It's no wonder none of the guys I knew ever wanted to be a shepherd when they grew up.

At the conclusion of the Christmas program that was held in the church sanctuary, all of the children retired to the basement Sunday school to await the arrival of Santa Claus. Once we were all seated in folding chairs, the Sunday school teacher hushed us all down. After a moment or two of silence a creaking sound could be heard coming down the stairs. Then, the anticipated deep baritone sound of YO-HO-HO-YO-HO-HO, and a disheveled Santa appeared, struggling with an oversized pillow case that contained the candy.

Every year, the same old guy played Santa. I recognized him in a flash, because he sat in the pew behind us at church every Sunday. The Santa suit he wore was kind of shabby and moth-eaten. But the false white beard was really a joke with chunks of cotton material missing here and there and exposing the bare backing cloth. It rested on his face at an awkward and unnatural angle, which made him look as though he had some unfortunate deformity. None of the children seemed to mind that Santa Claus had this affliction or the hint of booze on his breath because he busied himself handing out boxes of candy. The boxes looked like an animal cracker box with a string handle. Every year there was the same thing inside, hard-tack candy and one large cream-filled chocolate drop.

Easter was also a pretty big deal around our house. What with the Last Supper and the Resurrection of Christ, it's perhaps the most important date on the Christian calendar. As I recall from the paintings and stained glass windows at the church, Jesus and his disciples were sitting around in their bathrobes and really weren't all that dressed up. But, getting all dolled up at Easter was what it was all about when I was a kid.

Everyone, and I do mean everyone, had to have new clothes to wear to church on Easter Sunday. As a matter of fact, the Fifth Street Methodist Church was the site of a genuine fashion show every Easter. Mom would fret and fuss around for weeks over what outfits she, Virginia and Marge would wear on the big day. One year I got this two-tone, brown-and-tan sport coat, which I thought was pretty neat. Then Mom insisted I wear this matching clip-on bow tie. This made me look like a blond headed 'Alfalfa," that simple looking kid in Our Gang Comedies . As soon as I got to Sunday school, I took it off, intentionally breaking the clip and scolding Mom for buying me such a cheap tie.

Now anyone with an ounce of brains knows that the month of March can be colder than a well-digger's ass. One particular Easter, I remember Mom scurrying us all down Fifth Street to church while huge wet flakes of snow clung to our light clothing like meringue on a coconut cream pie. They were all on the verge of tears while it was all I could do to keep from laughing. This was the perfect kind of snow for big wet snowballs, but had I made just one, it surely would have pushed my Mom over the brink.

Naturally, holidays are special markers in the life of any grade school boy. These were special occasions, and for me the anticipation of the event held as much excitement as the arrival of the "Big Day" itself.

What made my years of elementary school different was that an on-going event was in progress. World War II was raging in Europe and Asia. Aside from some of the organized activities to help the war effort we had at school, the war touched our young lives in other ways.

One of the ways was through the rationing of certain products and foodstuffs that were deemed essential to the war effort. Items such as sugar, coffee, shortening and cigarettes were strictly controlled by the rationing board through plastic tokens that entitled each family to a certain quota of the rationed goods. There were no tokens for bubble gum, but it was a scarce and treasured treat for grade schoolers when we could get it. I would save it for days, planting it on the bed frame overnight until I could get a fresh supply.

Another item that was supposed to contribute to the war effort was bacon grease. I never knew for sure why we saved it, but at some point after the war, I was told it was used to manufacture explosives.

Butter was a rationed item, so we used margarine instead. Mom gave me the job of mixing up the margarine to make it look like butter. This stuff was nothing more than lard that came in a cardboard container. On top of the lard was a yellow capsule, the size of a pigeon egg, which I pierced with a fork and caused this runny golden liquid to pour out. Then I'd mash and mix it into the lard until all the white was gone. Now, this stuff may have looked like butter, but it tasted just like what it was: lard.

Even though cigarettes were rationed, the old man still smoked Lucky Strikes, which had a red circle on the pack. During the war the company had this advertising slogan that said, "Lucky Strikes Has Gone To War." They changed the color of the circle to green to demonstrate to nicotine fiends how patriotic they were and that Lucky Strikes was 100 percent behind the war effort.

When the old man had the dough for his favorite smoke, he would send me up to Chet's Confectionary with a plastic token and twenty cents to buy his Luckies. At other times, he would roll his own with a contraption that held cheap-cut tobacco and thin cigarette papers. All you had to do was turn a crank and a neatly rolled fag would come out the end of the cigarette roller. However, most of the time the paper wouldn't stick, so you had to moisten the paper with spit to make it hold. It really made me feel important if the old man let me roll some cigarettes for him.

Just about every adult I knew, except for my Mom, smoked cigarettes. Smoking was a natural right of passage to adulthood. All of the movie stars, sports heroes and anyone who wanted to act chic and with the times engaged in the cultivated practice of inhaling nicotine. Actually, smoking as portrayed on the movie screen was a glamorous and sexy ritual. Bette Davis and Lauren Bacall had the technique down pat. They'd take a deep drag of smoke into their lungs and slowly let it drift upward from slightly parted lips only to inhale it again through flaring nostrils. This way, a gal who really knew how to smoke could get two hits off one drag. This was known as French inhaling

The reality of this widespread addiction to cigarettes was that the ugly telltale signs of nicotine stains were generally visible on the fingers of the smoker. The thumb and forefinger of the old man's right hand had this permanent yellow stain that marked him as addicted to the weed. He would smoke these unfiltered "coffin nails" right down to the point where they were burning his fingers. That way he got his money's worth for the hacking cough that was also a side effect of this addiction. Strangely enough, nobody gave a second thought to the ill effects of smoking. If Joe DiMaggio, the "Yankee Clipper," could enjoy a "Chesterfield" and still hit a home run, maybe cigarettes would make us better ballplayers. Never mind if you developed a smoker's cough; the tobacco industry had a ready cure. Their answer was to smoke a mentholated "Kool." The advertisement showed a smiling, animated Willy the Penguin standing in front of an igloo in an army uniform, puffing on a "Kool."

The sacrifices we made at home concerning shortages of foodstuff, gasoline, and automobiles (which were not manufactured during the war) were nothing compared to the price paid by our men and women in uniform. I really did not have anyone close to me who was killed, wounded, or even served in combat. It was, however, a familiar topic of conversation among adults and many men from Steubenville served in combat zones in Europe and the Pacific. If a family had a member in the armed forces, they hung a sixteen-by-eight inch flag in their front window. Each flag had a blue star in the middle, but if their relative had been wounded, the star was silver. Gold stars were for the sons, husbands, and fathers killed in action. Whenever I saw a gold star, it gave me reason to pause and wonder about the sorrow the people in the house must have felt. Gold star mothers were treated with special deference and respect. These stars continued to hang in many windows years after the war ended. Maybe the war was never really over for the gold-star moms.

In the spring of 1945, the Germans surrendered and we celebrated what was called V-E Day. This meant that the war in Europe was over, but we still had those sneaky Japs to deal with. There was a special edition of the Herald Star on V-E Day and the Pathe News Reels at the movies showed us film of the destruction of Berlin.

Shortly after the Germans surrendered and places in Eastern Europe were liberated, the concentration camps were discovered. It was only then that the enormity of the Holocaust was disclosed to the public. Every movie theater in town showed films of the mass graves, bodies, ovens and the walking skeletons that were liberated. Many of my classmates at Garfield were deeply disturbed about what they saw and had nightmares fearing that this could happen to us. I never experienced these fears, but I just couldn't understand why the Jewish people were singled out for this horrendous treatment. I didn't know a lot of Jews, but they just seemed like regular people to me. Their church was on North Fifth Street, only two doors from where I lived. The rabbi had a long fuzzy beard and sometimes wore a weird-looking hat, but he allowed us to play on the front steps of the temple any day but Friday. I wanted to ask my friend Ieda Bernstein, who was the smartest kid in school, why this happened to all those poor Jews, but for once I couldn't find the right words to bring it up.

The task of beating the Japanese was never in doubt. It was just a question of how much longer they could hold out. Public sentiment in America against the Japanese was probably at its peak when they began the kamikaze attacks against our Navy. These suicide missions just reinforced our ideas that the Japanese were barbarians who placed no value upon human life. So, when we dropped atomic bombs on Hiroshima and Nagasaki, we all celebrated and cheered without giving a thought to the tens of thousands of Japanese kids who went up in flames. When we heard on the radio that the Japs surrendered and the war was over, everyone in our neighborhood went out on Fifth Street banging on pots and pans, and from somewhere the sound of fireworks and blaring car horns could be heard. I was just one month shy of my tenth birthday.

Even though the war was over, life went on as usual at home and there was never a time when Mom was free of money worries. She could not depend on my father to send money on a regular basis. He routinely made promises that were just as routinely broken. As a boilermaker, he was among the highest paid workers in the construction trades, but his wages were sacrificed to his drinking and gambling to the detriment of his wife and family.

The poor quality of dental care my Mom received was another sad chapter in her life. From a cosmetic standpoint, she didn't appear to have bad teeth, but routine check ups and corrections of minor problems were not part of her routine. Over time, these problems accumulated, but at forty-three years of age, were still clearly manageable by a competent dentist. The main hurdle in getting her problems resolved was the money it would cost to get the work completed. Once she found out the cost involved, she told her dentist she could not afford it. He told her it would be cheaper to have all her teeth pulled and wear dentures. Apparently, it didn't take Mom long to weigh the pros and cons of getting all her teeth extracted. So, without the benefit of a second opinion and with questionable reason to do so, she went ahead and had the procedure done. The dentures made for her were not the proper fit, which made wearing them a constant source of irritation. However, she had far too much pride about her appearance ever to be seen without her false teeth. Ignorance, poverty and an incompetent dentist all conspired to burden my Mom with painful gums for the remainder of her life.

I vividly recall a short period of time right before the old man left home for good when he appeared to abandon his reckless ways. He told Mom he had set aside enough money to make a down payment for a home of our own. I had never seen my Mom so happy and excited. She heard about some brand new brick homes that were being offered for sale up in Toronto, Ohio, which was only about five miles up the river from Steubenville. A neighbor of ours drove Mom and I up to Toronto one Sunday afternoon and we got a complete tour of one of these new eight-thousand-dollar homes. A three-bedroom home with all new appliances was beyond her wildest dreams. I was promised a room of my own, and there was even a fenced-in yard for Boogie. Well, of course it was too good to be true. The old man went on a bender and both he and the down payment were gone. These types of disappointments and broken promises took their toll upon my Mom and broke her spirit. She became very bitter and thought of herself as a victim. Even as young as I was, I felt as though I was an added burden to her life. So, I looked for every opportunity to be independent and earn money wherever I could.

Selling ice balls or shoveling snow was O.K. for seasonal work, but my first big break in the world of business came when my pal, Chuck Switzer, retired from his paper route. You had to be twelve years old to be a paperboy for the Steubenville Herald Star. Since I was eleven, Chuck and I made a deal. The paper route would stay in his name, but I would deliver all one hundred twenty-five papers, six days a week.

My route went from Ross Street, for about a mile, all the way to the Fort Steuben Bridge. Gill Hospital was on my route, so if I had any extras I would sell them for a nickel to the patients. The nurses at the hospital were always glad to see me and offered me a glass of lemonade or a cup of cocoa whenever I stopped by.

Every Saturday morning we'd collect 25 cents from each customer and Chuck went to the Herald Star to pay the bill. After paying for the newspapers, we generally had about ten bucks left, which we divided five bucks each. Considering the fact that I did all the delivering, this arrangement worked out well for Chuck, but I didn't care. I was just happy to make the five bucks.

When Christmas time came around, I found out that it was the usual practice for customers to give their paperboy a token of their appreciation for being prompt and reliable in his deliveries. Chuck said I should keep all the tips from the customers, since I did all the work and he had another job that paid him well.

Almost without exception, every customer on my route had an envelope for me that contained a one dollar bill. This was the most money I ever had at one time. Now came the problem: how was I going to spend it? Well, for starters, I bought my Mom a Toastmaster pop-up toaster and an electric percolator coffee pot. She was totally taken by surprise that Christmas morning to receive such elegant gifts, especially from me. I also got her a box of lace handkerchiefs that had a "T" on them. I can still remember that grown-up feeling I had and how very proud I was. I don't recall what my gift was that Christmas, but that special feeling I had was gift enough.

The Son of a Boilermaker

Chapter 6

Coming of Age
(1947–1948)

Seventh Grade at Grant School

I had wanted a bicycle for a long time before I ever got one. Other kids would let me ride their bikes, so I was an accomplished two-wheel bike rider by the time I was eight years old. Mom kept telling me I wasn't old enough, or that I might get hit by a car. Chuck Switzer had two bikes. Once he got his blue and white "Monarch," he let me use his old bike, but I really wanted a bike of my own.

It wasn't until my twelfth birthday, September 5, 1947, that I finally got my first bike. I had just started the seventh grade at Grant School, and when I got home, it was sitting on the front porch. It was a red "Dixie Flyer" with shiny chrome fenders and chain guard. It had white-wall tires and a red reflector on the back of the seat. The handle bars had a little bit of rust on them and one of the grips was missing, but on that day it was the sharpest bike I had ever seen. Mom told me that the old man had chipped in half of the money to buy it, so the gift was from both of them, which made me appreciate it all the more.

I rode my "Dixie Flyer" all over town, only curtailing my riding when the ground was snow covered. This, however, only lasted for a little over a year, because by the time I was in the eighth grade, riding bikes was no longer considered cool. So, with some reluctance, I set aside this youthful pleasure to bend to the will of the majority. Somehow, my bike disappeared after one of our moves, but even though I only had it a short while, my "Dixie Flyer" was the best gift I ever got as a kid.

During these awkward years, when puberty was just starting to get a grip on me, I was often confused and conflicted about the ways of the world. At times, I was self-assured yet self-doubt cast its shadow over much of my life. My horizons, however, were broadened considerably whenever I got an extended visit with Aunt Polly. Weeks before school let out for summer vacation, I'd jump the gun and begin to pester Mom about when I could go visit Aunt Polly. I could never get a straight answer, so I worried constantly about whether I'd be allowed to go. As it turned out, it was often a last-minute deal, but Mom gave in, motivated by her need to get some temporary relief from a troublesome son. So, she proceeded to make all the necessary arrangements for Uncle Walter to pick me up on a date certain.

Among the people I knew, there was no such thing as an annual family vacation. The closest thing to a vacation would usually mean spending a week with some relative who lived somewhere outside the city limits of Steubenville. If, per chance, somebody did take a vacation to some exotic place like Oglebay Park in Wheeling, West Virginia, this was reported in the Herald Star along with a picture of the fortunate travelers, grinning and posing beside the swimming pool. As for me, I was lucky; I got to visit Turkeyfoot Lake, home to Aunt Polly and Uncle Walter.

Aunt Polly, my dad's step-sister, was a striking beauty with platinum hair and milk white skin. She dripped with jewelry and wore big hats that matched her large and flamboyant personality. Uncle Walter was Aunt Polly's fourth or fifth husband. He was about fifteen years younger than she and was a paint salesman for O'Brien Paint Company. Uncle Walter was a tall man who was neither skinny nor fat. His brown hair was combed straight back from a receding hairline. The most prominent feature on his intelligent face was his long, hawk-like nose. A well-trimmed, pencil-thin mustache on his upper lip lent a certain sophistication to his appearance. These physical attributes, along with his natty clothes, made Uncle Walter just one brick shy of handsome. He had a dry sense of humor and I often had to think about what he said for a few moments before I caught the drift of his sarcastic remarks. Walter was a kook, but he was the smartest relative I had. He loved to play the horses, cussed a lot and was an alcoholic, but he treated me like I thought a father should treat his son. Uncle Walter was my first role model.

Walter picked me up and drove me to his and Aunt Polly's home on Turkeyfoot Lake for my summer visit. The drive from Steubenville was about eighty miles and we didn't get far before car sickness overtook me and I began to wretch. He had to stop the car three or four times for me to get out and throw up. This didn't get my visit off to a promising start. Nonetheless, Walter would make some choice comments about my lack of sophistication and question my heritage while taking it all in stride.

The turn off from the highway that led to their home was a gravel road about a half-mile long. At the entrance was a sign that read "Polly-Wally Drive." Their home was a two-story affair of wooden construction that faced the water and had a front yard that sloped down to a small wooden boat dock. The house was much larger and far better than anything I was used to. It was furnished with fine couches, comfortable chairs and fancy lamps with carpet on the floor, not the worn linoleum we had at home. Prior to leaving home, I had been warned to always wipe my feet before going inside, not to break anything and to try and keep my mouth shut. This last warning from my Mom was a big order.

There was no set time period for the length of my stay. Usually it lasted about three weeks or until they got tired of having me around. Along with Aunt Polly and Uncle Walter, the house was occupied by Grandma Twyford, or the "Old Lady," two parrots and a shepherd dog. During the week, Walter traveled, making his sales calls. He returned on weekends to do the cooking, drink and fight with Aunt Polly. He'd take me fishing for bluegills and rock bass, which he taught me how to clean. He'd fry these fish up for breakfast, which tasted much better than the cornflakes I got at home. Uncle Walter was the first person I knew who cooked on an outdoor grill. Only on rare occasions did I get steak at home. When I did, it was a tough cut of round steak fried in a skillet until it was black and difficult to chew. The first time I had a real steak, it was a medium rare T-Bone that Walter cooked on the grill. I got the whole steak for myself, which I could hardly believe. I asked if this delicious meat was really steak and if you could buy it in Steubenville. Walter had some choice remarks about my ignorance and unworldly lack of breeding as I gnawed the last bit of meat from the bone.

Aunt Polly had a large white domestic duck she kept as a pet. The duck's name was "Mrs. Quack Quack,' and had learned to respond to her name whenever called. Normally, domestic ducks have clipped wings to prevent them from flying away. However, Mrs. Quack Quack's wings were fully intact, so she was free to roam the entire environs of Turkeyfoot Lake.

Each evening, after Aunt Polly had polished off a few highballs, she'd go out in the front yard and summon Mrs. Quack Quack for supper. With a pail of corn in her hand, she'd repeatedly call in a shrieking soprano "Mrs. Quack Quack, Mrs. Quack Quack." Passersby in boats, fisherman and neighbors from across the lake were treated to this evening concert of duck calls. After four or five of these harsh communications pierced the tranquil lakeside scene, Mrs. Quack Quack came soaring in above the tree tops, quacking loud enough to drown out Aunt Polly. She'd land in the water with a big splash and then waddle up the walkway to be greeted by her proud owner and a handful of corn.

There came a time when Mrs. Quack Quack failed to respond to these evening calls, and Aunt Polly hollered for her until her voice was gone and dejectedly returned to the house. Finally, after two weeks and no duck, Aunt Polly gave up all hope of ever being reunited with her beloved fowl.

A short time later, I was fishing with my cane pole off a small bridge that spanned a lagoon a half-mile from the house. I'd let my red and white bobber drift back under the bridge and hook a bluegill every time. It was a quiet spot on this lazy summer afternoon when the tranquility was interrupted by a faint clicking and clacking sound coming from under the bridge. I climbed down to investigate and found Mrs. Quack Quack swimming in circles with a dozen fuzzy yellow and black ducklings. She wasn't the least bit afraid of me as I reached out a hand and gently stroked her head. I ran back to the house and got a wagon out of the garage. When I returned, I said, "Come on, Mrs. Quack Quack, it's time to go home." Without any protest, I loaded our missing duck and her brood into the wagon and pulled the family down the dusty road toward home. Just as I got to the house, Aunt Polly and Uncle Walter pulled up in the car. Aunt Polly got hysterical, crying tears of joy and Walter was laughing his ass off. "Wait right there," he said and went in the house to get his camera. He took my picture posing with the wagon load of ducks. For many years, this story would be told again and again by Aunt Polly and Walter.

The Old Lady had a small bony frame covered with parchment like skin that was wrinkled and dotted with liver spots. Had it not been for a set of dentures, her nose and stubbled chin would have surely touched. Upon my arrival at Aunt Polly's, she'd say in her West Virginia twang, "Tommy, come over and give your Mammy a big kiss rite cheer," as she pointed to a spot on her withered cheek with a skinny forefinger.

She had fine-spun gray and brown hair she wore in a knot at the back of her head. Occasionally she'd summon me to her bedroom as she readied herself for bed. Her hair hung down well below her waist. If she had already put her teeth in the bedside jar for their overnight stay, her appearance was drop dead frightening. It took all the courage a twelve-year-old boy could muster to approach her for her good night kiss on the cheek.

For the most part, she was very nice to me, and I'd run little errands for her. This would include going over to the store on the lake and buying her three bottles of beer. She swore me to secrecy about the contraband, and as I snuck the bottles to her room, she'd press two pennies into my hand and give me a sly wink. Her outward demeanor was that of a sweet old lady, but there was a side to her that was as mean as a copperhead.

Aunt Polly and the Old Lady were constantly bickering. The Old Lady would alternately take sides with "Pauline" or Walter in their never-ending disputes. Then, sometimes Aunt Polly and Walter would gang up against the Old Lady. One or the other of them was always trying to get me to take their side. Youthful as I was, I had enough sense to maintain my neutrality. Walter had taught the parrot to say, "Go to hell, Grandma." While some of their arguments were raging, the bird would be screaming this favorite epithet over and over. Then the other parrot would chime in with a chorus of "Glad-Ass-Happy Butt," (Gladys was Aunt Polly's middle name). This got her further pissed off at Walter, and before you knew it, it was pandemonium.

After one particularly heated argument between Aunt Polly and Walter, when they both had more than their fair share of booze, Walter stormed out of the house with his pistol. A few moments later there were two shots fired. Aunt Polly and the Old Lady went screaming out into the front yard, where they found Walter sprawled on the walkway, his chest covered with blood. They were hysterical and failed to notice that Walter had one eye open to take in their reaction to this suicide of their loved one. The blood, however, smelled like Heinz ketchup. Fortunately, Uncle Walter made a full recovery from the ketchup stains suffered in his suicide attempt. He would live to fight another day with Aunt Polly and the Old Lady.

One day I discovered, quite by accident, that the brush on both sides of Polly-Wally Drive was full of blueberry bushes. I didn't know a blueberry from a turnip and wasn't sure if they were safe to eat. So, I picked a handful and showed them to the Old Lady, who made an immediate identification. The taste was sweet and the berries were full of juice. The Old Lady told me she would bake a pie for me, so I set off for the bushes with pail in hand. The bushes were loaded and it didn't take long to fill up the container. That's when I got the idea that I could make some serious money from this lucky find.

It only took a day or two before I had set up a roadside stand on the highway. I made a sign on a large piece of cardboard which read "Blueberries For Sale-25 cents a quart." The blueberries were at their peak of ripeness and full of juice, and as I popped them in my mouth I enjoyed the sweet taste. The blue lips and mustache that I sported were a tell-tale sign of my new business venture. The berries sold as fast as I could get them picked, so I spent hour after hour hunched over in the underbrush, picking berries at a furious pace. When I set the price at 25 cents a quart, I didn't realize just how hazardous berry picking could be. The entire area was infested with snakes. I'm sure they were harmless, but I think their presence would have justified an increase of 10 cents a quart. The snakes were a minor inconvenience when compared to the chiggers and ticks. I was under constant attack from these blood-suckers. They were on my clothes, in my hair, on my skin, under my skin and driving me crazy. After a week of this torture, I closed the berry business for good. However, the rash, red marks and welts stayed with me for the rest of the summer. Once I got back home, I was denied admission to the swimming pool and declared a health hazard as a suspected carrier of some contagious disease.

As for Aunt Polly and Uncle Walter, their insane relationship continued until sometime in the mid-1950s, when Walter split for good. Aunt Polly didn't show signs of aging until she was well past fifty. She then came up with the idea of going to California and getting a face lift so she could marry some wealthy ambassador.

* * *

This was the summer that Puddy Robinson told me about the facts of life. Puddy was two years older than me and had been our neighbor when we lived at 930 North Fifth Street. We really weren't the best of friends, but it made him feel important to see that I was impressed by his stories and grown-up exploits.

Like most of my friends, I was under strict orders not to go swimming in the river. Aside from the water being polluted with raw sewage, the current was swift and the Ohio River had a reputation for tragic drownings. In spite of this, the lure of the river proved too much of a temptation. We had a special place where we went to swim which we tagged B.A.B. (Bare Ass Beach). As the name would suggest, we swam in the nude.

One day, I was hanging out with Puddy and he told me that he had been to B.A.B. and saw three women swimming naked. He said they came at about the same time every day and he'd hide in the bushes to watch them. He went on to describe every part of their anatomy in graphic detail. I told him I didn't believe it, but Puddy said he'd prove it to me if I wanted to come along. He swore me to secrecy and said I was the only person he had told about this erotic discovery.

For the next three days, we took off for B.A.B. at the E.T.A. and hid in the bushes, where we had a clear view of the swimming area. After the third day, I was convinced that Puddy was a bullshitter. There were no girls, clothed or otherwise. I decided to give it one more day and then call it quits. Sure enough, on the fourth day as we looked out from behind a clump of weeds, our quarry appeared strolling down the dusty path toward the river. There were three of them laughing and talking, totally unaware that they were being eye-balled by two sex-craved peeping Toms. Puddy had described to me what he'd seen so many times that I'd formed a definite picture in my mind of what to expect. As it turned out, Puddy's description was woefully understated.

They wasted no time in discarding their shorts, panties, halters and bras. Before they could get in the water, I got an eyeful. The vision of these voluptuous bodies made me feel good, bad, strange, excited and kind of crazy all at the same time. In a word, it was terrific. It was clear that they weren't mere girls, but real women. I guessed their ages to be about eighteen or twenty. One of the dark-haired women had the largest titties. They stood out just like the headlights on the 1936 Cord automobile that some guy who lived around the corner from me kept parked in the alley. I would have traded my entire comic book collection just to cup my hand under one of those beauts and give it a couple of jiggles.

It was a hot day and they seemed content to stay in the water, which was up to their necks. To my pleasure, however, every once in a while they'd bounce up and down, exposing a breast or two. They also performed this cute little dive under the water, which added a new dimension to the show. Finally, they got out of the water one by one and stood around drying their bodies in the sun. This reminded me of some pictures I once saw in Sunshine and

Health magazine, but the pictures couldn't compare to the real in the flesh thing.

For some reason, my eyes were drawn to their large patches of pubic hair. One of them had hair that was a reddish-blond color and looked kind of wispy. The other two had hair between their legs that was thick and black. They took their good old time getting dressed. We waited until they walked back up the dirt trail. Then we stood up, the show over.

We had been crouched down in the bushes and completely silent the whole time we were viewing the naked swim. As soon as they left, Puddy said, "Well, did that give you a hard-on?" I can't recall whether or not I gave him an answer. As we walked up the road away from the river, he said to me, "You're so dumb I bet you don't even know how babies are made." It was at this point that I got a crude explanation of the process of procreation. The only thing I could think of was that there was no way my Mom would do that.

What Puddy and I had just done must have fit into some category of sinning. I felt kinda guilty, but not so bad that I wouldn't do it again. This made me wonder if I'd feel any differently if I were Catholic rather than Methodist.

Catholics made up a large percentage of the population of Steubenville. Consequently, I had many friends of this faith and got to know some things about their beliefs. The Catholic kids I knew from the neighborhood possessed a blind faith and certainty about a God that would reward good behavior and exact harsh punishment upon sinners. The sins were even classified between mortal and venial, meaning big sins and little sins. However, Catholic kids had an out when it came to punishment for sins, big or little. All they had to do was go to confession and "poof" – just like that the sin was erased from their heavenly scorecard. I had a great admiration for the unwavering faith of Catholics.

A literal interpretation of the Bible was supposed to be the word of God, and there was no leeway given to pick and choose what you were to believe or not to believe. The way I understood it was that to be a real Christian, you had to believe it all. Now, I'm not saying I was ever a deep thinker when it came to theology, but I experienced a real problem making the leap of faith required to be the Christian I was supposed to be. This wasn't something that was ever discussed. I couldn't ask Reverend Peterson if Jesus really fed ten thousand Jews with one fish and one loaf of bread. Even to my young impressionable mind, I couldn't help but think that there would be one helluva lot of hungry Jews. But to be absolutely honest, I really didn't give the subject of religion a great deal of thought.

Although I didn't have a strong religious faith in the Almighty, I think my exposure to some of the things at Sunday school and church rubbed off on me. I had an acute sense of right and wrong, which came in handy since I was often left to my own devices in facing issues of fairness and morality. While I wasn't overly strict with my personal code of conduct, I seemed to know where to draw the line. Many times I found myself in situations that could have spelled serious trouble for me. With little or no adult supervision, it's a minor miracle that I didn't end up in reform school. Some of the trouble I dodged was just blind luck, but on some occasions, I made conscious decisions to take the moral high road.

One such situation presented itself when I was about 13 and a boy named Buzz Malloy moved to town from Pennsylvania. At first glance, he appeared to be fat, but he was powerfully built at about 170 pounds. He had a wide mean streak and bullied all the kids at the YMCA. Buzz was a natural athlete who used his physical strength and intimidation to acquire a position of leadership with the boys at the Y. Buzz joined our swimming team and exhibited talent as good or better than our best swimmers.

It was winter and five of us guys were just hanging out after leaving swim practice. As we walked up Franklin Avenue, Buzzy called our attention to a man coming out of the Field Club, which was a neighborhood bar. We were across the street and could see the man staggering as he made his way down the street. Buzz said "watch me" as he crossed the street and approached the drunk. He said something I couldn't hear, but all of a sudden Buzz delivered two vicious blows to the man's face, knocking him to the snow-covered ground. The man didn't move as Buzz drug him into a narrow alley and rifled through his pockets. He then just sauntered back across the street with a wad of bills in his hand. The rest of us guys were shocked and I, for one, was scared shitless. I had never been witness to such a violent act. Buzz was laughing and said that rolling drunks was an easy way to make money. I could see the man still lying in the alley and not moving. "I think we better go see if he's O.K.," I said. Buzz grabbed my arm and pushed me roughly on the chest. "Come on, we're leaving," he said and we all walked away. After we were a block or so away and around the corner, Buzz started to count the money he had taken from the man. He started to divvy it up with the rest of us. When I told him I didn't want any of that money, he threatened to beat the shit out of me, and probably would have. When the other guys also refused to share in the loot, he called us all chickens and we just drifted our separate ways.

I couldn't sleep that night, thinking about the man lying in the alley. The next morning, before school, I walked up to take a look and to my relief, the alley was empty. Did I refuse to share in the money because I knew it was wrong? Or did I say no to this thug because I was afraid I would get caught? Most likely, it was the combination of the two, but I would like to believe that somewhere inside me was a trace of goodness that rebelled against this cruel act.

* * *

Uncle Tom lived in Cincinnati. He and his wife, Aunt Marie, had two children, Sharon, who was two years younger than me, and Tommy, who was seven years my junior. We only saw Uncle Tom and his family about once a year, when they made their annual pilgrimage to Steubenville on Memorial Day to visit the grave of Grandma Woods. When they came to town, they stayed with friends who lived just outside Steubenville. Each year, Mom looked forward to these visits from her brother and his family with great anticipation. They'd arrive and we'd all go to the cemetery and stand around the gravesite while Aunt Marie took pictures of me posed with my two cousins Mom and Uncle Tom placed flowers on the grave of their mother.

I always thought of Uncle Tom as being our rich relative, and why wouldn't I? They drove a nice car, wore fancy clothes and I had seen pictures of their beautiful home with a fish pond in the backyard. Aunt Marie liked to "put on the dog" and I got a clear impression that we were viewed by them as their poor relatives. In point of fact, my Uncle Tom was most likely not a wealthy man, but when compared to us, it seemed that way.

Mom made sure to have a roast or chicken prepared in hopes that they would stay for dinner, but they were always in a hurry to get out of Dodge. Often they had just enough time for a cup of coffee. It must have been uncomfortable for them to sit down and share a meal with us in such shabby surroundings. This was very hurtful to Mom, but they had performed their duty and their good friends were expecting them. So much for our rich relatives for another year.

I cannot neglect to mention that when I was about twelve years old, Uncle Tom invited me to go with them on their family vacation to Canada. It was the only real vacation I had ever had, and it was to be a week's stay at a fishing lodge in Gracefield, Quebec. The trip started with me taking the train from Steubenville to Cincinnati. Even though I never lived more than a block or two from the railroad tracks, I had never taken an actual trip on a passenger train. It was pretty much an all-day ride, so Mom packed a lunch for me to eat on the train. I remember my shock when I went into the dining car to order a glass of milk to drink with my sandwich and was told by this black guy in a starched white coat, "That will be twenty-five cents, sir." The milk didn't even fill up the glass, which was sitting on a silver tray with a paper doily under it. He was standing there with the tray and staring at me, so I got out my change purse and dug out two bits and forked it over.

We left Cincinnati in Uncle Tom's Plymouth with me and my two cousins in the back seat. Cars were not equipped with air conditioning then, so it was a long, hot ride that took two days. It was interrupted every so often with my need to get out and puke. One good thing about it was I could always feel it coming on when excessive saliva began to accumulate in my mouth. Then, with a hand partially covering my lips, I'd give a mumbled warning and scramble out the back door just as the car was rolling to a stop. I could feel all eyes from the car staring at my back as I shuddered with the last wretch of vomit I could force up from my sour stomach. About this time, old Uncle Tom and Aunt Marie were probably having serious misgivings about extending the generosity of a summer vacation to their pukey nephew. We stopped in Ottawa, where I got my picture taken with a Royal Canadian Mounted Policeman standing on the steps of the Parliament Building. Lucky for me, I avoided puking on the Parliament steps or the policeman.

When we arrived at our destination, it was a classic, rustic lodge situated on a lake with water so clear you could see all the rocks on the bottom. We stayed in a comfortable log cabin not far from the lodge. At mealtime, a bell rang signaling us to the lodge. We spent the days fishing, swimming and playing ping-pong in the gameroom at the lodge. What sticks in my mind is that I caught a sturgeon, wrote my Mom a letter on a piece of birch bark and saw a river crammed for miles with logs floating downstream to the sawmill. Also, I seem to recall that I did something that got Aunt Marie pissed off at me. What it was I can't remember, but her aggravation was likely justified.

There must have been something about me that called out to folks, "Hey, take this poor kid on vacation," because when I was thirteen the preacher informed me that the congregation was coughing up the dough to send me to church camp for a week. It cost twelve bucks, but he didn't say why I was the only kid in the church they were sending to camp. I pretty much figured out that they were trying to do something nice for a poor kid. Now, to tell the honest to God's truth, I wouldn't have spent my own twelve bucks to go to church camp. I would have gone to YMCA camp, which cost the same amount of money. I thought church camp might be something like a week-long sermon, but there was no way I could refuse the generosity, and as it turned out, I'm darn glad I didn't.

The camp was located on a lake in Harrison County about forty miles from Steubenville. I had never attended a summer camp and was excited about the prospect of this unexpected opportunity. The place was just as I had imagined a summer camp to be. There were separate dormitory buildings which housed boys and girls, a large mess hall that doubled as a classroom, and several other buildings on the campgrounds for the counselors and the camp director. There was a large outdoor amphitheater built around a fire pit, where nighttime sing-a-longs and programs with religious themes were presented. Our mornings were devoted primarily to religious instruction. However, each afternoon was set aside for more traditional camp activities such as crafts, swimming, boating and soft ball. Predictably, I liked the afternoons the best. I would imagine that the whole idea of a Methodist church camp was to instill in all the campers some kind of pious thinking in line with

Methodist doctrine. I can't really say that this is what happened to me, and it made me feel bad that the congregation had wasted their twelve bucks on Tommy Twyford.

One memory I took home from church camp that was burned in my brain was the image of a girl named Bonnie. She was a saucy little blond with short hair, blue eyes and a compact figure that featured small but perky breasts. For reasons that still remain a mystery to me, she took a shine to me from the first day. Aside from her looks, what I liked about her was that she wasn't too overboard with this Jesus stuff. She and I swam together each afternoon and by the third day, we were holding hands. By day number five, we were swapping spit.

On the last night of camp, we were sitting together in the back row of the amphitheater during a sing-along. We were watching the sparks from the fire drift high into the summer night as we sang a camp song called "John Jacob Jingleheimer Schmidt." I had my right arm draped over her shoulder with my hand resting on the bare skin above the halter she was wearing. I could feel the heat from her sunburned shoulder against my hand. As she moved closer to me and smiled, my hand found refuge inside her halter. I was transported to heaven, but not by any spiritual awakening. My hand stayed on the edge of the gentle swell of her breast until the final verse of "John Jacob" was just an echo in the surrounding hills.

The next day was Sunday. It was time to go home and Bonnie and I promised we would keep in touch with each other. I never saw or heard from her again. Had the people from the church ever found out about my camp conduct, I would have been the first kid ever to be excommunicated from the Fifth Street Methodist Church.

Chapter 7

Life in Transition

1950 DuMont "Hanover"

There were two junior high schools in town. Harding was for the hilltop kids and Grant was for those of us who lived downtown. The seventh grade took kids from all the downtown grade schools, so I had new classmates as well as my old friends from Garfield.

Grant School was a more modern building than Garfield. The building had three floors with lockers that lined the hallways. I got my own locker, which was a really big deal to a seventh grader. Going to junior high was a major change since I now had a different teacher for each subject. I also had male teachers for the first time, which seemed odd to me. I soon adjusted to this new environment. There was a much wider ethnic diversity of kids at Grant and many more black kids than I had gone to school with before. Compared to the kids at Harding Junior High, we were a much rougher bunch. We called the kids who lived on the hill and went to Harding "cookie pushers." Part of the differences can be explained by the less favorable economic circumstances of the families of the Grant School pupils.

My academic performance in junior high was, in a word, lackluster. I seemed to have trouble with math and science. Report card day was as predictable as a full moon. Mom would drag out my sisters' and brother's grade cards she kept in a special box and show them to me, hoping it would spur me on to bigger and better things. She'd compare my report card, subject by subject, with those of her other three children. I'd just stand there with this blank look, or sometimes make a smart aleck remark and be threatened with dire punishment. There was space on each report card marked Deportment/Behavior, with a place for the teacher to make written comments. Most of the time they ran out of space and wrote "continued on back." Believe me, none of it was good. Report cards came out every six weeks and this same scenario was repeated so often it became sort of a family ritual.

Nevertheless, I did seem to inherit some family gene that predisposed me to acting and participating in plays, shows at school, church and elsewhere. I never had any fear of appearing before an audience. Most likely this had something to do with my need to be noticed. I got parts in plays at Grant School and by doing so gained Mom's approval. What was most important, however, was that teachers and classmates told me I was pretty darn good. This gave a boost to my confidence and self-esteem at a time when I needed it most.

One course I came as close to failing as any was shop. I knew from the first day that I was not a "shop guy." Being raised in a home with three women, the only tools we had were a pair of pliers, a screwdriver and a hammer. When something in our house was broken and needed fixed, we were completely stymied as how to remedy the problem. Whether it was a window, door, toilet, sink or furnace that needed repair, if the landlord wouldn't get a repairman to fix it, it stayed broken. When the accumulation of needed repairs in the house got too burdensome, we just moved.

Shortly after school started in the fall of 1947, when I was twelve, we moved again. This time we moved to the south end of town, back to the same old neighborhood we lived in when I was born. The house we moved to wasn't really a house, but a second-floor apartment above a vacant commercial brick building. The place was built on an incline. The front entrance from the street opened to a narrow, steep and poorly lit enclosed stairway. The back door opened to ground level, which was an alley. The apartment had two bedrooms, a living room, kitchen and bath. There was little natural light which made the place gloomy. What light there was was filtered through permanent grime that covered the windows.

Directly across the street built up to the level of our apartment were railroad tracks. At least fifty times a day, the building shook and windows rattled as the dust and soot was re-arranged throughout the apartment with each passing train. It was difficult to be heard over the vibration of the cars, hum of the tracks and the shrieking blasts of the whistle as the engine approached the overpass. Conversation was kept to a minimum, but I resorted to shouting if whatever words needed to be spoken couldn't wait, such as "GODDAMMIT, I HAVE TO USE THE CAN."

I actually liked being around trains, as there was something about them that I found exotic and exciting, especially passenger trains. This was undoubtedly connected with my yearning to travel to far away places. Whenever I saw a train, my curiosity about distant people and destinations was stimulated. This in turn made me discontent with the sameness of my life. I knew that somewhere beyond Steubenville there were mysterious and amazing places I'd one day visit. It troubled me somewhat that I was plagued with motion sickness, which could cramp my style when it came time to see the world. But, I told myself that by then, some brainy scientist would have found a cure, and I would be on my way free from any fear of blowing my beets in front of a bunch of foreigners.

One thing I didn't accept graciously was the sleeping arrangements. Think about it: Mom, two sisters and me. I suggested that since I was the only man in the house, I deserved my own private sleeping quarters. This suggestion was promptly overruled. Then I expressed my idea of at least drawing straws as my last hope of retaining some dignity, but this didn't fly either. As it wound up, my sisters shared a bedroom and I got to sleep on a cot in Mom's bedroom or out on the living room couch. I did, however, get my own dresser, where I could keep my clothes and other belongings, but this too had its drawbacks.

The bedroom I was to share with Mom and where my cot and dresser were located I called the "mildew room," and this wasn't because we ever had a President named Mildew. This place had steam heat that was erratic in providing warmth. The radiators located in each room popped and sweated as hot water and steam circulated through them. The walls would sweat and the rooms were either like steam baths or, at other times, freezing. However, dampness in this place was a constant, winter or summer alike. The corner of Mom's bedroom assigned to me was the worst. Mildew and other unidentified spores and fungus covered every surface. The decision to sleep out on the couch in the living room was an easy one to make.

Our new neighborhood in the south end was dominated by first and second-generation Italians. Most of the heads of household were employed in the steel mills, as was true of all neighborhoods in Steubenville, but the Italian influence was everywhere. There were lighted bocce courts where old Italian guys with fedoras on their heads and black stogies stuck in their mouths rolled the wooden balls on dirt surfaces in wooden enclosures. The corner grocery store was owned and operated by people whose names ended in either O or A and spoke in Italian or broken English to their customers. Balls of provolone cheese hung from the ceiling, as well as tubes of salami and bunches of fresh garlic, all of which combined gave off an aroma of the old country. On Saturdays, there were cages of live chickens stacked on the sidewalk in front of the store. These doomed fowls were purchased alive to be taken home where their necks were wrung and heads chopped off Often, I would see these headless birds hanging on clotheslines in back yards so they could bleed before the feathers were plucked. The smell of spaghetti sauce, garlic and olive oil drifted from the houses as I passed by. Sometimes the sound of an Italian vocalist singing an aria or folk song could be heard coming from an old Victrola.

The next-door neighbors at our new residence were Rose and Peter Lanzia. They had four kids: Mario was my age, Nino was a year younger, Linda was about eight, and the baby, little Pietro. They were great people and I quickly made friends with Mario and Nino. Naturally, they were Catholics, so they attended Holy Name School, but we hung around together after school and on weekends. I was always made to feel welcomed in their home.

Mrs. Lanzia kept a pot of sauce, or gravy as it was sometimes called, on the stove while she baked her own bread. Just the smell of this combination in her kitchen triggered hunger pangs in me, even if I'd just eaten. The kids hung around the kitchen asking when supper would be ready. To pacify everyone, and to tide them over until the meal was ready, she'd flatten out some leftover dough, spread a little sauce from the pot on it and put it in the oven. After ten minutes, it came steaming out of the oven and she'd shake some grated Romano cheese on top. This was the first pizza I ever tasted and I was hooked for life.

Mr. Lanzia was a man of few words. It was clear that he would tolerate no nonsense from his kids or their friends. He'd assign chores to Mario and Nino that I'd sometimes help them with so we could get on to the more important things we wanted to do. He stood tall and erect and was proud of his Italian heritage. Every few years he'd take a trip to visit his birthplace in Italy. On one of these trips, he purchased a large hand-cut crystal chandelier and had it shipped home. All the Lanzias were eager for the arrival of this new addition to their home. This splendid acquisition arrived from Italy in a huge box, completely intact. The facets of this one-of-a-kind ceiling fixture glittered and sparkled, bathing the living room in brilliant light. There was not one stick of furniture in the room to distract attention from this resplendent work of art. People came from all over the neighborhood and beyond to view this glowing light source. Mr. Lanzia gave a detailed narration in broken English of the history behind his acquisition of the chandelier and included the price he paid. At this point, everyone in the room let out a gasp as Mr. Lanzia smiled and nodded his head up and down. It was like some kind of shrine and I lived right across the alley from it.

* * *

It was easy for me to make friends and it wasn't long before I had acquired a wide network of friendships and acquaintances at Grant School. I made a conscious effort to be Mr. Personality. One tactic I used to gain acceptance was playing the role of the class joker. Wisecracking and clowning around often got me in trouble with the teachers.

Corporal punishment was used with a fair amount of frequency at Grant School to deal with some of the higher forms of misbehavior. Due to my practice of habitually tempting the rules, it was only a matter of time before I found myself on the receiving end of this physical reminder of who was running the show at Grant School.

Elwood Johnson and I were fooling around in the classroom before the bell rang to signal the start of math class. We thought it would be a good idea to grab Billy Quattrociocche and stuff him ass-first into the teacher's metal waste basket. Since Billy had small loins, the fit was perfect, if not somewhat tight. Everyone was laughing and Billy was raising hell and cursing me and Elwood just as Mr. Morrison walked in the room. Things quieted down in a hurry. Mr. Morrison didn't have to ask what was going on or who all was involved in this caper. He ordered Billy to get out of the waste basket, but there was no way that this was possible. He grabbed Billy's legs, which were sticking up in the air, and started tugging on them. It was a foolish spectacle– Mr. Morrison trying to win this tug of war and the rest of the class who were seated at their desks were cracking up. His face got redder and redder and finally Billy popped out of the can, like a cork out of a wine bottle. At this, he ordered me, Elwood and Billy to the principal's office. Billy was protesting his innocence, but it did no good. We were marched in the office before the principal, Mr. Snyder. Mr. Morrison explained in detail what had happened. When he finished, Mr. Snyder reached under his desk and pulled out a wooden paddle with round holes drilled in it and handed it to Mr. Morrison. At this point, Billy was crying and trying to explain that he was the victim in all this. It did no good. We were all ordered to bend over and put our hands on our knees.

Billy was first to get whacked. It was just one blow that sounded like a rifle shot and knocked him across the room, where he lay crumpled against the wall whimpering. I set my jaw and gritted my teeth as I knew I was next. It felt like I got hit in the ass by a lightning bolt and I found myself lying across the room on top of Billy. It was then that Elwood let out this big whooping laugh. Suddenly Mr. Morrison was talking real nice to me and Billy and consoling us in our pain. He told us to go back to the classroom, then turned to Elwood and told him to wait. Did I say that Elwood was big? Well, he was twice the size of either Billy or me. About ten minutes after we got back in the classroom, in came Elwood and he was no longer laughing. He remained standing, unable to sit at his desk, until class was dismissed for the day.

Steubenville had one policeman whose job it was to keep kids on the straight and narrow. His name was Officer Mavromates and he had a knack for reforming would-be criminals without the necessity of lawyers, judges, court hearings or probation officers. A well-placed crack to the side of the head, a backhand to stifle some wise guy, or as in my case, a forcible bounce against a wooden fence usually got his point across. When he told me some of the details of what a two-year stretch at B.I.S. (Boys Industrial School) would be like, he made a law abiding citizen out of me.

My one and only venture into a life of crime occurred when I was an eighth grader. Like most criminals, I didn't start out trying to make a big score, as I wanted to make sure I got the hang of it first. I'd start with "small stuff" then graduate to the big time when I had honed my skills as a thief. A lot of kids I knew at Grant School shoplifted stuff from the five-and-dime stores. Mostly, they stole cheap rings, bracelets or trinkets which they'd offer for sale at lunchtime or after school. This hot merchandise could usually be had at a negotiated price of anywhere from ten cents to two bits per item.

I'm not really sure I made a conscious decision to become a criminal; it kind of just happened. While I was bumming around in McCroy's Five & Dime, I found myself in the pet department. They had everything from goldfish to guinea pigs, as well as a full line of supplies and equipment for dogs and cats. What caught my eye was this red dog collar that had these shiny metal studs attached to the leather. My first thought was, "Wouldn't Boogie look great wearing this?" I checked out the price and it was obvious why it was the best looking dog collar I had ever seen; it cost three bucks. It was at that moment I began to formulate a criminal intent. I looked over my shoulder, walked around the pet department several times passing my target collar, pretending not to look as I went by. Finally, after making sure the coast was clear, I snatched up that sucker and stuck it under my shirt in a New York second. As soon as the heist was completed, I made a bee-line for the exit. Out on the street, I walked at a fast pace, looking over my shoulder to make sure I wasn't being followed. After about two blocks, I slowed down and breathed a sigh of relief. I was in the clear.

Just as I thought, Boogie looked like something special in this red leather collar with the shiny metal studs. She had been wearing the "hot" collar for about a week before my Mom even noticed it. I had forgotten to make up a story to cover my tracks, so when she asked me where the collar came from, I hemmed and hawed and said, "I found it." Mom took the collar from Boogie's neck, examined it, then gave me this funny look as she asked again, "Where DID the collar come from?" I knew I was busted and it was time to cop a plea. I fought to hold back the tears as the discussion turned to the possibility of me residing at B.I.S. The next day after school, I met Mom in front of McCroy's and we proceeded to the pet department, where she asked to speak to the manager. I had such a hangdog look that the collar would have looked better on me than it did on Boogie. As the manager approached, Mom took the collar out of her purse and handed it to me, saying to the manager, "My son Tommy has something to tell you." It was the ultimate humiliation. Mom and I walked home in silence and the incident was never mentioned again.

My actions in trying to enter a life of crime had made me deeply ashamed. I didn't look like a crook. However, I was acutely aware of projecting a sharp personal image. My God-given physical appearance dictated that I needed all the help I could get.

I'd stand in front of the mirror over the sink combing and re-combing the pompadour in my hair. When I thought I had the part and the swoop just right, I'd dip my comb in a bottle of this green-colored gooey liquid called "Dippity Doo" that Mom kept on the bathroom shelf, and comb the sticky gunk into my pompadour. Within a matter of seconds, the stuff would start to harden and after a minute or so, a category five hurricane wouldn't cause one hair to budge.

One or two-chair barbershops were located in most Steubenville neighborhoods. I knew a lot of kids at Garfield and Grant school who sported only homemade cuts. These homemade jobs were easy to spot, since any hair hanging below the rim of a cereal bowl was snipped off with sewing scissors. What was left after the bowl was removed was a round ring of hair, that I called a "Friar Tuck Haircut," a named I borrowed from the movie Robin Hood.

My first haircuts were at Ralph's Barber Shop, which was a two chair establishment. Ralph Marzocco was a close family friend, so my head was cut at a discount from the regular twenty-five cent price. The second chair was manned by a guy from the old country named Tony. Each time I went to the shop, it was my hope that Ralph would cut my hair. He had a gentler touch with the clippers than Tony and didn't hurt as much. However, when I heard the word "next" it was usually Tony beckoning me to his chair. He began by setting a board across the arms of the chair for me to sit on, which brought my head to eye level. He'd secure a ring of tissue paper around my neck with a white sheet, leaving only my head exposed. Then began the pinching of the tender skin of my neck between the dull blades of his hand clippers. An involuntary "ouch" "ooh" "OOO" came out as I squirmed and wiggled in response to this physical abuse. Old Tony never said, "I'm sorry," "Go to hell," "Kiss my ass," or anything but "HOLDA STEEL!!!" Occasionally, he'd draw blood, but was quick to stop the hemorrhaging with a blood-stained tip of a styptic pencil.

Mercifully, the haircut only took about two minutes. The finishing touch was a generous splash of lilac stinkum and a dusting of talc with a horsehair brush. Then he'd hold up a hand mirror to allow me to inspect his handiwork, and with a big smile say, "HOUSA DAT." Mom would nod her approval and I'd jump from the chair without waiting for him to lower it.

I kept the pompadour hair style from the sixth grade to my second year of high school. Being as short as I was, this particular hairdo was perfect for me, as it added two inches to my height. In about the eighth grade, I added a modification by allowing the sides to grow longer and combing them back to form a D.A. The D.A. was short for "Ducks Ass," and in 1948 and 1949, this was the coolest look in Steubenville for men's hair styling. When I walked in the Academy Pool Room down on Market Street with my pompadour and D.A, anyone could see I was hot shit. More importantly, the girls seemed to dig it.

The vanity I developed extended from the top of my head to the soles of my shoes. When I was really young, and I mean third or fourth grade, I had two pairs of shoes, one for school and play and a "good" pair for Sunday school. Mom took me to Thom McAnn's or Kinney's Shoe Store where they had this machine to X-ray your feet to see what size you wore. You could actually look down and see all the bones in your feet. Once it was scientifically determined what size I was, Mom would tell the clerk to give me a size and a half larger, so I could grow into them. Well, I was small for my age and a slow grower and my feet didn't grow any faster than the rest of me. Without fail, I would wear out the shoes long before I grew out of them. Mom thought it wasteful to get rid of shoes that still fit, even if they did have holes the size of a silver dollar in the soles. Shoe repairs were expensive, but she always found the answer at the five and dime store. They sold these do-it- yourself shoe repair kits for about fifty cents that consisted of two thin, rubber soles in various sizes and some glue in a nail-polish-type bottle.

There was always a considerable time lag between the time the hole first appeared and when Mom got around to buying one of these kits. This meant I'd get a hole in the bottom of my socks until the shoe hole was fixed. There was, however, an ingenious answer for this problem, and the answer was inside a box of Nabisco Shredded Wheat. There were four stacks of three biscuits in each box and these stacks were separated by thick cardboard dividers. Well, that's how the temporary problem of the holes in my shoes was solved. Unfortunately, we couldn't eat enough Shredded Wheat to keep up with the constant demand for the cardboard dividers.

When we finally got the sole repair kit, we could never seem to get the glue to hold for more than a day or two. When it started to give in the front part of the sole, it made this loud flapping sound when I walked. To avoid the embarrassment of drawing unwanted attention to myself, I learned to walk on my heels, kind of like a duck. As soon as I got my first job at eleven years old, I bought my own shoes and to this day have only worn the best shoes money can buy. When I reached high school, I was buying my shoes at Branigan and Punkie, which was the best and most expensive men's shoe store in town. The first pair I bought there was a pair of Florsheim wing tip oxblood cordovans. Those babies would really take a shine and I'd often spend an hour or so putting a spit shine on them you could see your face in.

Sometime during my junior year in high school, the pompadour and D.A. look was out, to be replaced with the crew cut flattop. I wasted no time in conforming to the short hair style. I kept my light blond hair even and standing up at all times. I was never without my tube of "butch wax," which I applied like a deodorant stick to the top of my head. I kept this style haircut for the next fifteen years.

During these awkward years of transition from boyhood to teenager, Mom had taken a job downtown as a clerk at Steiner's Curtain Shop. She worked five days a week until five p.m. On Saturdays she worked until nine p.m. when all the stores stayed open late. This meant that Sunday was the only day of the week Mom had time to prepare a proper meal. Sunday dinner took place in mid-afternoon after church. Typically, the main course was chicken, pot roast or Swiss steak. Along with this, we ate mashed potatoes and succotash, and one of Mom's dessert specialties. About twice a month, we were joined for Sunday dinner by Uncle Jimmy, who was Mom's uncle and my great uncle.

Uncle Jimmy was probably in his sixties, a widower who worked in the mill and lived alone in a rooming house. He took obvious joy in dining with his niece and her family on Sunday afternoons. Uncle Jimmy was a hunter, and in the fall he'd bring us squirrels and rabbits he had shot. Mom breaded and fried these rodents in a deep iron skillet. This was always considered a special treat, but when I took a bite of rabbit, I couldn't help picturing "Thumper," and somehow rabbit didn't taste so good.

I really liked Uncle Jimmy. After Sunday dinner, he'd pull out a plug of "Red Man" chewing tobacco and make a point of offering me a chew. When I declined, he'd give me a quarter and say, "Get some candy and share it with your friends." Uncle Jimmy was also very good to Mom and understood her plight. I'd sometimes see him slip her some folding money, which over her objections, he'd insist she keep.

I must have been a freshman in high school when I came home and Mom told me Uncle Jimmy was dead. He had just been to our house about two Sundays before and looked O.K. to me. However, he told Mom he was sick. I never found out what the problem was, but it must have been serious. When I asked Mom what happened, she told me Uncle Jimmy had put on his best suit and went up to Seventh Street and laid newspapers out on the ground next to the railroad track. To ensure he wouldn't get his suit dirty, he lay down on the newspapers, put a pistol in his mouth and blew out his brains. He left five hundred dollars to Mom, never got the suit he was buried in dirty, and we never ate squirrel or rabbit again.

* * *

By 1948, a few people in Steubenville began to acquire television sets. Even if a family was fortunate enough to be able to afford a television set, there were very few programs to watch. Before the novelty of the television wore off, people sat around watching a test pattern hoping that something more stimulating would appear. Because the reception of the video and audio signal was extremely poor, most of the time the black-and-white picture was covered with snow, rolling double images and audio static. The only television owners who got decent reception were the ones who had a tall antenna on the roof or on top of a separate pole erected in the back yard. Most of the television owners lived up on the hill where reception was at least a possibility. For anyone living downtown, a television set was worthless.

My neighbor, Mr. Lanzia, was the first person in the neighborhood to get a television set. It was a Du-Mont and it must have cost a lot of money, but Mr. Lanzia was determined to be on the cutting edge of this new technology. Living in the south end as he did, (which was perhaps the lowest elevation of anywhere in the city) the chances of him getting a picture were just about nil, so this beautiful new Du-Mont T.V. with the round picture screen just sat in his living room gathering dust under the gorgeous crystal chandelier.

Mr. Lanzia worked at Wheeling Steel and I happened to notice that he was accumulating a sizable pile of iron pipe stacked in his backyard next to the grape arbor. Over the weeks, this stack of pipe continued to grow in height and width until it covered most of the yard. Then, one Sunday morning after church, all these guys showed up at Lanzia's and began to rearrange the pipe and weld sections of it together. It didn't take long to figure out what was going on.

People from all over the neighborhood began to gather to watch the erection of this gigantic television tower in Lanzia's backyard.

A job of this magnitude took time and manpower, but as the day wore on, the tower stretched further and further skyward. Rungs for a ladder were welded to one side and sections of pipe were hauled up by handing a piece at a time from man to man. As the structure grew, more and more bodies were clinging to the rungs, high off the ground. This was undoubtedly an extremely dangerous undertaking. Mr. Lanzia was on the ground shouting up instructions and fortifying all his workers with glass after glass of his homemade dago red. As the tower continued to grow, Mr. Lanzia remained on the ground, shouting up instructions in Italian accompanied by constant hand gestures to his fellow paesanos whose courage was fortified by the considerable intake of wine. The volume and intensity of the instructions and hand signals grew as the mast increased its elevation. When this steel spire started swaying with the weight of an inebriated volunteer, the growing crowd of spectators started making sounds like a circus audience watching a high wire act. It was about this time that Mr. Lanzia indicated his satisfaction with a broad smile and shouted, "Mi piace" (I like it), "Fino in cima" (to the top), "Va bene" (O.K.), "Grazie Grazie" (Thank you thank you) and turned to the gathered crowd and executed a low bow just like an opera star. He did some quick figuring with pencil and paper and seemed satisfied with the height of the tower. It was then that he sent a lone climber to the top to place the antenna and run the wire. Once the antenna was in place, the spectators applauded, as Mr. Lanzia announced that it was just an inch or so above one hundred feet. He then and there proclaimed it to be the highest television antenna in Steubenville. Whether it was or not, its worth would be proven if the Du-Mont could pull in Saturday Night Big Time Wrestling.

An hour before the matches were to begin, there were at least fifty people sitting cross-legged on the floor in front of the Du-Mont. Mrs. Lanzia passed around bowls of popcorn and cups of lemonade. Since I was the next-door neighbor and almost a member of the family, I got a front-row seat alongside Mario and Nino. As the nine o'clock hour drew near, Mr. Lanzia switched on the set. For what seemed like forever, but in reality was only less than a minute, there was nothing but snow on the picture tube. Then the set made a belching noise and on came a perfect image of Gorgeous George stomping on the shaved head of Don Eagle. The match was on and everyone in the room cheered.

As far as my personal life was concerned, there wasn't much to cheer about. It was about this time I started to experience bouts of loneliness, feelings of isolation and sometimes depression. I occasionally regressed toward childish behavior only to assume adult responsibilities the very same day. Maturity and immaturity were like magnets pulling me in opposite directions, which caused me untold confusion. However, for the most part, circumstances dictated that I grow up as a matter of self preservation. Whenever I got hit with this double whammy of uncertainty, I gave myself a pep talk and thought about how Abraham Lincoln or Gene Autry would handle the situation. This generally made it possible to find a satisfactory solution to my predicament and enabled me to keep on trying.

The summer before I was to begin high school was winding down and we were still living in the south end next door to the Lanzia's A group of us guys decided we should have one last big summer adventure before school started. We hit upon the idea of a five-day camping trip out at State Lake, which was about ten miles outside of town.

Naturally, the guys had to convince their parents that this was a good idea and that being away from home out in the woods for five days would not place them in any danger. As for me, getting parental approval was not a problem. Once everyone got the O.K., we spent a week or more debating the menu, activities and what items of equipment would be essential to survival in the wilderness.

State Lake was a popular summer destination for picnics, swimming and hiking, but this late in the season we would virtually have the park to ourselves. The trouble was, we were all city boys with absolutely no camping experience and very little in the way of equipment. We had no tents, sleeping bags or cooking stove, but we each had a hunting knife, for whatever goddamn good that was going to do us.

Our plan was to use the shelter house as headquarters and sleep on top of picnic tables wrapped in our blankets. The cooking would be done over the iron grate at the far end of the shelter house. There were six of us: Mario and Nino Lanzia, Dick Patchen, Duke Swan, Babe Ansawini and me. Whatever other shortfalls we had in our preparations, we wanted to make sure we had enough food. So, with boxes loaded with canned fruit, vegetables, lunch meat, eggs and cheese, our expeditionary force piled in Mr. Patchen's car and headed for State Lake.

As soon as we unloaded all our boxes and meager gear at the shelter house, we decided on a swim. At a spot where the bank of the lake was high, a thick rope of hemp was tied to a tree branch that extended over the water. This made a perfect swing for us to do Tarzan-like maneuvers dropping from the apex of the rope's arc twenty feet into the water. Horsing around and playing grab-ass on the rope and muddy bank soon worked up our appetites for some good outdoor cooking.

The first night's meal was a minor success. We had cheeseburgers. The meat and cheese we wrapped in foil and put in the cool water at the spillway. I thought a can or two of beans and some canned peaches would go well with the cheeseburger entrée, but when we tried to find a can opener, no luck. The only solution to getting at those beans and peaches was our hunting knives. We each took a crack at trying to open the cans with these daggers, and only succeeded in punching holes in the tin, allowing the messy juice to ooze out of the can. When Babe Ansawini managed to take a nice slice of meat out of his hand, we decided to settle upon a one course meal. Of course, we gorged ourselves on toasted marshmallows, eating our five-day supply that first night.

Now it was time to turn in, and the sounds of the night were upon us with the constant chorus of katydids coming from the woods. I had one hell of a time trying to get comfortable with only a blanket separating me from the hard wooden picnic table. It didn't take long before the buzz of dive-bombing mosquitoes was ringing in my ears, and only seconds after that before they began to bite. The strong-smelling, oil based repellent that I had smeared all over the exposed parts of my body was definitely not working. It was one long miserable night, but we all survived as we finally welcomed the dawn.

Tom Twyford   95

I was dead-bang certain that Murphy's Law had jinxed our campsite when we discovered that our lunch meat, cheese and eggs had been eaten by some critters in the night. We weren't exactly facing starvation, but our food selection had been drastically reduced. Peanut butter and crackers proved to be our salvation for the next day and a half.

After another night of torture on the rack, otherwise known as the picnic table, we awoke with a renewed spirit when Duke suggested we raid a cornfield and get us some corn on the cob. In late August, the fields near the park were rich with corn, so we figured the farmer could spare a few ears for some boys who had overdosed on peanut butter. Once we scoped out the field, we left Nino behind on the road as a lookout just in case the farmer came on the scene. The stalks stood much higher than my head and blocked out the sun as I worked my way down the narrow rows. They were full of ears that looked ripe and ready for roasting. I was careful to pick only the biggest and best. In no time, we had more corn than we could eat in a week.

Back at the shelter house we shucked the corn and wrapped it in foil. Then we buried the ears in hot glowing coals of a wood fire. It didn't take long before we could smell the aroma of our roasting booty. We were hungry and started to argue about when to take them out of the fire, but when the smell became overwhelmingly delicious, we decided they were done. Using a long stick, I carefully fished our foil wrapped meal out of the fire and onto the floor of the shelter house. When we got the ears unwrapped, they were golden brown and steaming. Our butter by this time was digesting in the stomach of some raccoon, but we had plenty of salt, which I liberally applied as I sunk my teeth into the hot kernels.

The corn was as tough as the cob and absent any taste whatsoever. Chewing it was like trying to grind up tree bark and cardboard. Strands of stringy stuff the consistency of asbestos got caught between my teeth. There was no way we could eat this shit. To ingest one ear of this stuff would inflict permanent damage to the human alimentary canal. We tested several other ears and they were all inedible. As I said before, we were all city boys and trying to figure out this rural dilemma was beyond our realm of experience. But, Dick Patchen, the brainiest one of the bunch, hit upon the answer. He told us that what we had stolen and tenderly prepared wasn't "people corn." It was field corn used as animal fodder to feed cattle and slop hogs.

At this point, nobody said anything. We just looked at each other in a state of dejection, realizing that our hopes for a great outdoor adventure had been dashed. Just as the big letdown was sinking in, we saw the Patchen's car coming up the road. Dick's mom got out of the car carrying an enamel roaster pan, which she sat on the table. I recognized the smell of Italian spaghetti sauce even before she removed the lid. The rigatoni and sweet Italian sausage was still warm and we dug in, eating like it was our last meal before going to the electric chair.

All things considered, we agreed to cut short our intended stay in the State Lake wilderness and head for home. A full belly of homemade pasta and sausage had lifted our spirits as we joked and laughed about the great time we had. I would be fourteen in another couple of weeks and starting high school at Big Red. The other five guys would be moving on to Catholic Central and circumstances would cause us to drift apart as this youthful alliance came to an end. When I think about this camping trip, it's with bittersweet memories of these last days of boyhood.

Chapter 8

High School (1949–1951)

Steubenville High School

Steubenville High School occupied the whole city block between Logan and Dock Streets, just a few blocks north of the downtown business area. The building was only ten years old and was the first public building in the state of Ohio to cost over one million dollars. All the classrooms, gym, auditorium and other facilities were top notch and state-of-the-art. I liked the way it smelled. It had an aroma of something sweet, like the Beehee brothers' cinnamon buns coming out of the oven mixed with the clean smell of strong soap.

There were over a hundred boys in the freshman class at Steubenville High School in the fall of 1949. I wasn't the smallest guy in the class, but I was darn close to it. While most of my friends had growth spurts of several inches and filled out during seventh and eighth grade, I seemed to be shrinking. Of course, this was just my imagination, but just to make sure, I'd check my height and weight two or three times a week on the scales in the locker room. I formulated pictures in my mind of what it would be like to grow up to be a midget. I'd rather be blind in one eye, deaf in one ear and missing a few fingers and toes than be the "Tom Thumb" of the class of 1953. Was it wishful thinking, or did I actually pick up an inch and a half by Christmas 1949? After I confirmed this modest surge, it was a helluva load off my mind. I was perfectly content to wait awhile for that thick mat of black chest hair to appear.

My size didn't prove to be an obstacle to my thespian ambitions. I tried out for and got a part in a school play. It was then I realized this was a perfect outlet for my need to be noticed. Everyone told me how well I performed. I was not accustomed to being told that I was good at anything, so I was encouraged by this praise to continue my dramatic pursuits. I got a big part in a Steubenville Little Theater production called The Return of Peter Grimm. We put on two performances before sold-out audiences at the high school auditorium. The play was a hit and got a big write-up, along with pictures of the cast in the Herald Star. There was no doubt about it; I thought I was hot shit.

During my freshman year, I found out that Blum Brothers Wholesale Warehouse was looking for a part-time stock boy. The warehouse and office were located in an ancient-looking four-story brick building on North Street just three blocks from the high school. When I heard about the opening, I high-tailed it up there and talked to Mr. Arthur Blum. He was looking for a boy for every afternoon after school and all day on Saturdays. I told him that I would be just the ticket. He gave me several long hard looks, evaluating my puny physique, and said the job required lifting heavy cases of candy, canned goods and drug items. I told him that I was really a lot stronger than I looked and if he would give me a chance, I'd prove it to him. No doubt he felt sorry for me and, after some further hesitation, said he'd give me a try. The pay was seventy-five cents an hour and I'd be under the supervision of Mr. Grimes.

My first day on the job, I was introduced to my immediate boss, Mr. Grimes. He was a stoop-shouldered old guy who had this perpetual look of aggravation on his sagging face. I could tell right away that it annoyed him just to look at me. He had a whining, irritating quality to his voice. When he spoke I could tell he had the "red ass." I later came to find out that he did suffer with a serious case of chronic hemorrhoids.

He gave me a tour of this dark, dingy warehouse, which was lit with naked light bulbs hanging from the ceiling at none-too-frequent intervals. An old freight elevator required you to throw an up-and-down switch and tug on a rope to get it started. This was the means of getting from one floor to another. My job was to pick up orders on the first floor and, with the help of a dolly, fill orders from the cases of merchandise stored throughout the warehouse and bring the orders down to a loading dock for delivery. This meant I had to learn the location of the various categories and brand names of items so I could move about the warehouse and fill the orders without delay. In a very short time, I had the location of everything memorized and could fill an order in half the time it took my cantankerous boss.

Before long, the two of us reached an accommodation and the old guy began to genuinely like me. I helped him fill orders when it was difficult for him to reach cases on high shelving and otherwise made his work easier. Even though I was uncertain about what I wanted to do with my life, I was sure I didn't want to end up like poor old Mr. Grimes. Still, I was fourteen, had a job, was making money and life was good.

There was no way I was going to allow school and a job put a crimp in my social life. The YMCA was just a few blocks from the high school on North Fourth Street. In the basement of the Y was a gathering place where teenagers could dance and polish their skills at social intercourse. We called it Swing Haven and it was our hangout three nights a week–Wednesday, Friday and Saturday. The dance floor was surrounded by booths, a jukebox and snack bar. The lights were kept low, which created a night-club-type atmosphere. Swing Haven became as much a part of the high school experience as English, math and history.

From day one, I became a regular who rarely missed a night. My brother, Bill, had been the first student president of Swing Haven, which must have been quite an honor. Mom must have asked me a hundred times, "Did you know your brother was the first president of Swing Haven?" This was clearly a source of maternal pride, but I frankly felt it fell short of justifying his likeness carved in the granite of Mount Rushmore.

The early part of the decade of the 1950s, or pre-Elvis years, still had the feel of the forties. Big bands were not completely dead and male and female soloists still sang sentimental ballads of young love newly lost or found. Groups such as the four-this or three-that dominated the pop charts with a harmony familiar to teenagers a generation before. The clean-cut scrubbed look was still in, but was giving way to a scruffier, cooler image of the young rebel I so admired. This was a time of transition where I was caught between the respectable white bucks and the sometimes unsavory image of blue suede shoes.

As a freshman, I got right into the swing of things, so to speak, and enjoyed having the upper-class girls teach me to dance what was called Swing Haven style. Some of the popular recording artists of the time were The Four Aces, The Hilltoppers, Johnny Ray, Perry Como, Nat King Cole, Joanie James, Frankie Laine, Patti Page, Guy Mitchell, Jo Stafford and, of course, Steubenville's own Dean Martin. The words and the music of their recordings are embedded in my brain just as firmly as the youthful memories of all the fun I had at Swing Haven.

This was one instance where being short had some definite advantages, as I would rest my head upon a generous portion of the taller girl's anatomy as we swayed to the music of the Ray Anthony orchestra. Believe me, I took my good old time learning the technique of Swing Haven style.

There was .always a group of not-so-pretty girls standing around the edge of the dance floor. I'd look at them and try to imagine how it felt to come to Swing Haven week after week and never be asked to dance. So, I made it a rule that I'd ask at least two homely girls per night to dance. I can't be certain that dancing with Tommy Twyford made their night, but it made me feel good.

By the time I was a freshman, I had developed a serious interest in girls. Notwithstanding my youthful appearance, I had a strong urge to make a favorable impression on the fairer sex. One way to offset the shortcomings of my immaturity was to be a sharp dresser, and that's what I did. I was always particular about my appearance, but now it took on a sense of urgency if I had any hope of making a score. My job at Blum Brothers gave me the cash necessary to acquire the threads I needed to be successful in my quest for female companionship.

I became a regular at Myer & Stone Men's Wear on Market Street. One of the co-owners, Myer Pearlman, was one of the best guys you would ever want to meet. He gave me advice on all the latest trends in young men's fashions and even special-ordered things in smaller sizes especially for me. My shirts had the latest long collars that could be turned up in the back for that cool look. My pants had a fourteen-inch peg at the cuff and were made of the very best sharkskin wool fabric. Ole Myer really knew how to dress a guy. My shoes were white bucks, oxblood cordovans and blue suedes. When I wore my bucks, I'd carry around a bunny bag to dust off any smudges and for my suedes, a wire brush to keep that unblemished, smooth look.

As particular as I was about my wardrobe, I'd have sacrificed my left testicle to have a letter sweater. A black varsity "S" on a red knit cardigan from the "Target Shop" would have set me apart and made me more than just a spectator. It would have made no difference to me what sport the "S" was for, but letters were awarded to "doers," not "wishers," and my desire to be a jock could not compensate for my lack of athletic skills. Anyone could buy the red varsity sweater at the Target Shop, but without a letter on it, I wouldn't be caught dead in one.

Being the astute observer of nature that I was, I figured out that there must be a reason why male birds were more brightly colored than the female of the same species. Maybe, in some way, this was connected with my obsession to be a sharp dresser? Even though I wasn't the most robust looking guy in the world, my health was excellent. Although I wasn't sick in the usual sort of way, I was convinced that something serious was wrong with me. That is, I thought I might be oversexed. My thoughts seemed to dwell upon all matters sexual. I didn't know what testosterone was at the time, but I must have had an unusually high count. For instance, I found myself mentally undressing the nicest of girls in the most inappropriate places, such as church or the corner of Fourth and Market. Whenever I did this, which was fairly often, I'd feel guilty and promise myself not to repeat these sick thoughts. But the next thing I'd know, I was giving in to this lascivious thinking and "bingo"some unsuspecting girl was losing her underpants. Then there were frequent occurrences where some embarrassing anatomical change would take place for no apparent reason and I'd run for cover. There was also the question of how far one had to go to make a girl pregnant. That is, could a girl get that way if you didn't actually put the thing in the thing, but came close to it?

There was no one I could turn to for answers to these questions and more. With her Puritanical views, my mother was out of the question and I didn't know any man whom I could tell about my sex problem. I even went so far as to try and research some of this stuff in the school library. If the information I was looking for was there, I sure couldn't find it. Of course, I could have asked Ms. Rachel Freedman, the school librarian, for some help, but I'd have been kicked out of school on the spot. My only recourse was to bring the subject up with other guys in an off-handed manner. I didn't want to seem too dumb about such matters, but, at the same time, didn't want them to know I was a sexual deviant.

Along with sports and clothes, I suppose the topic of girls inevitably worked its way into most conversations when a group of guys got together. Some guys seemed obsessed with talking about girls and sex. To some extent I think we were all vocal about it, but some were more so than others. Whether hanging out at Swing Haven or at school, there was always some smart guy who could identify which girls "put out" and which ones were only "cock teasers." These poor girls' names would be bandied about from one group of guys to another, giving them a reputation whether or not the information was true. None of the guys I hung out with were attracted to a girl because she had a keen mind. They weren't looking for intellectual stimulation. According to some guys, concealed under every poodle skirt that traveled the halls of the high school was the pulsating crotch of a nymphomaniac.

Probably ninety percent of this talk was bullshit and I was smart enough to consider the source. There were times when I should have spoken up to defend some girl's honor, but most of the time my challenge would be a meek response like, "Just how do you know that?" and some big handsome football player who had all the scoop would angrily reply, "Because I've been there and had it." At that point, what the hell could I say without getting my teeth knocked out? I suppose it all had something to do with the rush of hormones in teenage boys and a need to brag about their imaginary conquests. The truth of the matter was that promiscuous behavior among the girls at Big Red was uncommon.

However, there was an incident that I recall not involving a football player, but some stupid guy who was a member of the "Shutter Bug Club" and an amateur photographer. Anyway, he convinced a freshman girl he was some kind of great photographer and could launch her successful modeling career. Being young and inexperienced, the girl was gullible enough to fall for his line of bullshit and agreed to model for this soon-to-be famous photographer.

For the sake of anonymity, I'll call our photographer Norman Swackhammer. Anyway, Norman showed up at school one day with dozens of eight-by-five inch, black-and-white photographs of our soon-to-be famous model, posed à la Marilyn Monroe, naked as a jaybird. Norman had no trouble selling these photographs to half the boys in the high school, including me. Old Norman charged twenty-five cents apiece. Even when he sold out, he was taking orders for more. Clearly stamped on the back of each picture was the name of the party who was responsible for this artistic photographic endeavor. It read "Norman Swackhammer Photography Studio," with the address and telephone number—really smart!!

Well, it didn't take long for the shit to hit the fan. Our model's mother was more than mildly pissed off and demanded that the school principal take immediate action. The very next morning, after the brisk sales day had by Swackhammer Studios, Mr. A.C. May was on the public address system to each home room, demanding that anyone possessing photographs purchased the day before turn them in immediately to the office. He went on to say that no consequences would be forthcoming so long as the photographs were turned in. Sadly, I, along with several of my buddies, sheepishly went to the counter in the school office and dropped our pictures in a box marked "photos" and signed our names to a sheet. We could have just destroyed the pictures, but we figured Norman for a squealer who would tell Mr. May who all purchased a photo. To be perfectly honest, that girl had one hell of a body and I would have liked to have kept her picture.

As for Norman, he probably wound up working for National Geographic somewhere in the depths of the Congo Republic, taking pictures of bare-breasted native women.

* * *

My high school yearbook is called The Steuben (Class of 1953). There is a full page in it with a picture of Clyde Higgins, which says "He Lives In Our Memory." He was a tall kid with reddish hair and freckles. He and I were in several classes together during my freshman year. We were always clowning around and just seemed to hit it off. I didn't have much contact with him outside of school, but did consider him a good classmate. Clyde was a member of an independent drum and bugle corps that performed at parades and functions throughout the tri-state area. I especially recall the elegant uniforms they wore, which were bright blue and yellow and had tall hats with feathery plumes

Clyde's parents were divorced and he lived with his mother and step-father. It was springtime and late in the school year when Clyde, without the benefit of permission or a driver's license, took his stepfather's car for a joy ride. The car was reported stolen and Clyde was arrested after being stopped by police. He was taken into custody and, rather than being thrown in jail, was locked in a courtroom at the Courthouse. It was reported that he was told he was going to jail, which scared him out of his wits. After being left alone and locked in the courtroom for a short while, the police returned to find him hanging from a sash cord at the courtroom window.

This happened at about four o'clock in the afternoon and his body was taken from the courthouse by the bus stop where dozens of kids were standing. I wasn't there, but was told that word of what happened quickly spread. The scene turned ugly with kids crying and screaming in shock at what they were witnessing. I went to see him at the funeral home, where he was lying in the casket dressed in his drum and bugle corps uniform with his hat at his side. This tragedy caused me to come to grips with the fragility of a human life and the reality of death.

I didn't do much more clowning around for the remainder of that school year.

I thought a lot about Clyde's death. Clyde was my age and I guess it created an awareness of how randomly death can visit anyone, even me. I had read about young soldiers dying by the thousands in the Civil War and I was aware of the deaths that happened during World War II. However, thinking about the wartime deaths of soldiers and school-aged children in Hiroshima, Dresden, Warsaw, and throughout Russia all seemed remote. These people had no faces I could visualize or relate to in any way. Clyde, however, knew me and I knew him. We talked, laughed and goofed off together—suddenly, he was gone.

It was a big help in shaking off feelings of sadness whenever my attention was diverted by some attractive girl. There was a girl I had my eye on in Spanish class. Her name was Betty Belfiore and I took every opportunity that presented itself to chat it up with her. The trouble was she was very quiet and never had much to say, so I usually did most of the talking.

Betty had dark hair, an olive complexion and a very pretty face, but was just a little on the plump side. Along with being quiet, another drawback was that she was half a head taller than me and two years older, but I was not easily deterred. After several weeks of carefully nurturing our friendship, I decided it was time to make my move. We were leaving class one day and I was talking to her a mile a minute. She was just nodding her head and smiling, not saying much when I blurted out, "Do you want to go to the movies with me Saturday night?" Before I could speak the follow-up lines I had rehearsed, she said, "O.K., what time?" I just about croaked. My mouth went dry and I couldn't think of anything else to say except, "I'll see you Saturday, seven o'clock," as I hurriedly walked away.

Over the next few days, I kept expecting her to tell me she had changed her mind, so I tried to avoid her along with the bad news I was sure would come. When Saturday arrived and I hadn't heard a word from her, I began to figure that our date had slipped her mind. Well, just in case she remembered, I was standing on her front porch knocking on the door Saturday night at 7 p.m. sharp. After I had knocked about five times and no one answered, I was about to walk away when the door opened and her mother said, "Yes?" She looked me up and down with a hint of a suspicious smile, like I was some kind of a salesman. Finally, I said, "Is Betty home?" and she invited me in and asked me to sit down. I was standing in the hall and didn't know where she expected me to sit, since the only thing in the entry hall was a hat rack. I told her I would just stand there and wait. Then I remembered I hadn't even told her my name or why I wanted to see Betty. Mercifully, Betty showed up before I had to explain to her mother that I wasn't trying to sell Betty anything, that we were just going to the movies.

We went to the Capitol Theater, which was about four blocks from her house. As we walked down the street, I tried to keep my distance from her so as not to make our difference in height too obvious. She asked me, "Why are you walking way over there?" I just told her it was a habit I had since I was a kid. Then she asked me what movie was playing at the Capitol. I really hadn't given much thought to selecting an appropriate movie for a first date. The name of the movie was "A Place In The Sun" and the stars were Elizabeth Taylor and Montgomery Clift. I didn't know it at the time, but the movie was based upon Theodore Dreiser's prize-winning novel An American Tragedy. Naturally, I hadn't read the novel, so how was I to know it was about some poor guy who gets a poor girl pregnant, then meets a rich girl and wants to marry her, so he drowns the poor girl, gets caught and goes to the electric chair? There was one mushy part after another, which made me feel very uncomfortable, but Betty never took her eyes off the screen. I think she forgot I was even sitting next to her. It was just her and old Montgomery Clift lost in the moment. If I had known all this beforehand, we would have seen the Randolph Scott western playing at the Paramount. That was my one and only date with Betty.

While my date with Betty didn't pan out quite as well as I'd hoped, I wasn't about to give up on girls. The "tingle" didn't go away, and there was no better way to impress some sharp-looking chick than to invite her to the prom. School proms were the really big deals. Committees were formed and detailed plans were made to make sure everything came off just right. Every prom had a theme and the high school gym was elaborately decorated to conform to the particular theme. For instance, the Christmas prom might have a theme of "Winter Wonderland" or "Holiday Hop."

Preparations were started weeks in advance, and it was important to line up a date as soon as possible.

Starting with my sophomore year, I never missed a single prom. The first prom I attended was a Christmas prom and I waited until just about the last minute to get a date. Her name was Judy Bloomer and I didn't really know her all that well, but she was a very sharp-looking girl. Judy lived up on the hill, so we couldn't walk to the prom. Since I didn't have a car, transportation was a problem. Even I was smart enough to figure out that putting her on a city bus dressed in a fancy gown would be a tacky move. I was rescued from this dilemma when a friend of Judy's who was also going to the prom and was being driven by her father volunteered to provide transportation for us as well. Now, all I had to do was rent a white sport coat and black trousers and buy her a corsage. It was customary to exchange dances with other couples by prior arrangement and note it on a dance card. In other words, I would get to dance with some other guy's date about every other dance. This was a welcomed relief for me because Judy and I didn't have much in common and were running short on conversation. She wasn't too much of a talker, and didn't find my jokes very funny.

Toward the end of the evening, it was time to get our prom pictures taken. There was a professional photographer who had each couple pose under this arbor decked out with fake flowers. Prom pictures were a very big deal to the girls and their parents. I wasn't too hot on the idea of spending five bucks, and anyway, I was very unphotogenic. However, there was no way I could get out of it. We were standing in line waiting our turn and as we got to the spot under the arbor, there was a flash and the photo guy said "Next."

Our ride was waiting for us outside after the dance was over and drove us to Judy's house. I got out of the car with her and walked her to the front porch, where I knew I was obligated to conclude the evening by giving her a kiss on the lips. I think she knew what was coming and leaned her head forward in a quick motion, causing the glasses we both wore to come together with a loud "click." So with my glasses hanging from one ear, I managed to plant a kiss on her mouth. She didn't swoon or even let out a sigh, but said thank you and good night. I felt a little let down and realized I would have to polish up my technique.

About a week later, the prom pictures came in. There were two four-by-eight inch prints in black and white, which came in an envelope. I eased them out very slowly in order to postpone my certain disappointment. Well, I wasn't just disappointed; I was sick. The picture was a disaster. I looked like a dead-bang ringer for the village idiot and Judy looked as though she were suffering some excruciating pain. The light reflected off both our glasses making two shining holes where our eyes should have been. There was no way I was going to give her this picture, but every day when I saw her in school she would ask where our prom pictures were. She said her mom wanted to show them to some relatives who were coming to visit from out of town. I kept trying to put her off, but it was no use, so I took the chicken way out and left the picture in an envelope with her name on it with her homeroom teacher.

I didn't have much further contact with Judy after that. She never said a word to me about the picture, but I can only assume that it was not prominently displayed in a place of honor at her home. Furthermore, I seriously doubt that any of her relatives ever got a glimpse of their pretty niece paired up with me in this disastrous prom scene.

I had a job, a sharp wardrobe and my ego and self-image was riding an adolescent high, but there was an incident that created a serious setback. It all started at Swing Haven on a Friday night. I had struck up a conversation with a girl in my class named Donna Rogers. The more we talked, the more interested I became. With the exception of my two dances with the homely girls, I danced every dance with Donna that evening. She was one of those real brainy kind of girls. Most of the time they were not much to look at, but Donna was an exception. She had dark hair with a fair complexion and an easy way of laughing at my clever comments that had me completely charmed. Her nose was small but looked just right on her pretty face. During the course of the evening, I couldn't help but take notice of her dynamite figure. As the evening was coming to a close, I asked her if I could walk her home, totally forgetting that she lived up on the hill. She reminded me where she lived and suggested I walk her to the bus stop which was a block away. Of course, I thought this was a good idea and, after the last dance of the evening, we left together, along with other kids who were headed for the same bus stop on the corner of Fourth and Market. As we walked along the street, she took my arm, which made me wish that bus stop would be miles away, instead of one lousy block. Anyway, when we reached the corner, a large group of kids, boys and girls, were gathered there waiting for the bus.

Located on that corner was the Union Bank Building, which was nine stories high. Things couldn't have been going better with Donna and me. She still had hold of my arm like I was some possession of hers. All of a sudden, there was a splat sound and I was in a whiteout, completely blinded by a gooey white viscous that covered my head and glasses. I heard a roar of laughter and some kid shout, "A pigeon just shit on Twyford!" By this time, Donna had let go of my arm and moved a safe distance away. I managed to get my handkerchief out of my pocket to wipe off my glasses, as all the boys on the corner were doubled over howling and in stitches. Donna just stood there with a look of shock. Now the stuff was running off my head and down both sides of my face and into my ears. My handkerchief was completely soaked. I was wondering how could it be possible for one pigeon to shit that much. Just then, the bus arrived and all the kids piled on, including my disillusioned and shell-(shit-) shocked companion. I could see her looking out the window with this forlorn look as the bus pulled away, leaving me standing alone on the corner mopping my face and feeling totally destroyed by a lousy pigeon with diarrhea.

This degrading experience only proved to be a temporary setback thanks to the advice and counsel of Chuck Switzer, who had been a pal of mine since second grade. Chuck was a year-and-a-half older than me. He was good looking, well built and very athletic, but had no interest in school. His primary interest was girls and getting his driver's license, which he did as soon as he turned sixteen.

Chuck was really a sharp dresser and a big hit with the girls wherever we went. I just kind of tagged along, trying to impress his castoffs and act as cool as he was, but I was never quite able to pull it off. Every weekend, Chuck would ask to borrow his dad's car. Mr. Switzer tried his best to refuse, but after a lot of bickering and wrangling, Chuck and I usually drove off with his old man's wheels.

My friend was always ready with advice for me about girls. He had a whole collection of what were referred to as "eight-page bibles." These were small, pornographic comic books which featured the likes of Popeye and Olive Oil, Dick Tracy and Tess Truehart and Little Orphan Annie and Daddy Warbucks, all graphically illustrated and engaged in some form of sexual activity. He only showed this prized collection to a very few of his special friends, and I was one of the honored few.

Chuck maintained that every guy should always carry a rubber with him, "just in case." He was kind enough to provide me with a special "French Teaser" in a foil package, which I kept in my wallet for over two years, "just in case." Unfortunately, my Mom washed my jeans with my wallet in the pocket and the Teaser must have come unraveled in the Maytag because she asked about it in a most casual way. I told her it was just something I needed for biology class. Believe it or not, I think she bought my ingenious spur of the moment explanation.

One Sunday afternoon in October, Chuck asked if he could borrow his dad's brand new Studebaker sedan. It had a bullet-nose front end that made it very futuristic in appearance. This model had just come out and his dad had only had the car for about a week. Chuck wanted to drive the car out to the country to buy some apple cider at Welday's Orchard. After many warnings and threats of dire consequences if anything happened, Mr. Switzer said O.K.

The first thing we did was stop at four different girls' houses to pick them up for a Sunday drive. Chuck had already made these arrangements even before his dad had given the O.K. Chuck was, of course, driving with two of the girls up front and I was sitting in the rear seat with a babe on either side of me. Chuck could hardly wait to see how fast this bullet-nosed Studebaker would go, so we had a wild ride to the orchard. We got there all in one piece and drank our cider in high spirits. We piled back into the car and continued our ride on the hilly, two-lane country road. One stretch was a series of hills very much like the course of a roller coaster. As we sped down one hill, Chuck would accelerate the Studebaker up the other side as fast as it would go. He did this several times and the girls were laughing and screaming as at times all four wheels left the pavement. Suddenly, Chuck shouted, "Oh Shit!" as a cloud of dust enveloped the car and the brakes squealed. The girls, on either side of me, were thrown to the floor and the top of my head hit the roof. Chuck had failed to notice that the road curved sharply to the left, as the Studebaker continued on a straight path through a barbed wire fence, finally coming to rest as it hit a low tree stump.

We all took a deep breath and felt lucky to be alive. I had a knot on the top of my head, but otherwise I was O.K. as were the others. When we tried to exit the car, we found that it was wrapped in strands of barbed wire. It was impossible to get out of the car without scraping the barbed wire over the surface, but that's what we had to do. The girls stood aside as Chuck and I struggled with the wire, trying not to inflict more damage to the shiny green finish. Finally, we got the car free and Chuck was able to back it on to the roadway. There was a big dent under the front bumper where we hit the tree stump; however, it was not readily visible. What were visible were gouges and scratches to the finish of the car on the hood, doors and roof.

We were all rather subdued on our slow ride home. We dropped off the girls and when we got to Chuck's house, he parked the Studebaker at the curb. Mr. Switzer must have been waiting for us, because he came out of the house before we could get out of the car. At that point, he didn't say a word. He just slowly walked around the car. His body was shaking and quivering with rage. Then he shouted, "GAWD DAMMIT CHUCK," and with tears in his eyes, walked into the house and slammed the door. Chuck turned to me and said, "Do you want to stay for supper?" I said, "No thanks, I'm not hungry," and I got the hell out of there.

Chuck and I continued to be bosom-buddies. His old man had to have a whole new paint job on the car, but it was pretty much restored to its former beauty.

In many ways, Chuck and I were as different as day and night. Maybe it was because he didn't feel threatened by me, since I presented no competition. Chuck's arms were sculpted with muscle. There was definition where mine were smooth and lacking the ridges, cords and prominent veins that showcased strength. Even if my triceps didn't pop out when I moved my arm a certain way, I liked to think of myself as wiry. I always wondered how all the football players got those knotted calf muscles that stuck out under their football pants. My Mom and sisters likened my physique to a string bean. Uncle Walter described my upper arms as strands of spaghetti with biceps the size of mosquito bites.

I was told that my brother had once signed up for the "Charles Atlas" course of "Dynamic Tension!! that was advertised on the back pages of many magazines. The ad was like a comic strip that showed this skinny guy at the beach with his girlfriend. Then some muscle bound bully comes along and kicks sand in his face, but the skinny guy is too weak to do anything about it. His girlfriend gives him a really shitty look and smiles at the bully. Disgusted with himself, the string bean looks in the mirror and says, "What the heck, I'm going to sign up for Charles Atlas." Then the ad shows this guy two months later, only now he's built like a brick shit house and giving the bully a swift kick in the ass. His girlfriend throws her arms around him and says, "You're the hero of the beach." The guy with the new body flexes all his new muscles and says, "Thanks to Charles Atlas."

From what I could see, I don't think my brother followed through with the course. I gave a lot of thought to giving it a try, but one of my friends with a very athletic build told me it was a rip-off. He said to me, "You either got it or you don't." That's when I decided to just be content with being the wiry guy I was.

While I was sure that neither my brother nor I had the physique of Charles Atlas, I was uncertain about my sister Virginia's perception of life. She was almost ten years older than me, and always somewhat of an enigma. Due to the difference in our age and gender, we had no common interests when I was growing up. She had a whole life of her own that had little, if any, relationship to mine. Not that Virginia was unkind to me or treated me badly, except when she wouldn't allow me in the bathroom. On these occasions, especially when I became a teenager, tremendous rows and quarreling developed over the use of the one-and-only john we had in any house we ever lived in. We were a house divided against itself when it came to the occupation of this essential room. Virginia would literally spend hours in there "putting on her face," while I banged the outside of the locked door on the verge of pissing down my leg or worse. When it came to this issue, my sister Marge wasn't great, but certainly not as bad as Virginia, who considered the crapper her exclusive domain.

The fights with Virginia over the bathroom got to be a matter of routine, but my biggest blow up came with Marge. I was trying to get ready for a night on the town and Marge must have passed out behind the locked door. I read somewhere that in times of dire emergency, people can get this super human strength which enables them to lift a two-thousand-pound tractor off some poor farmer trapped underneath. I believe the same thing can happen if you have to pee badly enough. Well, I completely lost it and ripped the door off its hinges, splintering the jamb and door itself. Marge was carefully applying her eyebrows with a Maybelline pencil as I stormed through the shattered doorway and bodily ejected her. Marge was screaming at me, Mom was screaming at me, but I didn't give a damn. I was blissfully relieving the pressure from my swollen bladder.

One thing about my sister Virginia that I'll never understand is how she got a very sophisticated English accent. Her diction was absolutely perfect as she dragged out each vowel of each word in a way that made her seem very bored with the conversation. She would say in this lofty manner, "RRReally Mother, does Tommy have to dOOO that?" Then I'd get a disgusted look from her which clearly indicated her displeasure at being such a close relative of mine. My friends would come to the house and, as they were leaving, would ask me, "How come your sister talks so funny?" Whenever I was asked about this, I would say that some doctor told Mom it was like a lisp, and there was no cure for it. Even though she did talk funny, her singing voice was pretty good. She never sang the kind of music I liked, but for classical stuff, I suppose it was all right. Virginia was a soloist in the choir at church and was a big hit with the congregation. I sometimes made fun of the way she cupped her hands together above her waist while she sang a song. I think this was some sort of an operatic pose, and just in case she got sick and barfed while singing, she was in a perfect position to catch it. Naturally, Virginia didn't appreciate my crude humor or comments about her singing stance.

In spite of our humble lifestyle and limited economic means, Mom never considered us common or part of the underclass. So, contrary to reality, she instilled in her children a certain air of social superiority. I have no idea where this notion came from, but there was little doubt that the Twyfords viewed themselves as being several notches above most of their neighbors and acquaintances in the social standing of the community. For some reason, I was not much taken by the idea that we were part of the upper crust. My Mom, sisters (especially Virginia) and brother all really believed this crap. Perhaps I was a bit more pragmatic than the rest, so before I could be convinced, I wanted to see some evidence that would justify our inclusion as part of the gentry. Unfortunately, no hard evidence was ever uncovered, but the idea, notion, feeling, or whatever you want to call it, was real. If a person can be a cut above the ordinary by believing it's true, then to that extent it is reality, and that part of Mom's philosophy rubbed off on me. More importantly, what I came away with, after casting aside all the bullshit, was a sense of dignity, which was a gift from my Mom.

I think Mom must have been born under a bad sign because somehow she always seemed to get the short end of the stick. Even when there was occasion to be cheerful or upbeat, there was a downcast aura about her that was unmistakable. She was more wistful than complaining, although there were a multitude of causes that would justify her voicing her unhappiness.

Mom had an uncommon fear of getting cancer. She often talked about people she knew who had died of this disease. In the fall of 1950, she began complaining of intestinal problems and abdominal pain. Finally it progressed to the point where she had a complete bowel obstruction that required surgery. A malignant tumor was removed along with a significant part of her intestines. At the age of forty-eight, she was diagnosed with the disease she had dreaded all her life.

This happened at a time when doctors were not under the obligations of full disclosure to their patients. The word cancer was never mentioned. As far as I know, my Mom was only told that she had a serious bowel obstruction. However, Marge was informed by the doctor the true nature of Mom's illness. She told me what the problem was and my reaction was one of resignation. It just seemed natural that nothing good would ever happen to my Mom, so I was hardly shocked to hear of one more thing to add to the long list of disappointments in her life. I suspect that she knew, but didn't want to believe it, so we all just went along with the story the doctor told her. She stayed in Ohio Valley Hospital for three months until January, 1951.

In late December, 1950, I visited Mom at the hospital each evening. She was steadily recuperating and her spirits were lifted as well as my own. At this time, Marge was working for the Steubenville Herald Star and my sister Virginia was working in Pittsburgh, so Marge and I were the only ones living at home.

One evening, not long before Christmas, I got home from work to find that the house was completely empty. By empty I mean everything was gone, save for the dust bunnies that were floating around the dismal-looking rooms. I searched each room looking for my belongings, or a note of some kind, but no such luck. I called for Boogie inside and out, but no dog. Perhaps Mrs. Lanzia, the next door neighbor, could help me solve the mystery. I went over and knocked on the door and Mrs. Lanzia answered, glad to see me as usual.

"What's going on at my house?" I asked.

"Oh, Tommy, you moved," she replied with a sad look on her face.

"Do you happen to know where I moved to?"

She hesitated a moment and said, "I think you moved somewhere up in the north end." Well, at least that was good news because it was my old end of town. I asked if I could use her telephone and even though it was late, hoped to catch Marge at work. Marge answered the phone and before she could say anything, I said, "What the hell's going on? Where's my dog and where's my stuff?"

"Do you mean Mom didn't tell you?" she replied.

I said, "Nobody told me a Goddamned thing."

I had no difficulty locating our new house. It was 808 North Fourth Street, which was only three blocks north of the high school and a short distance from my old neighborhood on Fifth Street.

This particular area of the north end was occupied by large old homes that were long past their prime. At one time, this part of North Fourth Street was considered to be one of the most prestigious neighborhoods in town. Some of Steubenville's most wealthy citizens lived in these grand old places. A few of these homes were still occupied by relatives of the original owners, but for the most part, these houses had been converted into multi-family rental units. What resulted from these conversions were awkward layouts that were passed off as separate living quarters. That's what we had moved into. We had the first-floor half of a much larger home with a separate apartment upstairs where another family lived. The landlady and her husband lived in the other half of the place.

Our part of the larger house consisted of four rooms and a bath. The entrance was on the side of the house, down a narrow walkway, which was crammed between us and the house next door. However, on the bright side of things, there was an extra little nook in the front that passed as a room and had formerly been part of an entry hall. It was a stretch to call this space a room, as it measured about eight feet by ten feet, or the size of an average walk-in closet. It had a door that opened to a porch and the outside. There were brass bases of old gaslight fixtures still attached to the ceiling and wall. These fixtures had lit the porch and foyer a century before the room became my new bedroom. This was the cozy den assigned to me and where I would spend my sleeping hours for the next four years.

Contrary to what you might think, I liked my space. The space was large enough to accommodate a daybed and a cardboard "shiffrobe," which held my clothes and all my personal effects. Yet, the thing I liked most about the place was that I had my own private entrance and key, which made it possible for me to come and go as I pleased, undetected by inquiring eyes.

Had it not been for that door to freedom, I would have felt like an inmate confined to a cell in a woman's prison. Having left the mildew room behind for a better address, I looked upon this unannounced move as a stroke of good luck.

Chapter 9

High School (1951–1953)

High School Graduation Picture 1953

During my high school years, I kept up my church and Sunday school attendance and was an active member of the Methodist Youth Fellowship. When I think about some of the other crap I was doing at the time, there is an obvious inconsistency with my church involvement. But, what the heck, I needed all the help I could get spiritually and otherwise so I didn't stray too far from the flock.

It was my continued participation with the church that created a defining moment in my life. The month was September 1951. It was at a Methodist Youth Fellowship meeting that I met Dorothy Parks and the course of my life was irrevocably changed. Dorothy was a striking fourteen-year-old beauty with dark hair and a slim figure that captured my attention immediately. Her eyes were dark with heavy eyebrows and her skin was tanned and flawless, giving her the exotic look of a Polynesian girl I had once seen in the movies.

During the course of the meeting, which was sparsely attended and chaired by Mrs. Peterson, the preacher's wife, the topic focused on matters of religious importance. However, my mind wandered to thoughts far removed from religion as I stared at the girl across the room. After the meeting had adjourned, several of the members were milling around and talking in Reverend Peterson's study where the meeting was conducted. In attendance was Jay Peterson, who was the pudgy and obnoxious twelve-year-old son of the preacher. His offensive behavior was directed toward the girl who had been the object of my attention during the meeting, Dorothy Parks. Jay was hitting and pushing her in a way that was causing her obvious distress. Well, in a flash, Tom Twyford came to her rescue. Since neither the preacher nor his wife was present, I kicked Jay's fat ass out of his father's study and threatened to report his conduct to the Reverend. He mumbled a few words and exited the door with the benefit of my not-so-gentle urging. The girl smiled at me, said thank you and I asked if I could walk her home. She nodded O.K. and we left the church. We had only gone a few steps and I had just started to tell her about her heroic savior, when she said, "Here we are." How the hell was I to know she only lived a few doors from the church? Anyway, we talked outside her house for a few more minutes and I said, "I'll be seeing you around," as she went in the house and closed the door. I wouldn't go so far as to say it was love at first sight, but I knew right there and then Dorothy Parks hadn't seen the last of Tom Twyford. We had our first date a short time later: a movie at the Capitol and hamburgers at a place called "Stans."

* * *

I had been attending Big Red football games two years before I entered high school, and had listened to the radio broadcasts as far back as I remember. The participation and attendance of the student body at Big Red games was nearly one hundred percent. On Thursday nights, we had big pep rallies that featured the band, cheerleaders and sometimes a bonfire. The players and coaches were introduced one by one to the deafening roar of the crowd. The rally concluded with the band playing and marching down Fourth Street toward downtown, followed by mobs of student cheering and yelling their lungs out, getting hyped up for the game the next night.

The success or failure of the Big Red on the gridiron meant everything to the community. The players were adopted by the fans and their performance was viewed as an extension of the level of achievement we all could share. When the days became shorter and a chill filled the air, a feeling of anticipation gripped the hearts and minds of the Big Red faithful.

At kickoff time, a thin mist of smoke and fog gathered beneath the lights. The second the kicker's foot struck the pigskin, a roar erupted from ten thousand voices that was loud enough to wake the dead in Union Cemetery just beyond the stadium fence. Then a chant arose from the student section, "Hit em in the belly, Kick em in the jaw, Throw em in the graveyard, Rah, Rah, Rah."

My junior year was a banner year for the Big Red. Our football team routinely had all the state powerhouses on their schedule. The teams from Canton McKinley and Massillon Washington were legendary in Ohio high school football. As some indication of just how seriously football was taken, every baby boy that was born in Massillon, Ohio was given a regulation football as a gift from their Chamber of Commerce.

That season of 1951, we destroyed the Canton McKinley Bulldogs at Faucet Stadium before 20,000 fans. We were undefeated and ranked number two right behind the Massillon Tigers when we met them late in the season at our Harding Stadium. Massillon was loaded as usual. They dressed close to eighty players for the game. Watching them take the field wearing the Tiger colors of orange and black would have been enough to intimidate the Pittsburgh Steelers. However, when the Big Red came charging onto the field behind our high-stepping band, all hell broke loose.

The game was a low-scoring struggle with Massillon substituting players freely after every other play. Few, if any, of their players played both offense and defense and with talent three or four-deep at every position, they had fresh players on the field throughout the game. Our starting eleven was not to be denied. Led by Calvin (C.J.) Jones, Eddie (Punkin) Vincent, Benny Bunch and Frank (Shaggs) Gillium, they gave the fresh-legged Tigers all they could handle and more.

By late in the fourth quarter the score was Big Red-12, Massillon 7, with the clock on the scoreboard showing two minutes and thirty seconds. The Tigers got the ball on their own twenty-yard line when, from the Massillon bench, came a two-hundred-twenty pound fullback in a clean uniform whose name was Ace Grooms. It was rumored that Massillon had recruited him from Pennsylvania when they got his old man a good job in Tigertown. Anyway, this guy was awesome as he ripped off yardage in eight and ten-yard chunks through our exhausted line. Then with just time for one more play, our weary guys lined up, full of determination on the seven-yard line. Grooms was hit in the back field as everyone was screaming in anticipation of victory. But this bull broke two tackles and carried two defenders with him over the goal line as time ran out. Final score Massillon-13, Steubenville-12.

The basketball team that season proved to be just as successful as the football team. The coach was Angelo Vacarro who also coached the baseball team. "Ange," as he was called, was a popular and well respected coach at Big Red for many years. The team he put on the court in 1952 was certainly one of the best ever. Big Red went through the entire regular season without a loss, knocking off some very good teams in the process. The biggest obstacle in our path that year was Wellsville, a team from just up the river. To be more specific, it was their star player, Bevo Francis, who at six foot nine became a basketball legend of the 1950s.

We had played Wellsville and Bevo during the regular season, coming away with a victory by a narrow margin. When we met them again in the district finals, the press was touting this as the game that would determine the state championship. Coach Vacarro assigned the job of guarding Bevo Francis to our bruising center Calvin Jones, who was to become the most famous football player in Big Red history. C.J. stuck to the much taller Francis like glue, making him miss shots he normally made. A few well-placed elbows to big Bevo's ribs had the big man off his game and we chalked up another win. After breezing through the regional finals, we headed to Columbus with a record of twenty-eight wins and no losses to meet Middletown for the state high school championship.

I had never been to Columbus, which lies one hundred-fifty miles west of Steubenville. Everyone in town who could find a way headed for Columbus and the big game. My friend Chuck Levy had an old station wagon in which six of us made the trip.

The game was on Saturday night, but we arrived the day before on Friday afternoon. I was in awe of downtown Columbus, which had wide streets, big hotels, fancy restaurants and the State Capitol Building right in the center of it all. Fans from Steubenville crammed every hotel and crowded the downtown streets. Here we were, sixteen year old boys on our own in the big city looking for adventure. Half of the rooms at the elegant Deshler-Wallack Hotel were occupied by people from home. We wound up checking out the pre-game parties that were in full swing on every floor of the high-rise hotel. Of course, our group of guys was not the only one, as teenagers were in and out of rooms and roaming the halls, raising hell throughout the hotel. At one point, a house detective chewed us out and ordered us to vacate the premises.

Somehow, I wound up in a very sophisticated and dimly lit cocktail lounge in the lobby called The Hour Glass Room. There was a bar that circled around a large sparkling and revolving hour glass. Along with a couple of my friends, I bellied up to the crowded bar and ordered my favorite high-ball from home, a sloe gin fizz. I really hated the taste of the stuff, but I liked the name and the way it sounded as the words "sloe-gin fizz" rolled off my tongue. I half expected the bartender to call the "house dick," but he set down my drink in a tall glass. I sat there in the semi-darkness sipping my drink, smoking a cigarette and watching a couple of babes table hop around the room—what a life!

The next day was Saturday and it rained all day. The gloom of the weather settled over Big Red as we lost to the Middies, but being state runners-up wasn't too shabby.

* * *

After his sophomore year in high school, my friend Chuck Switzer browbeat his parents to sign so he could quit school and join the navy. He had been driving a grocery truck for Mar-Kay Market, so, once again, I went after Chuck's old job. The Mar-Kay, which stood for the name of the owner, Maurice Katz, was on the corner of Fifth and Ross Streets. I was well acquainted with these folks because it was in my old neighborhood and we had bought groceries there for years. Maurice had a younger brother Lou who had the assignment of training me to be Chuck's replacement. I had just started a driver's training course at high school, but Lou needed to teach me the finer points of driving a Ford panel truck all over town.

This was in 1951 and before the days of the supermarket. Customers could, of course, come to the store to buy their groceries and take them home, but they also had the option of having their grocery order delivered. There were perhaps six or seven grocery stores that delivered at that time and Mar-Kay was one of the oldest and best.

In addition to mastering the driving, I had to learn the routes, all the customers' names and any peculiarities about deliveries to their homes. For most people, I unloaded the groceries on the kitchen table and put dairy items in the refrigerator. Some customers paid upon delivery, while others did not, but I had free access to their homes, usually through an unlocked back door, where I would loudly announce my presence by yelling out "Mar-Kay."

I kept the same schedule at school that I had while working at Blum Brothers. I got out of school last period each day at 2:30 p.m. and worked until the deliveries were made. Then I stocked shelves or took orders over the telephone for the next day's deliveries. Customers called the store and I wrote up in detail the items they needed. For instance, a customer would order "two nice pork chops, a pound of lean bacon, three juicy grapefruits and a case of cold beer, and make sure it's cold when delivered." I usually got off work by 6:30 p.m. On Saturdays, which was our busiest day, I worked about ten to twelve hours. I really liked my job and Maurice and Lou Katz were very good to me.

My starting pay was twelve dollars a week, which enabled me to be financially independent. That is, I bought all my own clothes and had my own spending money. I continued to buy the best of threads from the best haberdasher in town, old Myer Pearlman. All I had to do was walk in the store and say, "Myer, make me look good," and he would say, "Tommy, have I got the one-button roll perfect for you."

A one-button roll" was a suit jacket that had wide padded shoulders, long lapels with a narrow taper at the hips, and a single button waist high. Any other kind of suit was unthinkable for a sharp guy like me. Of course, the pants had to be "pegged" to fourteen inches at the cuff.

I was as particular about my customers as I was about the way I dressed. It was important to me that they like Tommy Twyford and my employer, Mar-Kay Market. At times, I had to beg-off talking with them, explaining that I had to get a rib-roast delivered to so and so, in order that dinner could be served on time.

Many of our customers were C.O.D., so when I delivered the groceries, they paid me on the spot. The bills were made out at the store and put in the grocery box. When I collected the money and made change, I soon noticed that several of our customers had grocery bills for as much as a thousand dollars. However, they only paid the current bill and the balance was carried forward. After making some discreet inquiries about these large bills, I found out that these balances were fifteen to twenty years old. During the Great Depression of the 1930s, Maurice never ceased providing food to customers who were out of work and couldn't pay. The charges still appeared on the bills years later, but I don't think Maurice ever expected payment.

My salary of twelve dollars a week was enhanced by the enjoyment and sense of satisfaction that couldn't be measured in dollars. On cool summer mornings before the neighborhood was fully awake, I'd hose down the sidewalk in front of the store and sweep it with a push broom. Using a long metal crank, I lowered the green-and-white awnings that shaded the storefront from the afternoon sun. Then I carefully arranged boxes that contained peaches, plums, grapes and apples under the awnings for display. The stickers on the wooden fruit boxes had colorful pictures that bore the likeness of fair-skinned maidens wearing scooped-necked blouses and carrying baskets of fruit from the orchards. Family names were part of the unique logos that also indicated the far-western origins of the fruit. It was a quiet time of the day and I enjoyed performing this routine before the fast pace of filling orders and deliveries began.

Christmas at the Mar-Kay was a bonanza for me. Just like the customers on my paper route took care of the paper boy, the customers of Mar-Kay remembered their delivery boy. We had a wide cross-section of customers ranging from very poor to very rich, and they all extended their generosity to me at Christmas. However, not all my gifts were money. Many people gave me scarves, neckties, shirts, handkerchiefs, candy and homemade cookies or Christmas cakes.

One customer in particular, Mrs. R.C. Williams, was a very wealthy and sophisticated older lady, who would come into the store once a week in the company of her chauffeur, an old black man named Clyde. Clyde, who always dressed in livery, escorted her into the store and then waited by the door while I accompanied her up and down the aisles, picking out the items of her choice. Then we went to the butcher who presented, for her approval, two lamb chops. It never failed that they were "just right." She graciously thanked everyone as she left with Clyde carrying the groceries. As he drove away, she sat in the back seat of her black 1938 Packard Touring Car. The day before Christmas, Clyde dropped by the store in the Packard and handed me a white envelope with beautiful handwriting on it which said, "Merry Christmas Tommy Twyford from Mrs. R.C. Williams " Everything from the presentation to the envelope and the generous personalized check inside was top drawer and classy as hell. I thought that someday I would like to have a chauffeur like Clyde, but I would let him sit in the back seat while I did the driving.

There were several other full-service markets in Steubenville, and I got to know the delivery boys from the other stores. We always gave a friendly honk when we passed each other in our trucks. Sometimes we stopped and shot the shit with each other for a while. One such guy who became my close friend was Richard Harrison, who, at all times, had a wad of bubble gum in his mouth. We called him "The Bubble Gum Jew."

Richard worked for his uncle's grocery store and was my age, although a year behind me in school. I had also known him from hanging around the YMCA, where he was a star basketball player in a league comprised of much older guys. Richard was small and slightly built, but a natural athlete who could shoot and dribble rings around guys much bigger and older. He was only on the high school team for a very short while. Once he asserted his independent attitude to coach Angelo Vacarro, the Bubble Gum Jew was out the door.

Richard was also an accomplished pool player. We hung out at the Academy Pool Hall and Hat Cleaning establishment. This place was owned at one time by Jimmy "The Greek" Snyder, the famous gambler and odds maker who moved from Steubenville to Las Vegas. Anyway, Richard and I put our money together and set up a kitty, which we wagered on Richard playing against any sucker dumb enough to take him on at a game of eight ball. Sometimes, Richard would let the patsy win a game or two to build up his confidence, but when the bet was raised, the Bubble Gum Jew ran the table. More than once we had to make a hasty exit in order to avoid getting beat up by some pissed-off loser.

Richard had an old Chevy and when we weren't out cruising around, we could usually be found at Herbie Goodrnan's Cigar Store, which was downtown next to the Ft. Steuben Hotel. The baseball scores came in on the ticker tape at Herbie's and Richard and I would mark the inning-by-inning results of each game on a blackboard that covered one wall. Herbie gave us free cokes and snacks for performing this service. All evening long, guys dropped by to check the scores and see how they were doing with the bets and parlays they played earlier that day. Men, women and even kids would come in to play the numbers or try their luck on the punch boards. Occasionally, Herbie actually managed to sell a cigar or two.

After all the baseball games were over, we drifted across the street to the Hi Hat Tavern to get one of their meatball sandwiches. The meatball sandwich at the Hi Hat Tavern was famous throughout the upper Ohio Valley. The owner of the Hi Hat was "Stogie" DeSarro who invented this sandwich and was a good friend of my Uncle Tom. A half loaf of crusty Italian bread was hollowed out and three steaming meatballs and a generous portion of sauce were put inside the warm cave of crust. It was impossible to get your mouth around this meal in a loaf, but with the aid of a knife and fork, I could usually put a big dent in it.

Along with the Hi Hat meatball sandwich, Steubenville had another culinary claim to fame, Primo DeCarlo's Pizza. Primo's pizza shop had humble beginnings in a small storefront on South Third Street. He had four stacked ovens where rectangular trays of dough with "filetto di pomodoro" topping baked until the sauce was bubbling and the thick crust was crisp. As the steaming trays were taken from the oven, the pizza was covered with a shredded mozzarella cheese and handfuls of sliced pepperoni. Since the pepperoni was put on after the pizza was baked, there were no pools of grease on top. Then the tray of pizza was cut into twenty squares that cost ten cents apiece. A slice of De Carlo's pizza was a slice of Steubenville itself. Most of the town's population had a conditioned response to the De Carlo name and would salivate upon it's mere mention. "Primo" in Italian means the best and De Carlo's was the "numero uno" pizza in the world.

A short way down the street from Herbie's was a place called the Musical Bar. The management of this place wasn't too particular about the age of their patrons. Word got out that if they weren't too busy on a week night, a thirsty sixteen-year-old might just be able to enjoy a brew at the piano bar. A lot of my friends had taken advantage of this opportunity, so I finally succumbed to their urgings to participate. I was indeed sixteen years old, if barely, but I had the appearance of a very mature looking twelve-year-old. Everyone said that they never turned anyone down at the Musical Bar, but guys were laying bets that I would be the first. It was my idea to wear this snap brim pork-pie hat turned down over my forehead so I might look something like a younger version of Humphrey Bogart in "The Big Sleep." If the truth be known, I didn't much like the taste of beer and would have preferred a coke, but this would have ruined the bets, so I shocked everyone and told the barmaid in my deepest voice I wanted a Sloe Gin Fizz. She never flinched and mixed up this concoction that tasted like cherry cough syrup for which I laid down a buck and told her to keep the change.

There were about five of us guys sitting at the bar, which surrounded a piano being played by a talented old pro who was singing one dirty ditty after another. I was fascinated by this live entertainment and clever lyrics that had us all laughing till we hurt.

The lyrics to one of the more memorable numbers were, "I love to nibble on her cupcakes just like her mother's their just right and left."

My Mom wouldn't have approved of the way I conducted myself, but I figured what she didn't know wouldn't hurt her. With her health continuing to be a matter for concern, if somehow she found out about some of my antics it would cause her more anxiety. While I sometimes felt guilty and had all the best intentions, it wasn't enough to cause me to undergo a miraculous transformation. After her initial bout with cancer in the fall of 1950, it was an on-again, off-again situation. She did regain enough of her vitality to return to work at the curtain shop, but her periods of work were intermittently interrupted by relapses and additional surgeries. While she did have her good days, for the most part, she never felt quite well. As could be expected, this nagging illness took its toll upon her personality and temperament.

At some point, she started to get hooked on faith healers and some of these kooky radio and TV preachers. One of these charlatans sent her a "prayer cloth" for a modest donation, which she was to place upon the afflicted part of her body to affect a cure. She swore to high heaven that this piece of fabric blessed by some self-ordained phony baloney actually helped her. I never took issue with her in this regard. If it made her feel better, who was I to argue?

There was this woman faith healer from Pittsburgh named Katherine Kuhlman who my Mom saw on television. Sister Katherine announced that she was having a crusade to be held at Steubenville High School auditorium. Mom insisted that I attend this gathering of the faithful with her. It was on a Sunday afternoon and bus loads of the sick and lame converged upon the high school. The only prayer I uttered was that I wouldn't be seen by anyone who knew me. The place was jammed to capacity with people lying in the aisles, crying and talking in tongues. I shrunk down in my seat as far as I could go, but I could see from the corner of my eye the tears on my Mom's cheek. She reached over to me and held my hand. When she did this, tears also came to my eyes, so I sat up straight and realized I had to be the man she could depend upon.

The Old man
(center) with 2 other
boilermakers

The Twyford Kids,
Virginia, Marjorie, and
Billy with Aunt Marie
before I came along

Mother and Father
circa: 1925

"The Old Man" somewhere
at the crossroads

Tom Twyford   131

Fifth Grade class, Garfield School (1945)

I'm looking for
a curve ball

Catwalk

Panhandle R.R. Bridge
and two not-so-smart ideas!

Anything for a smoke

Seventh Grade at
Grant School

Fishing in Canada with Cousin
Tommy Woods

Tom Twyford   133

Fifth Street Methodist Church

Naples Spaghetti House
"A Taste of Italy"

Dorothy all dressed up
for Christmas on
"Prom Night" (1954)

"Check out that one button roll"

Lieutenant Twyford
standing "AT EASE" in
front of quarters

On the boat to Alaska
before I developed
a severe case of
seasickness

My first new car—a 1958 Impala convertible

Lieutenant Twyford at his desk. Headquarters and Headquarters Company, First Battle Group, 23rd Infantry, Fort Richardson, Alask

Dorothy as a fashion model.
"What did she ever see in me?"

Dorothy as a hula dancer
at officer's club party

Elegant in dress blues

The difference between right and wrong was no mystery to me. However, my resolve to be "mister goody-two-shoes" did not fit my image. The good and bad in me continued to blow hot and cold as I teetered between good intentions and the reality of my conduct.

The houses "down the line" were a seven-day-a-week business and, in spite of the unsavory line of work conducted there, they were notorious and widely known. In a way, "the line" was something like a tourist attraction that lacked the sophistication of a string of art museums. Before I swore off making any more visits "down the line," I can't forget a series of events that made this a part of a memorable Christmas Eve.

I had gone to the candlelight services at church with Dorothy and Mom, and Virginia sang a solo of "O Holy Night." After church, I went up to Dorothy's house and all her relatives were there. Her mom was serving coffee, cocoa and fruitcake. Since she had all this company, I didn't think I should stick around too long, so I said good night at about 9:00 p.m.

It was too early to go home, so I wandered down to the Academy Pool Hall. There were a few guys there that I knew, among them Bob Spenski. He was a year older than me and a member of the senior class. Bob drove a red Ford Sunliner convertible and lived in a big white brick house in Brady Estates. His old man had plenty of dough, and it was no secret that he owned several whorehouses.

Well, nothing much was going on at the Academy, so Bob suggested we go down under the Market Street bridge to pay a Christmas visit to one of his old man's places. There were five of us guys and we were welcomed by the Madam like we were long-lost friends. It being Christmas Eve, there was no business, but there were still five or six girls on duty. Anyway, what kind of pervert would be in a cathouse at 10:30 p.m. on Christmas Eve?

Once inside one of these whorehouses, we found they were actually very nicely furnished. The couches and big overstuffed chairs would make a person feel right at home, except the stuff we had at my house wasn't nearly so nice. Considering that these girls were in what some might regard as a dirty business, I can tell you that the houses were clean as a pin. As a matter of fact, most of the houses had a sweet scent of some kind of floral soap that smelled like the cosmetic department in The Hub department store.

The girls were in the kitchen making salad, dressed in bathrobes. They insisted that we have some, along with a bottle of beer they cracked open for each of us. We just sat around in the kitchen shooting the breeze and enjoying our salad and beer. I had just started on my second beer when I checked the time: it was 11:30 p.m. Holy Shit. I had promised the Laffertys to go to midnight mass with them at St. Peters. I thanked the Madam and the girls for the salad and the beer and hot footed it up to St. Peters through a light snowfall just in time to meet Mrs. Lafferty and Chuckie at the bowl of holy water in the church entrance.

* * *

I had a pretty good idea that Dorothy's parents didn't consider me as any trophy for their daughter—far from it. Most likely, they suffered in a quiet state of resignation and hoped for the best. Come to think of it, there was probably no set of parents in all of Steubenville that would have had Tom Twyford's name on any list of most eligible catches.

Toward the end of my junior year, Dorothy and I started to "go steady." I was sixteen years old and she was all of fourteen. My Mom gave me a small onyx ring set in gold that she had had since she was a girl, and I gave it to Dorothy as a "going steady" ring. A part of me really tried to resist this idea of exclusivity as far as girls were concerned. However, whenever I tried to develop an interest in anyone else, like Linda, Mary Jane or Gloria, none of them could come close to Dorothy in my eyes. Also, there were other guys who were predictably attracted to her and the thought of her dating anyone other than me made me ill.

One on occasion, I learned that a boy in her class named Bob Quinn started putting the moves on her and walked her home from Swing Haven. Even though we weren't yet going steady, I cornered Bob at school one day and told him to stay away from "my girl." Just to emphasize the point, I slammed him up against the wall lockers and added some warnings of dire consequences. I felt safe in taking this gallant action, since Bob was a brainy type with no taste for physical confrontation.

While Dorothy and I were captivated and enamored with one another, I think it was different for me. Dorothy came from a stable home with loving parents and relatives. I had never felt the security of being openly loved, nor had I ever been touched in a loving way. It was hard for me to believe that another person could feel such love for me, much less this beautiful girl. I didn't believe this really could be happening to me, but I would never allow myself to let her know how deeply I was touched by her affection. I felt that I had to maintain this tough exterior, but by doing so, I'm sure that she often felt that I was indifferent to her loving words and gestures. Nothing could have been further from the truth, but this was a mechanism I used to protect myself from being hurt. In spite of my hang-ups and immaturity, we fell in love.

My scholastic progress remained in the doldrums. I made a half-assed effort at most of my subjects, but I had yet to make an effort to excel. Toward the end of my junior year, I was nominated to be a member of the Key Club, which was an organization sponsored by Kiwanis International. Only the top male students were invited to join. I'm certain my invitation was based solely upon my popularity and not because of any academic achievements on my part. When the faculty advisor got wind that I had been proposed for membership, he put the kibosh on that in a hurry, so I was turned down for admission. This incident got me to thinking that it was time I got my ass in gear.

Many of my classmates were talking about going to college when they graduated. Some of them made visits with their parents to college campuses and were excited about the prospects of entering a profession. I had no idea what I wanted to do, and my "C" average grades did not make me a good prospect for any institution of higher learning. Besides, the courses I had been taking were not in the college preparatory curriculum. I talked with my boss, Maurice Katz, at the grocery store, along with Miss Helen Brown, the math teacher, and Miss Eleanor Giles, my speech teacher, and they encouraged me to consider college after graduation. Without any firm plan or any idea what career path I wished to follow, I made up my mind that I was going to college. This meant that I would have to get really serious about my studies from here on out, and that's exactly what I did. My class was loaded with brainy guys and gals. Out of a class of two hundred students, I started my senior year buried well down in the lower half. Just studying hard would not get me where I wanted to be. I had to repair my credibility with the teachers and shed my reputation as a goof-off.

I had developed a fondness for poetry and verse, especially ballads. The poet who was my absolute favorite was Rudyard Kipling. I have recited "Gunga Din" over and over again since the tenth grade and though my army years, mostly while quite drunk. Kipling struck a chord with me that gave me a sense of harmony. His famous poem "If" ends with the lines:

"If you can fill the unforgiving minute
with sixty seconds worth of distance run,
Yours is the earth and everything that's in it,
and what's more, you'll be a man my son."

The words of this poem I thought to be the most meaningful and inspirational of any lines in all of English verse. I have, in times of personal trouble and anguish, read selected lines from this poem, much as a religious zealot would read a prayer or a passage from the Bible. My love of poetry was a guide that helped me formulate a set of personal values that continue to sustain me.

Even though I was working at the Mar-Kay Market about twenty-five hours a week, I would never miss out on being part of any theatrical production put on at school. I got one of the leading roles in the Junior Class Play and Lou Katz was kind enough to cover part of my route for me so I could attend play practice. In keeping with my natural propensity for being a ham and a show-off, I continued my theatrics all during my senior year. I had the spotlight and the time of my life as the master of ceremonies for the senior assembly, which was a variety show of senior talent. I recited Casey at the Bat and injected all the emotional gestures I could contrive right up to the final verse and Casey's disappointing strike out. I wasn't the right type to get the male lead in the Senior Play, but I did manage to get the role as the leading character actor. The cast members of these plays and shows formed a close bond and some of the best times I can recall were at play practices and cast parties.

True to my resolution to turn over a new academic leaf my senior year, I managed to crack the honor roll for each grading period. In spite of my best efforts, I was no threat to the real brains of the Class of 1953, who were Stanley Freedman and my old friend from Garfield Grade School, Ieda Bernstein.

More often than not, we fail to appreciate how very good we have it until our situation changes for the worse. Not so with me. During my senior year in high school, I was well aware that this was a magical time in my life. Everything just seemed to fall into place for me. The excitement of all the activities and the fact that I had finally gained some measure of respect and achievement gave me a newfound confidence. Still, in a small corner of my mind was a lingering doubt that I tried to ignore, a voice that said this good time wouldn't last.

In the early spring of 1953, I was invited to go to New York with Dorothy and her parents for Easter vacation. Her uncle Bill and Aunt Babe lived in Seaford, Long Island. Their home was a Cape Cod that backed up to a canal and was situated on a quiet street. I had never before seen the ocean. Uncle Bill had a 36-foot boat he parked in the canal behind the house. He worked for the Long Island Railroad and he and Aunt Babe opened their home as a vacation destination to all the relatives back in Steubenville. Aunt Babe was a native New Yorker and a marvelous hostess. She stuffed me with seafood and her homemade cheesecake and I was treated as one of the family. The room assigned to me was in the attic with a view of the canal and the smell of fresh salt air. Nobody had to tell me that I was a long way from home.

Dorothy and I spent the better part of a whole day strolling along a near-deserted boardwalk at Jones Beach. The weather was raw with a cold wind conning off the ocean, which stimulated the romance and excitement of the day. I can't remember what we talked about, but I'll never forget that feeling of youthful joy. There are perhaps a handful of days in a lifetime that stand out in my mind as being perfect, and this was one of those days.

It was Easter weekend and I had never been to New York City. After getting detailed instructions from Aunt Babe and Uncle Bill, Dorothy and I boarded the commuter train for the ninety-minute ride into New York City. As I looked out the window of the train, I was fascinated by everything I saw. I was a slack-jawed rube trying to take in everything at once, while still making an attempt to impress my girlfriend with a faked worldly demeanor.

We had tickets to see the Easter show at Rockefeller Center. This, too, was a first for me, seeing the world-famous Rockettes perform on this grand stage in this beautiful theater. After the show, we had hot dogs, which we bought from a street vendor, and just walked around taking in the sights until it was time to catch the train back to Long Island. It was dark inside the train, and we sat side-by-side holding hands as the lights of the city flashed by two kids who were in love and perfectly contented in a world of their own.

That spring was like none other. The pale green of the new leaves on trees between home and school had a fresh smell that prompted me to reduce my normally quickened pace to a stroll. Even the rain had a special softness and good feeling, so I didn't care if I got wet or if my white bucks got dirty. This heightened awareness of what was just normal for April and May was a first for me. All things were possible in that spring of 1953 in the weeks before graduation.

The theme for the senior prom was Evening in Paris. In the weeks preceding the prom, the popular "Song from Moulin Rouge" was piped over the school's public address system along with the daily announcements. Although I'd never been much farther than Paris, PA, the music and colorful posters of Paris street scenes plastered in the hallways had the intoxicating effect of the real thing.

When I knocked on the door at the Parks' residence in my rented white sport coat with a pink carnation, Mrs. Parks ushered me in the living room to wait for Dorothy to come downstairs. In just a few minutes, Dorothy walked in the room followed by her beaming parents. She was wearing a strapless white evening gown with the corsage I sent her on her wrist. For a moment I was speechless, totally dazzled by this gorgeous girl who stood before me. How in the hell could I be so lucky?

By this time, Dorothy and I were spending a good part of every day in each other's company. At school, I would meet her outside each of her classes and walk with her to her next class. I would take detours in the grocery truck and park in the alley behind her house just long enough to run in and get a kiss while the ice cream melted in the truck. There was seldom a night that I wasn't at her house, and we would linger at her front door clutched in an embrace until the third or fourth reminder that I should leave was shouted down from upstairs.

I didn't think anything could put a damper on that magical spring of 1953. However, Boogie's black muzzle was now completely gray and she had a field of fatty tumors on her chest and belly. These were things I chose to ignore until she began to have seizures, which increased in frequency to be a daily occurrence. Mom said it was time to spare her any more suffering and she called the veterinarian, Doctor Haverfield.

On a warm morning in early June, I stood on the back porch holding Boogie, with tears streaming down my face, as Dr. Haverfield put a needle in a vein of Boogie's front leg. She cocked her head, looked at me and dropped like a rock. That same evening, I graduated from high school.

My sister Marge was in Germany at this time visiting with my brother George and his wife, Diana. He was in the Army and living the good life in Bavaria. Virginia was also away and I don't know where my old man might have been, but he didn't make it to my graduation. So, my Mom, Dorothy and both her parents were my rooting section at the graduation ceremonies.

It was a perfect evening in June at Harding Stadium where the diplomas were handed out by our principal, A.C. May. There were two hundred and two graduates, one hundred one boys and one hundred one girls. After everyone was called by name to get their diploma, the Valedictorian, Stanley Freedman, and Salutatorian, Ieda Bernstein, were given special recognition and each gave a short speech. Then special awards were given to individual graduates who excelled in some particular areas of study or endeavor. Names were called, and awards were presented to the most outstanding graduates in the fields of math, science, English and several other areas of scholastic achievement.

I was barely paying attention when my name was called to come forward to the presentation stand. My first thought was that it was some mistake. As I took the long walk to the front, I was racking my brain trying to think how I could possibly be honored and for what? When I reached the stand, I saw Miss Giles, the speech teacher, step forward from where the faculty was seated. She was smiling at me as she spoke into the microphone: "And the award from the Carnegie Institute of Technology for Outstanding Achievement in Speech and Dramatic Arts goes to Tom Twyford."

I didn't know any such award existed and when she said, "Please accept this award of five hundred dollars for your fine efforts," this outstanding speech guy was speechless. As I got back to my seat with the envelope in my hand, the guy sitting next to me asked if I was going to count it. "No," I said, "It's probably a check," but I peeked inside the envelope just to make sure.

After graduation, I began working full time at the Mar-Kay. I needed to save all my money because I had made the decision to go to college in the fall. Ten of my classmates had applied and been accepted at Ohio University located in Athens, Ohio. Several of them showed me the literature they had on the school. The pictures in the school catalog made the campus appear like scenes from New England. Since it was a state-supported school, the tuition wasn't nearly as expensive as many other colleges and universities. With very little further investigation on my part, I sent in my application to Ohio U.

About a month after graduation, I was hanging out with some of the guys at Coes Drive-In, munching on burgers, when someone suggested that it would be a swell night for a swim. Immediately everyone agreed that this was a great idea, and the Steubenville County Club wasn't far away. It was about midnight when two carloads of us took off for the swimming pool by the golf course. There were eight of us in the two cars as we cut the lights and parked under some trees near the entrance to the club. The July sky was lit up with stars and a full moon as we made our way giggling and pushing each other toward the eight-foot fence which surrounded the pool. The moonlight reflecting off the water made it look all the more tempting, and the fence was no big deal to agile seventeen and eighteen-year-old trespassers.

We quickly shed our clothes and quietly eased into the pool buck naked. The water was cool and invigorating as I lay floating on my back staring up at the sky. Then I saw one of the guys bounce off the high board in a cannonball tuck, crashing into the water with a loud splash. It wasn't two seconds later before the pool area was lit up like a Christmas tree. The harsh lights were momentarily blinding as we all scrambled out of the water and threw our shoes and clothes over the fence. It must have been an interesting sight for the watchman as he emerged from the club house to see eight bare asses humping over the fence and running out of the light on to the golf course. I could hear the old watchman mumbling as I crouched behind some bushes a safe distance from the pool. I was starting to shiver as I jerked on my pants and ran barefoot through the wet grass, carrying my shoes back to where the cars were parked. We all got there about the same time and the cars took off, throwing gravel in their wake.

Everyone in the car was laughing and someone suggested we get some beer, but somehow I just wasn't in the mood and asked to be dropped off at home. I had lost my shirt and as I got out of the car, one of the guys said we should do it again next week. "Count me in," I said, as the car pulled away, but I knew a night like that would never happen again.

On July 31st of that summer, Dorothy had her sixteenth birthday. Her dad was kind enough or crazy enough, I don't know which, to lend me his car to take her to Myers Lake Amusement Park in Canton, Ohio, for her birthday. He had a canary yellow 1953 Hudson Hornet convertible, a car before its time. I seriously doubt that lending me the car was his idea. He most likely succumbed to the pleadings and pressures of his daughter and wife, but it sure was generous of him. Having the car was a real treat, but my most vivid recollection of that night was Dorothy in a red-and-white, candy-striped dress, seated side saddle on a carousel, radiating pure beauty at sweet sixteen.

Chapter 10

Low points, Gut Checks, and Moving On (1953–1954)

A good place to work

Before I knew it, that wonderful summer came to an end and it was September and time to leave for college. I hadn't visited the campus at Ohio University, so I really didn't know what to expect. The university had sent me a large packet of confusing information about orientation week, which raised more questions than it answered.

Ten members of my graduating class were attending O.U. and I had planned to be roommates with two of them, Jerry Kindsvatter and Al Ludlum. In the final days before our departure, we got together to discuss this new phase of our lives. Both of these guys were excellent students and were eager to get going. They had visited the school, so they could speak with authority about the ins and outs of college life. Jerry and Al had the word on everything from how to dress to what fraternity they were going to pledge. I soon got caught up in their enthusiasm and was excited about the prospect of being a college man.

Dorothy's parents insisted that they drive me to school and invited my Mom to come along. As the days grew short before it was time for me to leave, Dorothy started moping around and tearing up every time the word college was mentioned. Any enthusiasm I had about embarking on this sea of higher education was soon drowned in waves of my girlfriend's tears. I began to have serious doubts about the whole idea of going to college. However, I had told everyone about my big plans for college and I had sent in my tuition, so I was committed; it was too late to back out.

We left on a Sunday in September for the one-hundred-twenty mile ride from Steubenville to Ohio University in Athens. Somebody had given me a Samsonite suitcase for graduation, which I had packed with most of my worldly possessions. Mr. Parks was driving his new DeSoto automobile with Mrs. Parks beside him and Mom, Dorothy and I in the back. Mrs. Parks tried to keep a light conversation going, which was hard to do, what with the frequent loud sobs coming from her daughter in the back seat. I had my arm around Dorothy while I whispered reassuring words in her ear, but I needed reassurance myself. It was a long, miserable ride.

It was a bright and sunny day in early autumn and the campus had a picture-book appearance. As we turned onto the street where my dormitory, Scott Quadrangle, was located, cars were parked on both sides of the street unloading new freshmen with all their belongings. We had to park way down the street, but since I only had the one suitcase, unloading was no problem. I asked everyone to wait in the car while I went in to check things out.

The place was a mass of activity with parents, students, luggage and boxes crowding the entrance and hallways of the dorm. I found my way to the second floor, third wing where my room was located at the end of a long hall. When I got to the room, the door was open and Jerry and Al were there unpacked and firmly entrenched, looking like they had been living there for a year. Due to my late arrival, I was informed I got the top bunk and the dresser was already taken. My roommates had graciously saved shelf space in a closet where I could put my clothes. It really didn't matter since they each had three times the stuff I did. Besides a bunk bed, a single bed, and dresser, there was a two-man study desk that held Jerry's lamp, Al's name plate and both their books and other supplies in the drawers and on top. I didn't have to ask who got the desk.

In order to drag out the painful goodbye, I rode out to the edge of town where Dorothy and I got out of the car and locked up in a prolonged embrace. Finally, we pried ourselves apart and as the car drove away, I made the long, sad walk back to the dorm, where I arrived five minutes too late to get dinner.

The summer weather of 1953 lingered well into fall. The Harris Tweed sport coat that was the focal point of my collegiate wardrobe was far too heavy for the unseasonably warm temperatures. But, since that was the only jacket with the collegiate look I needed, I sweltered through my first month of college. However, by the time autumn weather finally arrived at Ohio University, my enthusiasm for playing the role of "Joe College" had also cooled off considerably.

Ohio University was a great place to launch a college career, but I never gave it a fair chance. All I could think of was the next time I could get home and see Dorothy. Two weeks after arriving, I hitchhiked home for the weekend. When it was time to return to school, I had to force myself to leave. She wrote me a letter every day, which I would reread time and again, and instead of cheering me up, it kept me in a perpetual state of anguish and longing. I went home every weekend the opportunity presented itself. So, I never really got into the swing of things. Other than a few guys who lived on my floor at the dorm, I made no friends, nor did I become involved in any campus activities.

I was an emotional wreck, unable to function or concentrate on my studies. I had made up my mind by mid-semester that I would not be returning for the second term.

Notwithstanding my delicate mental state, I did manage to attend most of my classes, two of which were drama classes. I was nurturing a vague idea that I wanted to be a drama major and someday pursue a career in radio or television as a sports announcer, or perhaps even a career as an actor on stage or in the movies.

The students in the drama courses were ninety percent girls. The gender of the remaining ten percent was in serious doubt and they made no bones about swishing through role playing identities with a gusto I couldn't muster. I actually enjoyed the classes, but felt sure

I would be identified with the ten percent of animated tight butts who had much more confidence in their acting ability than I had in mine. Since I purposely held back my inhibitions, I failed to make a favorable impression on the instructors, who were not encouraging about my potential for a career in show biz.

I reasoned that if only I could get home, all would be well. I counted the days until the semester was over and I could leave this place for good. At that point, what I needed was someone to give me a good kick in the ass and get me thinking straight. But there was no one to do it, and left to my own devices, I was destined to fuck up, which I did in a big way.

Finally, I was at home and could see my girlfriend every day, but my status had abruptly changed. My high school class had moved on to other things and I was no longer part of the high school scene. Having told everyone that I was going to college, I now had to explain what I was doing at home. Was it my imagination, or could I see them thinking: "Umm, this guy only lasted one semester at college?" I thought everyone looked upon me as a failure.

Dorothy was totally involved in her studies and numerous activities at school, and my hanging around only complicated her life. She did everything she could to cheer me up, but I just felt like I was in the way. My life was a tangle of wire coat hangers that I'd never straightened out. After sitting at home for a couple of weeks feeling sorry for myself, I knew I had to find a job, and jobs were hard to come by that winter.

The prospects for an untrained drop-out were not too promising. Searching help-wanted ads and filling out applications for menial jobs was embarrassing and demeaning. I felt despondent and disgraced because I had acted like a love-sick jackass, never allowing myself to give the college experience a fair chance.

After several weeks of an unsuccessful job search, I finally took a job out of desperation as a driver/salesman for Ace Dry Cleaners. The owner was a guy named Eli Rabb. He owned a jewelry store in town as well. He was about 35 years old and appeared to be very well fed and wore expensive suits with French cuffed shirts and gold monogrammed cuff links. Eli was a smooth talker with greasy skin and wore a diamond pinky ring on his pudgy finger that was painted with clear polish. He was definitely not my kind of guy, and I was not taken in with his bullshit about the promising career this job held in store for me, but it paid a buck an hour, so I went to work.

Ace was a pick-up and delivery dry cleaning service. My job was to make the deliveries and pick up dirty clothes. If that's all there was to it, it wouldn't have been so bad, but I was also expected to go door to door and sell this service. Eli gave me a morning briefing, assigning me specific streets of town to cold canvas for new customers. All of my efforts were to be concentrated on more affluent areas of the hilltop where people could afford the service. At the end of each week, I had a meeting with Eli where I was to present him with a list of the new customers I had successfully solicited that week. My weekly lists were so short that it was not accurate to call them lists at all. In a good week, I would have two names on my "list." I included "maybes" and "I'll think about its." Otherwise, I would have nothing to report for my week's efforts.

My heart just was not into it and I soon found out that I had a low tolerance for rejection. When I rang a doorbell, I would pray that no one would answer. Sometimes, if the person who came to the door had a hostile or irritated look, I would just act as though I had a wrong address. To my way of thinking, it was no big deal for a person to drop off their own laundry or dry cleaning. There were dry cleaners all over town, so only some incredibly lazy person with money to burn would be interested in what Ace had to offer. What I dreaded most was knocking on a door where someone knew me. "I thought you were away at college," they'd say, and I'd reply with some story about gaining business experience as I tried to disengage myself from the situation as fast as possible. It got so bad that I'd park the truck at the end of some street and hide out for a couple of hours reading a book and smoking my pipe. I felt guilty about being a goof-off, but I reached the point where I couldn't knock on another door. If there had been something tangible to sell, I don't think I would have had a problem. But trying to convince people to turn over their dirty skivvies to me just seemed like a bogus idea.

My dad was living and working in Pittsburgh at this time. He was a "pusher" on a big boiler repair job at Jones and Laughlin Steel. He supervised the work of about 12 other boilermakers, which meant he did next to nothing and got an extra two dollars an hour. The old man did have a good deal of clout within the union local and was trying to get me a job as a water boy, a position he created. He had to get the approval of the union business agent before I could get on the payroll. The job would pay a whopping three bucks an hour, so it was worth waiting for. Meanwhile, I had to hang onto my job at Ace.

By this time, the old man had married a woman named Marion. She was a barmaid in her mid-thirties whom he met while working in upper New York State. She was a hefty woman, just short of being fat. Her hair was dark brown, in contrast to her milky white complexion. Marion had an easy way about her and was quick to smile or laugh, which made her immediately likeable. When she spoke, it was apparent she was not an educated person. However, having worked in restaurants and bars all her life, she was wise in a worldly way. I was immediately taken with her and could, see that while she was a complete opposite of my Mom, she was a good choice for the old man.

Finally, I got the word from the old man that it was cleared for me to start work in Pittsburgh as a water boy on the job. I wasted no time in telling Mr. Rabb that I had come to the realization that a dry-cleaning career was not for me. I think he agreed with my assessment and I thanked him for giving me a job.

The old man had made arrangements for me to get a ride from Steubenville to Pittsburgh with a guy called Burley, one of the boilermakers who made the forty mile commute each day. The arrangement further provided that I pay Burley five bucks a week for giving me the ride. This was, of course, O.K. with me and Burley picked me up at 6:00 a.m. each morning for the drive to Pittsburgh.

Burley was anything but burly. He was a skinny guy, about the same age as my old man, with a bald head. When I tried to get a conversation going with him on our rides to and from work, it didn't take long to see we had little in common I gave every subject I could think of a try, even Pirate baseball, but all I could get out of him was an occasional grunt. After the first week, I figured it out: Burly had a hangover every morning and was in no mood for chit-chat with me.

About halfway to Pittsburgh on Route 22 was a truck stop where Burly pulled in every morning at 6:30 am. While I drank a cup of coffee, Burley drank two Ashia Japanese beers with two shots of whiskey on the side. When the waitress saw us come in the door, she sat the two shots and two beers on the counter. Appropriately, a shot and a beer are known as a "boilermaker." Why Burly was partial to the Japanese version of the boilermaker, he didn't say. It only took him about fifteen minutes to knock down these drinks and he was out the door. We'd get about ten miles down the road and Burly pulled over, got out and stood behind the car and pissed like a race horse. This routine never changed the whole time I rode with him.

My job as a water boy really wasn't much of a job at all. I had a portable canister strapped to my back, which had a tube of paper cups attached to the side. It looked very much like a fire extinguisher.

This particular job was primarily an outside job, working off a tank one hundred feet high. This required some climbing up and down the scaffolding both on the inside and outside of the tank. It was early April and still quite cool, so the demand for my service was not great. Basically, I just hung around on the top of the tank shooting the shit with the operating engineer who ran the crane that lifted materials up to the workman. All the guys on the job called me "what-a-boy," or "Gunga Din" and I answered to other less complimentary names as well. I was the brunt of all kinds of practical jokes. They sent me on errands down to the tool room to ask for a "left-handed monkey wrench" or a "sky hook." The tool room guy would tell me all the sky hooks and left-handed monkey wrenches were signed out. When I came back, out of breath from climbing up the tank, to relay this information, all the men would crack up with laughter. How the hell was I to know they were just making a horse's ass out of me? Anyway, if I didn't learn anything else, I sure learned how to take a joke.

The boilermakers and ironworkers used some of the most colorful language I had ever heard. Every sentence they uttered was peppered with obscenities. Not long after I started, the men in the white hats started to come around on a daily basis. These guys were engineers and management men from J & L who were evaluating the progress and quality of the work. Whenever the foreman saw these guys coming, he ordered me to "go fuck the dog"; in other words, get lost, go hide. I found an out-of-the-way cubby hole in a deserted building where I set up my secret headquarters. It was there that I spent the greater part of each day reading Ian Fleming's James Bond novels and smoking my pipe. (To tell the truth, I would much rather have had some real work to do rather than engaging in canine intercourse all day long.)

One day, Burly announced that he was "pulling the pin." This phrase was interpreted to mean that he was quitting, and that's what he did without fanfare or notice. I really wouldn't miss all our stimulating conversations, but I would miss my ride to Pittsburgh.

The old man and Marion had a large furnished apartment in a nice old neighborhood on Pittsburgh's north side. They both insisted that it would be no problem for me to sleep on the couch four nights a week. Another boilermaker would drive me to Steubenville on Fridays after work and back on Monday mornings. This worked out well, except that I needed something to do or somewhere to go on the nights I stayed in Pittsburgh.

There were a couple of movie theaters not far from their apartment where I took in a flick a couple nights a week. One evening, Marion asked me to go to the drug store, which was only a few blocks away. The drug store had a soda fountain and, since I was in no hurry, I sat down at the fountain and ordered a milkshake. The girl who waited on me looked to be about my age and was very friendly. Beside that, she was one sharp chick. She asked where I was from and told me her name was Janet Marx. We talked for quite a while and she asked if I planned to stop by the next evening. I said I would and my visits to the drug store got to be a regular thing. Each night when she got off work, I walked her home. Janet was a high school senior who planned to go to Thiel College at Greenville, Pennsylvania in the fall. I would be lying if I said I didn't enjoy her company, but at the same time, felt pangs of guilt since I had a steady girlfriend.

Naturally, I didn't tell Janet about Dorothy, nor did I think it would be a smart move to tell Dorothy about Janet. Somehow, I doubted that Dorothy would approve of my having a friend in

Pittsburgh who just happened to be a girl. If I could have shown her a picture of some really ugly female, it might have been O.K., but Janet was a far cry from being ugly, so I thought it wise to keep my own counsel. Anyway, our relationship never blossomed into anything too serious, although it probably could have, had I let it. She invited me to her senior prom, but I begged off. For the next year, she occasionally corresponded with me while she was in college. Janet was a lovely girl and certainly deserved somebody better than a two-timing philanderer like me, who, incidentally, was in love with his steady girlfriend.

The job at J & L Steel ended in June, and I was back at home without a job. But, not to worry, the old man was trying through the union to get me a helper's card. This would clear me to work at a repair job that was soon to start at Wheeling Steel in Mingo Junction which was just a few miles down the river from Steubenville. At this time, unless you knew someone to put in a word for you, the chances of getting a job through a trade union were absolutely nil.

I had to wait until July before I got the O.K. to start work as a boilermaker's helper on a temporary permit. The job was for the repair of a boiler. The boilers were needed to produce steam to turn the turbines that generated electricity. It was never explained to me how this fit into the steel-making process, but no one seemed to care if I had an understanding of the big picture. I just performed whatever immediate tasks I was told to do.

The first thing that I noticed upon crossing the pedestrian footbridge and entering the mill was the noise and the heat. All kinds of machinery, cranes, belts and gauges were in operation, and red warning signs were all over the place that said "Danger." I followed along behind our work gang, up several metal catwalks, to the location of the boilers. The one that needed the work was, of course, shut down, but it was in between two other boilers that were fully operational. The heat coming from them kept the temperature in our work area in excess of 110 degrees.

For the first few days I was on the job, they didn't know what to do with me. Any instructions I got had to be shouted loud enough to be heard over the constant din in the mill. Half the time I failed to understand what I was being told, so a pantomime or hand signals were necessary for me to get the message. This was frustrating for me as well as the guy trying to make himself understood. Since I didn't know enough to self-start, all I wound up doing was carrying an end of some heavy piece of metal from the boiler that was being dissembled. The guy on the other end was twice as strong as I was, so he frequently cussed me out for not holding up my end. When the other boilermakers weren't laughing at me or subjecting me to some form of crude humiliation, they just gave me a disgusted look and shook their heads.

These guys came in all shapes and forms, but there was a predominance of guts that protruded below their belt line. For the most part, these men had no education beyond high school and they took delight in making lighthearted mockery of higher education. I was intellectually much smarter than my fellow workers, but on their turf, I didn't know my ass from first base about boiler making. That just might be the reason I answered to the name of "Einstein." It was their way of letting me know that, in some respects, they knew a hell of a lot more than some wise-ass, would-be college boy.

My salvation from this degrading treatment finally arrived when it came time to install a part of the boiler called "the mud drum." The mud drum had a long tubular shape' and looked like a big submarine with holes all over the top, measuring anywhere from eight to twelve inches in diameter. Long metal tubes had to be inserted in these holes. These tubes extended up to the next drum or main part of the boiler that was forty or fifty feet above the mud drum. The long tubes had to be secured into the holes in the mud drum to make an airtight fit.

In order to do this, someone had to get inside the drum to use caulking material and a tool that belled the edges of the tube inside the metal casket of the drum. There was only one way in or out of this drum. There was a hole in one end that was no more than eighteen inches across and a foot high. My twenty-eight inch waist was at least ten inches smaller than the next smallest belly on our work gang. I was the only guy who would fit inside the drum. At last, there was an indispensable job that only Tommy Twyford could perform, and all these big, strong guys knew it.

This was a tough job that had to be performed lying on your back inside a claustrophobic metal sphere at temperatures of plus 120 degrees. Even if these beer-bellied guys could have fit in the hole, I don't think any one of them would have volunteered. Belling tubes inside the mud drum was, without a doubt, the nastiest job a boilermaker had to perform. The heat was so intense that I could only stay inside fifteen minutes at a time. Then I'd swallow a handful of salt pills to replace the saline loss from perspiration, wait ten minutes and squeeze back inside. It took a week or more to stick all the tubes, but when the job was finished and tests proved all the tubes to be air tight, heads no longer shook at me in disgust. I was one of the guys and an honest-to-goodness boilermaker.

158   The Son of a Boilermaker

Chapter 11

Becoming A Buckeye

Fort Steuben Bridge and Ohio Horseshoe

After the abortive attempt to launch my college education at Ohio University, and my experience in the dry cleaning industry, I came to the realization that I needed an anchor in my life to halt my aimless drifting. With no sense of direction or stability, how was I ever going to get wherever it was I wanted to go? I knew that neither my Mom nor the old man could point me in the right direction because their aspirations for me, while unspoken, were far below what I had for myself. At least if I was going to drift, I would be headed in the right direction, and I decided to set my course in the direction of The Ohio State University.

My brother George was out of the Army and was attending law school on the GI Bill at Ohio State. He and his wife Diana had a one bedroom apartment not far from campus. He invited me to stay with them until I could find something permanent. I took him up on his kind invitation.

On a warm September day, I hitchhiked the one hundred fifty miles to Columbus. I had one suitcase and thirty-five dollars in my pocket. Since this was kind of a spur-of-the moment thing,

I hadn't even communicated with the university. It was a week before the start of classes, so there was still time to get enrolled and set up my schedule. However, my first priority was to find some kind of a part-time job.

The second day I was in Columbus I scanned the help wanted ads in The Lantern, the official school publication. I needed a job that didn't require transportation, so I confined my search to campus. An ad caught my eye for a job as a busboy/waiter at the Terrace Dining Room, which was located in the student union building.

It was the middle of the afternoon and not yet time for the dining room to open. However, the door was open and I walked in. All of the tables were set with monogrammed flatware and silver service upon white linen tablecloths, with napkins to match. There were two gray haired waitresses in white uniforms with blue caps and aprons putting the finishing touches on the table settings. I asked where I might find the person in charge and explained that I was there to apply for the job that was advertised in the Lantern. Both of these women were much older than my Mom and they gave me the once over twice as they pointed to an enclosed divider that separated the dining room and kitchen.

As I looked around, one wall of the room was made of floor-to ceiling windows overlooking the campus. Silver-trimmed signs on some of the tables read "Reserved for Faculty" and "Reserved for Alumni." Oh boy, I thought, maybe this place is too fancy for me; I started to get cold feet. This was a helluva far cry from Naples Spaghetti House back home. But, what the heck, I was already there, so I might as well go ahead with it.

I pushed the swinging door to the kitchen open and I saw a glassed-in office with a sign that read "Head Dietitian–Georgia Miller." Seated at a desk behind the glass enclosure was a heavy-set middle aged woman dressed in a white uniform, minus the cap and apron. She had a stern look as she waved her arm and motioned me to come ahead. She introduced herself and I could tell that she was a no-nonsense kind of person. I was nervous as hell and, in a calm voice, she asked me to tell her about myself. I wound up talking for half an hour. Then she asked me about school and if my tuition and books were paid for. She said it was a rule that student employees were forbidden to eat on the job. Finally, with a warm smile, she told me I was hired and I was to report for work the next day at 4:00 p.m. As I got up to leave, she called me back and told me that tomorrow was pay day and that I should pick up my check at noon. I hadn't worked one day, but sure enough there was a check for two hundred dollars waiting for me per the authority of Mrs. Georgia Miller, Head Dietitian. That was the beginning of a relationship that would span more than thirty years.

I went to the admissions office the same day I got my check and paid my fall quarter's tuition. This still left me with more than enough to buy my books. Also, I was faced with the unexpected choice of deciding whether to enroll in the Arts College or the Business Administration program. There was no language or math requirement for the Business School, so my decision to become a businessman was dictated solely by my inability to understand algebra or conjugate verbs in Spanish.

Most of my classes were in Hagerty Hall, or Hagerty High School as it was commonly referred to. There were required courses in economics, business organization and English composition. Also, all male students were required to take at least two years of ROTC (Reserve Officers Training Corps). While the college curriculum was somewhat challenging, I soon found out that I was just as academically prepared as the next guy. Of course, I was also working at the dining room about twenty-five hours a week, so I had a busy schedule.

I was sleeping on a cot in George's living room, which made for an awkward situation, so I only used it as a place to sleep. I'd be out in the morning and not return until midnight. As an employee at the Ohio Union, I finagled a way to use a shower at work. I got off work by 8:00 p.m. and the black cook, Louise, never let me leave until she cooked me a hot meal. Mrs. Miller knew what was going on, but she just smiled and looked the other way. Upon leaving work, I went to the library and stayed until closing time.

Some friends of mine from home were staying at a rooming house on 14th Avenue. There were ten guys in the house. It was the home of a middle-aged couple named Mr. and Mrs. LaMont. They had no children of their own, so the guys at the house were treated like the sons they never had. Mrs. LaMont put me on the list as first in line for a room as soon as one became available. Other rooming houses near campus were run as businesses, but at seventy-five dollars a quarter, the LaMont's weren't in it for the money. Finally, during the winter quarter of 1955, there was a vacancy and I got to share a large attic room with my friend from Steubenville, Joe Shanton. We each occupied one end of the room. Each end was furnished with a bed, dresser and study desk. In between was an overstuffed sofa and easy chair. The quality of my existence underwent an immediate transformation from miserable to sublime. I was never made privy to what sort of celebration George and Diana had upon my belated departure, but they must have been as happy as I was that this ordeal ended.

While all was going well for me at college, back at home the situation wasn't so good for Mom. My sister Marge was married in November, 1954 to a guy named Jim Bedortha. He worked in management at Weirton Steel as an industrial engineer. Shortly after they were married, my Mom's health deteriorated to the point that she could no longer work or live on her own, so she moved in with Marge and Jim.

Now that Mom had moved out of the place on North Fourth Street, for all intents and purposes, I no longer had a home in my hometown. Once again there was someone there to come to my rescue. Mrs. Lafferty was quick to offer me a room in her home, where I had spent so many happy hours as a boy. When I was fortunate enough to get home on a weekend to visit my Mom and, of course, Dorothy, I now had a place to go. The following summer, my home was at the Lafferty's. I had to insist to Mrs. Lafferty that she take rent from me as I convinced her it was a necessary element in my education and preparation for life.

Being a student at Ohio State meant that football and the fortunes of the Buckeyes became a part of my life. Alumni of Ohio State never lose their zeal and Buckeye mania keeps pace with the formation of wrinkles, stiffening joints and other symptoms of the aging process. Buckeye fans decorate their homes in scarlet and gray, name their firstborn after Woody Hayes, and plan their vacations around the Buckeye's schedule. Christmas, New Year's and birthdays pale in importance when compared to the anticipation and excitement of the Michigan game, while a loss to Michigan is just as traumatic as a death in the family.

On game days, when the noon-time dining room rush ended, I'd high-tail it for the stadium. Usually I was able to get there before kickoff. The horseshoe stadium was a vast sea of red where the sound of ninety thousand fans ebbed and rose again like waves with each play, only to climax with a crashing roar when the Buckeyes scored a touchdown.

Attending my first game in Ohio Stadium was an experience I'll never forget. It was hard for me to believe that there were more than twice as many fans at the game than lived in all of Steubenville, including Wintersville and Mingo Junction. Watching the scarlet and gray charge onto the field, followed by the marching band forming "Script Ohio," makes a permanent impression upon the mind of every Buckeye. The passage of time cannot erase the image of a tuba player dotting the "i" as the final gesture of this grand performance.

A football Saturday at the Terrace Dining Room was a mad house. It was my job to get the meals out to the dining room and at the tray stations for the waitresses to serve. The faster I accomplished this, the better, because everyone was in a hurry to eat and get to the game.

I had perfected a technique of loading a tray with twelve dinners stacked three high. I could balance the tray on one shoulder, steadying it with one hand, while racing through the dining room dodging tables, chairs and crowds of people. Because of my speed and agility, I had never dropped a tray or spilled a dinner. Well, one particular football Saturday, I was moving like Howard "Hop-A-Long" Cassidy, our All-American half-back through the crowded dining room with a fully loaded tray when this distinguished looking older gentlemen, decked out in scarlet and gray, suddenly stood up from where he was seated. A violent collision between his forehead and the edge of my tray made a sharp crack that silenced the room as all heads turned toward the sound. The tray never budged from my shoulder. As the old guy sank back into his chair, his face was as white as the tablecloth. All eyes were on me as I set the tray on the stand and turned to the aid of my victim.

I began to mutter an apology and could see this huge goose egg forming on his forehead. His face turned from white to red as his eyes flashed with anger and I knew I was in deep shit. Just then, the five men who were at his table began to laugh as it became clear he was going to survive. This immediately relieved the tension and some sparse applause could be heard throughout the dining room. I ran and got a towel full of ice, which I applied to his head. He was a great sport and placed all the blame for the mishap upon himself. As for me, I worried the rest of the day that he might have a delayed reaction and drop dead at the game. But Ohio State won, so I guess that soothed the injury to this beleaguered fan. Still, I wondered if that grotesque pump knot ever went down or if he was deformed for life.

That June of 1955, Dorothy graduated from high school. Her graduating class was much larger than mine, with over three hundred students. Dorothy ranked in the top ten percent of a class that was full of brains. Undoubtedly, she could have had her choice of top colleges. Her striking beauty had given her the opportunity to do some modeling with the local department stores, which had attracted the attention of modeling agents in Pittsburgh and New York. They had made serious inquiries with her mother about her availability to go to New York and attend modeling school, but her mother made it clear that she was cool to the idea.

I took Dorothy to her senior prom and presented her with my graduation gift, a diamond engagement ring. Mom had given me a diamond ring that I had re-set at Shanton Jewelers. Since Mr. Shanton was my roommate's dad, he gave me a great deal on the ring. As diamonds go, this was no rock. I'd say it was more like a "speck," somewhere between the size of three or four chips. Mr. Shanton used all his skill as a long-time jeweler to mount the speck in such a way as to create the optical illusion of size. Nonetheless, Dorothy was thrilled and all thoughts of her pursuing her own career went out the window with our engagement.

Although I had gotten engaged, I had no immediate plans to get married. I still had three years of college to go, we had no money, and at nineteen, I had a hard time thinking of myself as a married man. It just didn't seem that long ago that Chuckie Lafferty and I spent hours on end playing with matchbox cars and lead soldiers.

I felt like I had to be the luckiest guy that ever lived. This beautiful girl was crazy about me. She laughed at all my jokes, even the ones that weren't funny. She always agreed with everything I said and hung on my every word. I could always count on her to come to my defense even when I was wrong. She lavished me with attention and affection, which was something I'd never experienced. When she touched me, even in the most casual way, my spirits soared to new heights. I should have let her know she had this effect upon me, but I never did. In one way I thought all of these grand feelings would last forever, but another little voice inside warned me to be cautious where happiness was concerned.

My first year at Ohio State was winding down that spring and I knew I was going to need a job for the summer back in Steubenville. I needed more than a part-time job and depending on my old man to get me on with the boilermakers was a hit-and-miss proposition, so I was looking for a more definite situation. Spring quarter came to an end and I still didn't have a job, but two of my Steubenville friends from the rooming house, Joe Shanton and Dick Lodge, had been hired for the summer by the State of Ohio Bridge Commission to work at the Fort Steuben Bridge. They thought I might be able to get hired on as a spot painter. Since I had no fear of heights, climbing all over the bridge with a wire brush and paint can posed no problem for me. I went in to meet the bridge manager. He more or less hired me on the spot, but told me I would need the signature of the Jefferson County Democratic Chairman on my application before I could go to work. That same day, I beat it downtown to the office of Mr. Hugo Alexander. He signed it and said that everything was in order, but I would need one more signature before going to work.

I was directed to see a man named Cosmo Quattrone. I asked where his office was and Mr. Alexander told me to go to the Venetian Café and ask for him. Well, I was familiar with the Venetian Café because it was a hangout of the old man's, so I walked up to Sixth Street to find Cosmo.

It was the middle of the afternoon and my eyes had to adjust to the dim light inside the café. I asked the bartender where I could find Mr. Quattrone and he pointed to a table in the back where four men were seated drinking red wine. A jug of dago red was in the middle of the table.

My approach to the table was tentative as I said, "I'm here to see Mr. Quattrone."

One of the men spoke up, "Thatsa me boy, whatsa your name?" "Tommy Twyford and I want to go to work on the bridge," I said.

He took his time in answering and then replied, "Uhmm, don't I know your daddy?"

"Well, he comes in here sometimes," I said.

"Are you a college boy?" he asked, and when I said I was, he smiled and said, "Thatsa good, you get the education."

He held out his hand to me and I gave him the application signed by the County Chairman. He glanced at the paper and handed it back. Then he motioned to another guy at the table who handed him part of a paper napkin. With the stub of a pencil he wet on his tongue, he wrote on the scrap of paper and gave it to me. With that he said, "Good luck and tell your daddy to drop by and see me sometime." He shook my hand and I thanked him as I left.

When I got outside in the sunlight I looked at the torn piece of napkin in my hand. It read "O.K. COSMO."

My duty, along with three other college guys, was to attack the rusty sections of the metal bridge with a wire brush and then spot paint it with a rust-resistant paint. This was a big bridge that had a lot of rust on it, so it was a formidable job. Beside that, it was a long way down to the river from the superstructure of the bridge, so it got a little hairy from time to time. Anyway, this was what the job consisted of for the first half of the summer until we finally got all the rust off the bridge.

At that point, the manager told me I was going to be a ticket taker for the rest of the summer. I was to report for work in a clean white shirt. The toll to cross the bridge was ten cents per car. For commercial trucks, the toll was ten cents per axle. The bridge was part of Route 22, which was a major east-west highway with Pittsburgh, Pennsylvania only thirty-five miles to the east. On the immediate east side of the bridge was Weirton, West Virginia and the Weirton Steel Corporation. Most of the mill's employees were from Steubenville, so they had to cross the bridge to travel to and from work each day. Since this entire area was heavily industrialized, the semi-tractors and trailers were a big part of the traffic. As an accommodation to the local traffic, we sold tickets in strips of 20 for $1.00. That way, people who bought a strip could cross the bridge using only one ticket that cost five cents rather than the usual ten cent toll.

The toll booth had two attendants, one for eastbound traffic and one for westbound. There was also a bridge officer on duty at all times. The first time I worked the afternoon shift, I was working with one of the regular full-time employees. Most of these guys were in their thirties and forties and got their jobs by virtue of some political favor and were a small part of a much larger patronage system.

No sooner had we began our shift than this rat-faced guy I was paired up with said out of the side of his mouth, 'Aren't you going to buy a few strips of tickets?"

I wondered, "Why would I want to do that?"

Then this guy repeated himself with a knowing wink and asked me if I had five bucks to buy five strips of tickets. I was still trying to figure this out and just gave him this dumb look. "Look kid, do I have to spell it out?" he asked. Then he said, "Just watch how I do business for a while and you'll be O.K." Since I was new at this and didn't want to make any mistakes, I figured I'd better listen to what this guy with the red beady eyes was telling me.

It never dawned on me that he would steer me wrong, so I did as he said and watched him do business for a while. A four-axle truck approached the booth and the driver gave him forty cents, ten cents for each axle, which rat face stuck in his pocket. There was a counting device in the road that counted the number of axles as a vehicle passed over it. As the truck pulled away, my new role model took two tickets from his other pocket, put them in the drawer and rang up two passenger cars on our register machine. Wait a minute I thought, that was a truck, not two passenger cars. Then the light bulb lit up. Those two tickets cost five cents apiece. Somebody just made themselves thirty cents on that truck and it wasn't the State of Ohio.

"Now do you get it, kid?" he asked.

"Oh sure," I said, but I was dumb-founded to learn that my sharp faced mentor was a thief.

I soon discovered that all these guys were making themselves fifty to one hundred dollars a shift using this scam. Just who all knew about this, I wasn't sure. However, it presented no moral dilemma for me. My life of crime had ended with the theft of Boogie's dog collar some six years earlier.

For awhile, all the guys I worked shifts with would ask me when I was going to wise up and start buying tickets. To get them off my back, I told each one of them that I was a real religious guy and was planning on becoming a Methodist minister. Apparently, this worked to dissuade them from trying to make me a part of their criminal enterprise. From the time I was in Garfield Grade School, I had learned not to be a squealer, so I never seriously considered turning them in. Anyway, I wouldn't have known who to squeal to and then there was a distinct possibility that I would have wound up with broken knee caps.

My shift schedule was the same as Sergeant Dembowski, who was the man in charge and occupied a small office attached to the toll booth. I have no idea what work he might have done during the eight hour shift. Every time I saw him, he had his feet up on his desk with his nose in a girlie magazine, thumbing through the pages, looking at the pictures.

Dembowski, who insisted he be called by his military rank of "Sergeant," was a balding, thick-bodied "Des, Dems and Does Guy." He wore a tan-colored uniform with eagles on the epaulets of his starched shirt, and what looked like medals pinned on the front. He reminded me of a character from some comic opera out of a Marx Brothers movie.

At the end of each shift, I was required to fill out a form that summarized the traffic activity for the eight-hour period. There were various blocks on the form to be checked off such as "traffic heavy or light" and a tally of the amount of money taken in and number of vehicles during the shift. At the very bottom of the form was a space marked weather," which I filled in with the appropriate description such as fair, sunny, cloudy, etc. I then gave the form to Dembowski for his signature. Without fail, he'd study it with his little pig eyes taking forever to review the checked off information. Then he would slowly get up and step outside and sniff the air like a Labrador retriever. With that he'd say, "I tink we're going to have a tunder shower, put dat in your report." "Yes, Sergeant," I replied, as I stared up at a clear blue sky. This idiot said the same thing every day, but would be upset if I tried to beat him to it and wrote "tunder" showers on the report before he had the chance to sniff the air for the telltale scent of an impending storm.

Chapter 12

Sadness, Loss and Relief

Union Cemetery Steubenville, Ohio

Mom's cancer was raging within her by the summer of 1955. She had been in and out of the hospital for various conditions that were symptomatic of her cancer, but she was beyond any hope of recovery. Her bowels were no longer functioning, so she had a colostomy, which meant she wore a bag on her side. She talked as though this was a temporary thing, but I knew differently. I don't know how much medication she was taking, but it was not enough to relieve her pain.

Dorothy and I visited with her often and it was apparent that Mom enjoyed Dorothy's company. They would hold hands during our visits as we did our best to try and cheer her up. I always spoke in terms of "when you get better," but it was clear that she was severely depressed. Once, she was taken by squad to the emergency room, where they pumped her stomach for taking overdoses of all her medications. It was never specifically referred to, but she had attempted to end her suffering.

I returned to school in mid-September to begin the fall quarter, but due to Mom's worsening condition, I hitchhiked home every weekend that I could manage to take off work.

Tom Twyford   171

If we were having a home football game, it was not possible for me to take off. However, Mrs. Miller was most understanding and sympathetic to my situation and allowed me to take off as many weekends as possible. By early October, Mom was back in the hospital. My visits became more and more painful as I was overcome with feelings of helplessness, pity and even anger. Why did she always have to be sick? Why couldn't things just be normal? Why couldn't she just get better? These thoughts haunted me and made me feel guilty and ashamed.

The third weekend in October was a football weekend but something told me I had better go home. I went to Mrs. Miller and told her how I felt and she told me not to worry, that I was needed at home and to go.

I have always hated hospitals because of the smell. The smell in my Mom's room was something that attacked my body and mind, as well as my senses. She had tubes and bags hooked up to her frail body that were draining out yellow, green and brown fluid. I sat by her bedside, giving her ice cubes to hold in her mouth since that's all she could tolerate.

I was twenty years old and my Mom and I had never been able to put into words that we loved each other. I always assumed that I was loved the least of any of her four children. But during my last few visits with her, I came to a realization that she loved me deeply. Not that she actually said so, but I could tell by the way she held my hand and looked into my eyes.

It was a Sunday evening and I had to get on the road before dark if I expected to get a ride. I said I'd see her next weekend and as I exited the door to her room, I turned back toward her and she smiled and raised her hand as far as she could with the tubes in her arm. The next morning, I was walking into the student union when George caught up to me and told me Mom had died during the night. It was like a huge weight had just been lifted from me, and I was swept with relief. I didn't shed a tear until much later.

Mom's funeral was held at McClaves Funeral Home, which was located in the north end, only a block or two from where I grew up. I knew all the men who worked at McClaves. They sat behind the mortuary facing the alley where we kids played every evening during the summer.

Mom was also a regular at McClaves, so to speak, as a result of her regular visits with Mabel Mayhew to view the departed. Only this time, she was the object of the viewing. After many months of wasting away from the relentless progress of her disease, she barely made a ripple in the pink comforter that covered her body. Her face had the color of chalk and her long, thin fingers folded on top of the cover didn't look real. I had to bite my lower lip to keep from weeping when I looked into the open casket. Dorothy was at my side during the visiting hours and funeral, but there was no way I would let her see me cry.

My Mom's existence could best be defined by her sacrifice and devotion to her children. The old man never showed up at the funeral, but there was a basket of flowers from him with a card that said "Everett." The burial plot at Union Cemetery was next to her mother, Mabel C. Woods.

I returned to school after the funeral and, at the end of fall quarter, I came home for Christmas vacation. Mrs. Lafferty had my room at her house ready for my arrival. She made me feel right at home and comfortable with no thought that I should spend the holidays anywhere else but in her home. My exams were completed early in December, which gave me more than a month off school before the start of winter quarter. I was hoping to get a job over this vacation period to take care of expenses. The day I got home, I stopped in at Myer & Stone's Men's Wear to say hello to Myer Pearlman. He asked if I would like to work at the store over the holidays and I jumped at the chance.

Mr. Pearlman, or Myer, as he preferred to be called, had hired six other college guys as part-time Christmas help. His store was a very popular and busy place, but no way did he need seven extra clerks in addition to his regular help. I think Myer just liked having us around, and liked the idea of lending a hand to college guys who were always hard up for cash. All of us were sharp dressers and created a certain collegiate image for the store as we stood around in our tweed sport coats, flannel pants and striped regimental ties.

Most nights, the store stayed open until nine o'clock, as did all the stores during this time of year. Christmas decorations were in the windows and lighted garlands hung over the streets. Uniformed Salvation Army people stood on street corners stomping their feet in the cold beside iron pots, ringing bells and hoping for a donation from a passerby. Christmas music could be heard on the streets as well as in the stores.

The lights from the stores and Christmas decorations cast a reflection on streets wet with the mixture of rain and snow. Shoppers maneuvered through the crowded sidewalks holding tightly to packages and children's hands while avoiding slush and puddles accumulated at curb side intersections. Knots of adults and kids formed several rows deep to get a glimpse of Santa's animated elves busy making toys in the windows of the Hub Department Store. Old Santa himself occupied a throne on the fifth floor, listening to the gift wishes of children lined up one by one to sit upon his lap. Norman Rockwell could have used this scene as the subject for the cover of The Saturday Evening Post.

That whole Christmas vacation, there seemed to be constant talk about showers, weddings and honeymoons. I was not really an active participant in any of these talks, which were mostly between Dorothy and her mother. They also went over details with Grandma Conn and several aunts. I just kind of stayed on the sidelines, being swept along by plans that I thought were in the somewhat distant future.

However, when specific dates started to be bandied about, I took an immediate interest. I thought, "Wait a minute here what's the hurry? Nobody's pregnant," but before I knew it, the big day was set during spring vacation, March 17th, 1956, just three months away.

I was ambivalent concerning marriage. My first-hand observations of married people did not give reason for much optimism. Yet, there was the "sex thing" that urged me in that direction. It was strong enough to cause me to overlook a helluva lot of drawbacks, such as having your girlfriend hanging around when you had to use the bathroom, or me being right there when she had to go. That kind of stuff really bothered me, but I didn't have the nerve to bring it up. I wondered if I was the only guy who ever thought of using biological necessities as an excuse to stay single?

Chapter 13

Wedding Bells
or How I Learned to Live on Love

Eyes closed, fists clenched. Is it a wedding or a firing squad?

While I was at school, preparations were going full speed back in Steubenville for the wedding. Dorothy kept me up to date with daily letters explaining the progress. It was to be an evening wedding at the Fifth Street Methodist Church, with a reception to follow at the Fort Steuben Hotel. Our honeymoon was to be a motor trip to Virginia, with our destination being Colonial Williamsburg, where we had reservations at a restored tavern. As weddings go, this was not a large affair. The guest list was primarily family and a few close friends. Since my personal financial condition was its usual hand to mouth, Dorothy was financing the whole shebang from her earnings as a telephone operator.

Our wedding day of March 17th was also Saint Patrick's Day. It dawned overcast and cold as snow began to fall by noon in the Ohio Valley. By late afternoon, the snow had begun to accumulate. George picked up my charcoal suit for me at the cleaners in Columbus and was to bring it to Steubenville. At five thirty, I was hanging around Lafferty's house in my underwear, waiting for

George to get through the snow storm with my wedding suit. I made the mistake of calling Dorothy's house and telling her Aunt Mary that my suit was missing. This threw the whole bunch of Dorothy's family into a panic, which prompted talk of a postponement of the nuptials. Finally, at six fifteen, George arrived with the suit.

The ceremony went off without a hitch, except I stumbled over the words "for richer and for poorer," and hoped this slip of the tongue wasn't some foreboding of future economic woes. Dorothy looked terrific in an aqua-green dress as she marched down the aisle on her father's arm. She told me later that just as the organ hit the first note of the wedding march, her father whispered to her, "It's still not too late to call it off." You can tell that he didn't put much stock in the old saying, "I'm not losing a daughter but gaining a son." Uncle Walter was loaded and his colorful comments could be heard over the sound of the organ. Despite all odds against this being a lasting union, the deed was done and the good Reverend declared us man and wife.

It was a subdued wedding reception held in a party room at the Fort Steuben Hotel. There was no live music, wild dancing, or plenty of booze to stretch the party on to the wee hours of the morning. The featured refreshments at our reception were tea sandwiches, bowls of nuts strategically placed around the room, wedding cake and a tasty fruit punch. However, there were some in attendance, like Uncle Walter, my dad and brother George, who had a thirst for a more substantial beverage, so they found their way to the bar off the lobby. Feeling in a festive mood, I thought it would only be appropriate if I joined them for a drink. Now that I was a married man and one of the guests of honor at this shindig, I was confident that serving me a shot of booze would be no problem. I sat on an empty bar stool next to my kinfolk and told the barmaid to "fill them up and pour me a double." Without any hesitation she said, "Sorry sonny, but you'll have to wait a few more years." I tried to tell her that it was me, Tom Twyford, the groom at this reception, but that only made things worse as she told me I didn't look a day over twelve. Not able to endure any further humiliation, I beat it back upstairs to my wife Dorothy, and we shared a glass of that tasty fruit punch.

With an absence of alcohol, the reception broke up early, allowing us to begin the honeymoon. Mr. Parks graciously volunteered the use of his new red-and-white Plymouth for me to drive on our motor trip to Virginia. By the time we got the car packed and pulled away from the curb in front of Dorothy's house, there were eleven inches of snow on the ground. Everyone tried to talk us out of leaving that night because of the weather. However, I wasn't too worried because we were only going as far as Pittsburgh, where we had reservations at a fancy motel near the turnpike entrance.

At that time, there was no interstate highway system, and our route was over old Route 22, which was a narrow two-lane road. The heavy snow had created hazardous driving conditions and the traffic was barely moving. Many cars were off the roadway and in ditches. Somewhere up ahead, a semi tractor-trailer had jackknifed, backing cars up to a standstill. At the rate traffic was moving, we wouldn't get to our motel until 2:00 a.m., so I decided we had better get off the road and try and get a room at the first place available. Up ahead I could see a flashing neon sign in large letters that read WILLIAM PENN MOTEL. As I pulled in, I spun the car on ice, almost getting us stuck in a snow bank.

The place was a one-story affair with perhaps twenty rooms. I think the snow had covered up its shabby rundown condition so it didn't look too bad. There was a dim light in the front where a sign said "Office." I went in and got a room for four bucks. It sure wasn't what we had anticipated for the first night of our honeymoon, but that was it.

Dorothy was wearing boots that went half-way up her calf, and my shoes were already wet, so in an act of utmost chivalry, I had Dorothy carry the luggage into the room. It would be a request I would come to regret for the rest of my life, as my honeymoon gallantry would be recounted hundreds of times by my wife in the ensuing years.

The room had a well-worn look to it, but it had all the basics. Not having frequented motels, I had nothing but pictures from a brochure of the hotel where I had made reservations to compare it to. The pictures in the brochure sure didn't look anything like the grim surroundings of the William Penn. I could tell by the look on Dorothy's face that she was disappointed, but she was a good trooper and didn't complain.

It was late and we were both tired as the tensions of the day caught up with us. The moment was awkward and as soon as we opened the suitcases, my bride said she was going in the bathroom "to get ready." I had purchased a pair of red and green plaid jockey shorts for the occasion. Maybe I reasoned that something other than plain old white ones were required for the wedding night. Anyway, there I sat on the edge of the bed in my tartan underwear, waiting for her to emerge from the bathroom. All at once she let out a scream and the bathroom door flew open. She came out wearing a beautiful negligee and pointed to a giant cockroach scurrying across the floor in my direction. Since I was in my bare feet, I thought better of trying to squash it with my foot. The only thing handy was a Gideon Bible that was on the night stand and I nailed the cockroach with the Good Book on the first try. Leaving the body smashed on the floor in full view would certainly detract from any romantic moment we could salvage, so I opened the door and kicked it out into the snow. Although our first night was a far cry from anything we had planned, we were young, in love and the consummation of our marriage was successful in all respects.

The next morning, feeling well rested and excited about going to Virginia, we closed the door on the William Penn without a backward glance. Realizing that we were hungry, we stopped at a Howard Johnson's, where we sat at the counter and each ate a fried chicken dinner at 11:00 a.m. Some truck drivers, along with others at the counter, were staring and smiling at us while we ate. I'll never know how they guessed it, but as they got up to leave, they asked if we were newlyweds. Dorothy eagerly stuck out her hand to show them the "rock" she was wearing on her finger, as we accepted their congratulations.

The bed at the colonial tavern in Williamsburg had a canopy over it, and sat up so high there was actually a three-step ladder to assist those who needed the help. We splurged one night and had dinner at the Williamsburg Inn. Beyond a doubt, it was the most high-toned place I'd ever been in. The waiters wore white jackets and their skin was as ebony as the baby grand in Brettell's living room. Our waiter had a southern accent that was similar to something I'd heard in the movie Gone With The Wind. In order to take some of the edge off the formality, I started to tell him that I, too, was a waiter and busboy. The minute I shared this bit of information, I regretted it. This was clearly more than our waiter needed to know. He probably thought he was waiting on some wealthy "high roller" until I let the cat out of the bag. Some of the items on this sophisticated menu required his patient, drawled-out explanation. I made sure that I left him a generous tip, with Dorothy's money, of course.

After returning to Columbus, I resumed my schedule and things went on as usual with classes and work. Being a married man didn't make me feel any different, although some of the guys at the rooming house kidded me about it. I tried to get home on weekends whenever I could, but I had a responsibility to be at work. When I was absent, there was a greater burden upon everyone else to make the dining room operation run smoothly.

When I did take off for the weekend, I tried to get a ride with another student from Steubenville who had a car, but most often I had to depend on my thumb.

There was a certain art to hitchhiking, which I had perfected to a science. First of all, you had to look the part of a college student. I wore my tweed sport coat, khaki pants, button-down collar, tie, and my white bucks. For most of my college years, I was a big fan of white buckskin shoes. It was considered cool to allow them to get dirty, but I generally carried a "bunny bag" to apply white powder to the smudges. Along with a wool cap (à la the 1930s), this completed the uniform necessary for successful hitchhiking. Also, I made sure that the grip I was carrying had a prominent Ohio State sticker on it visible to oncoming traffic.

Only on one occasion did I ever encounter someone who gave me reason for serious concern. The guy picked me up just outside Columbus. He was probably in his thirties, well dressed and looked quite respectable. As soon as I got in the car, he made some comment like, "I bet you college guys get a lot of good pussy." Well, I knew right off this guy was a strange one. I told him that I didn't have much time for girls since my participation on the OSU boxing team took up all my spare time. This lie was calculated to discourage any wrong ideas this guy might be having. When he asked if all the guys on the boxing team were as good looking as I was, I knew I was in trouble. My response to that leading question was to tell him I had four knock-outs in my last five fights. Even this didn't discourage the unwanted topic of conversation. He said, "If you want to see something interesting, look in the glove compartment."

"Oh, that's all right," I said, not wishing for any more surprises. He kept insisting, so I opened the glove box, which contained a thick packet of photographs. "Oh, Jesus, Mary and Joseph," I thought. The pictures were of him, twisted like a pretzel, in various kinds of erotic, homosexual contortions with a person who was, obviously, a very close friend. I didn't think it necessary to go through the whole pack of pictures, as I caught the drift right off the bat.

"What do you think of that?" he said. I said,

"I think you are very photogenic and should send those pictures to Sunshine and Health," a popular nudist magazine. Just then, we were approaching a red light in Zanesville. When he stopped, I opened the door and got out.

"Hey, I thought you were going to Steubenville," he said. I replied, "I changed my mind. Good luck with your modeling career." This was my only encounter of this type, but from then on I made sure everyone I got a ride with knew that my hands were lethal weapons.

* * *

At the end of spring quarter, I knew it would be necessary for me to find a good-paying summer job in order to help see us through the next school year. Good-paying summer employment was hard to find.

It was my good fortune to have Mrs. Lafferty as my friend and mentor. Through her good graces and a word to the right person, I got a job at Weirton Steel. The Lafferty name at Weirton Steel had a lot of influence. Although Mr. Lafferty had been dead for over ten years, there was no request from his family that would be denied by management. If Mrs. Lafferty wanted to get a summer job for Tommy Twyford, it was a done deal.

Dorothy and I lived with her parents in Steubenville during that summer. It was our plan that she would request a transfer from Ohio Bell in the fall and we would get our own place in Columbus beginning autumn quarter. For now, I started my summer job at Weirton Steel working in the sheet mill as a "catcher" on the galvanized line.

Ever since I was a kid, I've been an animal lover. There have been only short intervals in my life when I have not owned a dog. All kinds of wildlife and birds have been a life-long fascination for me. Perhaps the Disney movie Bambi made more of an impression upon me than I realized. I wasn't a hunter and never intentionally killed a living creature other than a fish.

The one and only exception to this love of animal life was my aversion to rats. I made the mistake of mentioning this to some of my fellow workers at the mill, as the biggest free range rats in the western hemisphere roamed at will throughout Weirton Steel. Since they were primarily nocturnal, they worked the night shift with regularity.

I carried my lunch in a black metal box that had a thermos for coffee inside the lid. It usually consisted of one or two sandwiches wrapped in wax paper, along with a piece of fruit and an Old Moon Pie or a Tip Top devil's food cake. On the graveyard shift, we took our lunch break about 3:00 a.m., where the guys on the galvanized line sat around the tool room to eat.

These veteran steel workers were always scheming up some prank to play on the "college kid." I'll not forget the surprise and revulsion that awaited me as I unwrapped my salami sandwich to find a nest of squirming, sightless, hairy, red, newborn rats. As I screamed out and threw the boiling pile of tails and flesh in the air, I could hear all the heehaws and, "Who packed your lunch for you?" Getting or staying angry would do no good, but afterward I thought if only I had had enough guts to bite the tail off one of the disgusting creatures, I would have put those sick bastards in their place. Another favorite trick that continued off and on all summer was for me to catch a sheet of steel that came through the rollers with a squashed rat smeared all over the surface. Any rat trapped in the mill was destined to be flattened and ultimately scraped off the steel by yours truly.

I had some difficulty adjusting my sleeping habits to working a swing shift. When I had to work nights, I often came to work with little sleep because I couldn't sleep during the day. My job as a "catcher" was to manually guide the sheets of steel through the rollers and stack them according to number, gage and quality. The guy on the other end of the line fed the sheets on the conveyer, where they would dip down into a well or pot to get a coating of the galvanizing material. The conveyer ran the entire length of the building and it was our job to keep the steel sheets moving without hesitation or delay. A sleepy "catcher" at the end of the line was not a good thing.

It was about two hours into the graveyard shift when I began to feel drowsy. This had happened to me many times before, but I was always able to fight it off. I don't remember dozing off, but I was roughly awakened by two bosses shaking either side of me, yelling and cursing in my ear. When I looked up, I saw that the line had come to a complete halt as sheets were bent and tangled in the rollers. As a result of my catnap, the line was completely shut down for six hours of the shift. At this point, I was in deep shit. There was no telling how much money my nap had cost the mill. Of course, the bosses were the ones who had to answer for this monumental screw up. There was no doubt this was a serious enough infraction to get me fired. After all the chaos and confusion was over and the line was again in operation, my boss told me with a sly smile on his face, "Tommy, tomorrow you dross the pot."

I had no idea what the hell he was talking about, but the next day was Sunday, and I reported to work to "dross the pot." I soon found out that drossing the pot was one of the hardest, dirtiest and hottest jobs in the mill. Once a week, the pot or well of hot molten galvanizing material had to be cleaned of all the sludge and impurities that accumulated on the bottom of the pot. This stuff was referred to as dross. It was removed by large ladles manually scraped across the bottom of the pot and then shoveled off the ladle into cooling molds.

A labor gang usually did the job of drossing the pot. My assignment to this task was my punishment for screwing up. I found myself working alongside five muscular Nubians whose bulging muscles gleamed with sweat. Two of the big dogs easily scooped up a ladle full of the dross and the other three shoveled it from the ladle to the forms. I, in turn, dug my shovel into the hot bubbly mass. As I attempted to lift the shovel, I staggered backward from the unexpected weight of the boiling liquid, spilling it from the shovel and splashing it all over the legs of my co-workers. They yelled and hopped around as their pant legs began smoking and burn holes peppered their smoldering trousers. The scene resembled some sort of tribal dance as these black giants with smoking legs jumped up and down frantically beating themselves with both hands, while emitting painful screams. Once the fires were out and the dancing and yelling had ended, they all just stared at me and began to move toward me with an unmistakable intent to commit violence. "Sorry, boys" was all I could say as I backpedaled in retreat. Luckily, none was seriously burned. They grabbed me, stuck a shovel in my hands and instructed me to only take a third of a shovel full at a time. I followed their instructions to a tee, but even so, after a full shift of drossing, I could not lift my sore arms more than waist high for three days.

Fall quarter began the third week in September, so I had to find a place for Dorothy and me to live. Her transfer to Columbus had already been approved by the telephone company. With her salary and what I earned at the Ohio Union, we figured we would have just enough to get by. The problem was finding a suitable apartment we could afford. I knew that most of the furnished apartments for rent in the campus area were nothing more than dumps, but we were determined to be together, even if we had to live on love. Dorothy thought this was really a possibility, but I wasn't enchanted with this romantic notion.

My job at the Ohio Union was primarily working in the Terrace Dining Room, but I frequently worked nights and weekends at numerous big banquets that were held at the Union. Some organization affiliated with the university was always having some big shindig and our banquet rooms easily accommodated up to five hundred people. Serving meals to this many people required quite an effort, so it was necessary to have part-time help. The women who did this job were referred to as banquet girls. The word "girls" was a misnomer, as the average age of these women was about sixty.

One of the banquet girls I knew very well was Anne Marling. Anne was a thin woman with pure white hair, and I would guess her age at an even sixty-four. She was a widow who never had children and you could tell she had been very attractive in her day. For some reason, she took a shine to me and was always inquiring about my welfare. When I told her about my search for an apartment, she lit up and started rambling about the perfect apartment she had in the upstairs of her home. What would it hurt to take a look?

Her home was a well-kept older home on the near west side of Columbus, which was a fair piece from campus. She lived in the downstairs. The upstairs had a bathroom at the top of the stairs, and spacious bedroom off the hall. There was a cozy sitting room with a small kitchen and eating area under the slant of the roof, which made me stoop just a little to keep from bumping my head. Everything was clean as a pin, from the carpeted sitting area to all the older furnishings. Actually, the place was perfect for us, and the rent Anne charged made it a bargain. I didn't hesitate in taking her up on the generous offer. The week classes started for fall quarter, we moved in with nothing more than our clothes.

Dorothy was scared about riding the bus to work in such a big city, but soon became adjusted to the routine. I bought a "new" car, a 1941 Studebaker, which looked like an exotic foreign model. It was green with bright red wheels and cost us two hundred fifty bucks. We also bought a maple coffee table with green stamps, which made a nice touch in the sitting area. We were now all set playing house in the first ever place of our own.

It wasn't long before Anne, with all the best intentions, began asserting a maternal attitude toward us. She looked upon us as her children and I soon realized that she was very conservative in her views with a Victorian sense of morality. She kept a keen eye on our comings and goings, often asking questions about where, why and how long. It really didn't bother me too much, but Dorothy soon became resentful of her intrusions.

What did present a rather delicate problem was the cramp it put in our love life. We had only been married for six months, we were young and our passion and thirst for sexual activity seemed insatiable. The problem was the noise that inevitably accompanied our love making. We were certain that Anne kept a sharp ear to everything that transpired on the second floor.

I was constantly being shushed up by Dorothy. "Who, me? I'm not the one making the noise," I would say. This would be followed by giggling and then a passionate groan. "She can hear everything that's going on," one of us would say. "I don't care," the other would reply. "Neither do I." Try as we may, we were never completely successful in stifling the clamor. This went on with a degree of frequency that I'm much too modest to relate. To make matters worse, the squeaks in the bed springs and banging of the headboard on the wall would shake the old house to its foundation. At least that's what I thought. To avoid creating all this reverberating racket was the option of the goddamn floor which was awkward and uncomfortable. When we were leaving in the morning after an active night, Mrs. Marling would always be at the bottom of the stairs with a forced smile and a knowing look. This made me slink out of the house feeling like a sex-craved rapist. I wanted to turn around and shout, "We're married!" but I suffered this indignity in silence.

We lived at Mrs. Marling's house until spring quarter of 1957, when we moved into a brand-new apartment at the end of 15th Avenue, right next to the railroad track and the Ohio State Fairgrounds. It was a simple, one-story concrete block structure with one apartment next to ours. We moved in without a stick of furniture, save our maple coffee table and an army cot.

It may seem inconceivable that two adult people were able to fit on an army cot, but we were both narrow, skinny people who had the appearance of being somewhat undernourished, which we really were not. Dorothy had done some modeling for a department store back in Steubenville and had the shape, bone structure and carriage that fit the perfect image of the top models of the 1950s. As for me, I was more what one might call scrawny, but I preferred to describe myself as "spindly."

Even though this apartment was brand new, it was cheaply constructed and there was thin sheet rock that separated our apartment from the one next door. Now the guy that lived there was a bachelor who definitely held the notion that variety was the spice of life. He paraded a different girl through his apartment every night. I guess it was poetic justice that Dorothy and I were subjected every night to grunts, groans, and yes, even screams coming from our neighbor and his bevy of partners in the throes of orgasm. I often saw him and his past night's companion leaving in the morning. This guy didn't look anything like a stud, but he must have had something very special going for him. He never said much, just nodded and said hello, but I couldn't help having a great deal of admiration for the guy.

We really had to watch our dollars if we were going to make ends meet, so our diets didn't consist of meals that were likely to make us outgrow the army cot. Saturday was the one day each week that we would splurge and treat ourselves to the extravagance of two cream puffs from Albers Super Market.

About a month after moving in, Dorothy's parents arrived one weekend with a trailer load of furniture. I guess they didn't approve of their daughter living under such meager circumstances. The rocker and horsehair wing chair were welcomed additions to our enjoyment of the twelve-inch, black-and-white television set, which needed tinfoil wrapped around the antenna to bring in three channels of snowy reception.

Chapter 14

Disease Detective—U.S. Public Health

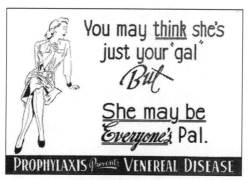

You may **think** she's just your 'gal'
But
She may be
Everyone's Pal.

PROPHYLAXIS *Prevents* VENEREAL DISEASE

Vintage advertisement

In the fall of 1957, Dorothy and I were at the Ohio State Fair walking through the horse barn and spied a Dalmatian bitch with a litter of pups in one of the stalls. The pups had just been weaned, but they were still all squirming around their mother trying to get at a teat. Naturally, we had to stop and look. Next to the beauty of the female form au natural, a speckled pup runs a close second in its attraction to my sense of charm and delight.

We talked with the horse trainer who owned the dog, and he informed us that they were AKC (American Kennel Club) registered with an impressive pedigree and asked, "Which one would you like to take home?" It didn't take but a minute to pick out the largest pup in the litter, a male with a black patch that completely covered one eye. I quickly struck a bargain with the owner, and, as Dorothy lifted him out of the straw, I gave the guy every dollar I had, which was seventy-five bucks. So, without any prior intention or design, we became a family of three. There was absolutely no discussion or debate about what his name would be. His official name on his registration papers was "Patch of the Fair." We just called him "Patch."

With graduation right around the corner, the university was bestowing a Bachelor of Science degree in Business Administration upon me, with a major in personnel management. What the hell did that mean? I knew that I would never be a business administrator, much less a personnel manager. It took every bit of effort I had by hook or crook to manage my own affairs, much less be a manager of some corporate pussies. Somehow, this whole program was not my bag, but whatever they wished to call it, I would be a bona fide college graduate, and that's all I gave a damn about.

Prior to graduation, at the urging of the college job placement program, I had several interviews with corporate representatives looking for sharp young guys for their management trainee program. Before the interviews, I was told by the placement counselor to never ask the interviewer how much the job paid. What the hell were they talking about? This was probably the most important thing I wanted to know. All the interviewees were instructed to play this phony game with the interviewer, expressing how much a career opportunity with their corporation meant to them. What a bunch of bullshit this was. The interviewer always asked, "Why did you want to interview with us?" Of course, the obvious answer was, "Because I need a job." Unfortunately, you were supposed to say, "Because I have always wanted to be a part of the Scott Paper Company team and sell your toilet paper, which I know is on the cutting edge of wiping technology."

Another question that you needed to be prepared to answer was, "Where do you expect to be in another ten years?" I really don't think they were looking for a specific geographic location, but expected you to tell them of your aspirations in climbing the corporate ladder. This was just more crap; how in the hell did I know? Along with most other graduates, I was subject to the draft, and there was a distinct possibility that I could wind up with my ass shot off in Korea or some other Asian hellhole.

When classes ended and before graduation, I said goodbye to my friends and supervisors at the Terrace Dining Room. I had worked there for over three years and had become somewhat of a legendary busboy and waiter. I know this sounds crazy, but what I gained from this work experience proved just as valuable to me as all my classroom work at the university. The ability to understand

and successfully deal with people on a day-to-day basis was a skill that I was weaned on as a delivery boy at the Mar-Kay Market and something that I cultivated as a student employee. I don't recall a course in the business school that taught this subject, but I think I learned it well.

Graduation day was a big day for the Twyford family. George got his law degree at the same ceremony in St. John's Arena where I got my Bachelors degree. Of course, Dorothy's mom and dad were there, as well as many of my co-workers and supervisors from the Student Union, so when I walked to the platform to receive my degree, I could hear a small cheer from the depths of the large arena. The best thing about my graduation day was that my old man showed up. He did have two sons who were receiving degrees, but knowing his history for commitments, I wasn't sure about his appearance until I saw him face to face.

I got offers of employment from Parker Pen Corporation, Hallmark Greeting Cards, Jewell Tea Corporation and Ohio State Life Insurance. All of these offers involved starting in some sales trainee program and then being assigned a territory somewhere. I respectfully declined all of these wonderful opportunities and took a job with the U.S. Public Health Service as a venereal disease interviewer and investigator. This was something I was born to do.

The guy who interviewed me for the job was a career public health service veteran from South Carolina. He was in his mid-forties, tall and lanky, with a fringe of hair that surrounded a shiny bald head. He wore a suit that was way too small for him and just as shiny as his noggin. When he crossed one leg over the other, he exposed a sagging black stocking and the white hairless skin it was meant to cover. He had such a thick southern accent that I had difficulty understanding some of his words. His name was even one of those southern names like Beauregard, Beauchamp or Beau-something. I assumed by the way he looked and talked that he wasn't too bright. Nothing could have been further from the truth. This guy explained the mission and the responsibilities of the V.D. Service in such an articulate and passionate way that I was reminded of Spencer Tracy playing the role of Knute Rockne and giving his half-time speech to his Notre Dame players. If Mr. Beau-something could arouse such enthusiasm about fighting this nasty social disease, I can't even imagine how successful he could have been recruiting for some popular disease like measles.

I could tell he was concerned about how young I looked since he asked my age at least three times. The last question he asked me was, "Now, do you have any objections to working around Negras?" "Oh, no," I said, "I've done it for years." He said he would be in touch. As I left the shabby hotel room where the interview was conducted, four or five guys stood in the hall waiting their turn to get the V.D. pep talk. One of them was a black guy. Two days later, I got a call telling me I could have the job. I accepted and was instructed to report to Detroit, Michigan for three weeks' training.

When I told people about my new job, I had a hard time convincing them it wasn't a joke. Skipping over the technical fine points, I worked out a simple explanation of the job that everyone could easily understand. It went something like this: "Some guy does it with some girl and within a day or two his pee-pee starts hurting. The guy has no money to get it fixed up, so he comes into the free clinic. I then interview the guy about who he had relations with. We won't fix his pee pee until I get her name. I then go out and convince her to come in to see if her pee-pee is dirty. She, in turn, is interviewed to see how many other guys she might have given dirty pee-pees to. Then I go out and find these guys, interview them and so on and so forth ad infinitum. Then I fill out weekly/monthly reports on the number of interviews conducted and the number of dirty pee-pees discovered and treated. My job performance is rated by the number of dirty pee-pees I can find. One very promiscuous guy or gal with a very dirty pee-pee can make my month. That's it in a nutshell."

At the training school in Detroit, we were taught how to conduct interviews that would elicit this delicate information from a stranger who was infected with gonorrhea or syphilis. These interviewing techniques were designed to extract the names of "contacts," or people who had sexual exposure to the person infected. It was also vital to learn the whereabouts of these contacts. Since all of our efforts were concentrated in the urban areas of medium-to-large sized cities, the vast majority of our clients were black.

Establishing rapport and gaining client confidence was crucial to our success. There was a whole series of questions pertaining to their sex life, such as how often they engaged in sex and how many different sexual partners they had during a given period of time. Basically, our interview questions were designed to provide the interviewer with a pattern of the person's sexual activity. Of course, if the answers to our questions were untruthful, the whole process was rendered worthless. But, we had a hammer to get at the truth, and at VD. school I was taught how to swing it.

First and foremost, we were taught to use fear and pain to get the truth out of people who routinely lied about everything, especially to a white person in a position of authority. Typically, a guy in obvious distress, suffering from gonorrhea, or "clap" as it was usually called, would present himself at a treatment clinic. The pain associated with an untreated dose of clap in a male subject is often excruciating. It was my job to make it clear to him from the outset that I wanted to help him. However, he was told that before I could help him, he had to help me and truthfully answer some questions.

The setting in which I was asking questions about the most intimate details of the person's sex life made some of these dudes very uneasy. Their eyes darted around the room, they developed facial tics, their legs were in constant motion and they were in a hurry to get our chat concluded. I was trained to spot gaps in their stories which, when filled in, usually gave me the name and address of their last piece of ass. Then and only then did our interviewee get his shot and relief from the stabbing pains in his groin. It was all I could do to contain the power surge I felt as I exercised my will over these poor bastards. What a job!!

This is an example of just one interview technique we were taught to use: "Now I'm going to ask you a series of questions about your sex life. After each question I ask, I'm going to write down a number on this piece of paper on my desk. The number I write down will depend on the answer you give me. So, if you give me an incorrect answer, I'm going to write down the wrong number. After I'm through asking you all the questions, I'm going to add up all the numbers and give that total number to the doctor. This total number will tell the doctor the correct dosage of medicine to inject in your butt. So you see, if you give me wrong answers, I write down wrong numbers and the Doc gives you the wrong dosage. Do you know what can happen to you then? Your dick may eventually fall off or at the very least, you've had your last hard on."

Depending on the suffering and intelligence level of the bastard, this technique worked wonders to give a habitual liar the veracity of a saint. If I was satisfied that I got the correct names and addresses of his contacts, he got a shot of penicillin and was sent on his way, cured and feeling horny as ever within a day or two.

A good portion of our training was in the field, actually knocking on doors in the Detroit ghettos trying to convince persons thought to be infected to voluntarily come in for treatment. Women don't have the same painfully acute symptoms of gonorrhea that a man does, so often they may have the infection for months and not know it while they spread the disease to multiple partners. In order to give me an air of authority, I wore a white coat, carried a small black bag and had a large official badge pinned to my wallet, which I flashed just like "Boston Blackie," the movie detective I saw as a kid at the Rex.

Quite a bit of time in my initial training was devoted to record keeping and how to fill out all the various forms that had to be sent into the headquarters of the U.S. Public Health Service in Atlanta. The VD. Service was really big on statistics. You name it, we kept numbers, percentages and statistics on everything from a common dose of clap to blue balls or some exotic venereal disease such as "lympho-granuloma venerium." If a person could get the disease by screwing, you can bet we kept statistics on it.

At conferences we had to attend, some big shots in the service would embellish these statistics to make V.D. sound like the biggest health threat to the country since the Spanish Flu Epidemic of 1918. Everyone knew the numbers were grossly exaggerated, but they were close enough for government work, and the job I had was more exciting than selling greeting cards for Hallmark.

Another aspect of the program was to conduct mass blood testing in selected areas of the country. The purpose of these tests was to determine whether the person tested was infected with syphilis. We sat up street corner stands within crowded areas of inner cities offering free blood tests to anyone who agreed to be tested. Mention the word "free" and it immediately captured the attention of curious onlookers. Then I was taught to go into this spiel about how some "bad blood" had recently been discovered in Cleveland, Detroit, Cincinnati or Philadelphia or wherever I happened to be. I was surprised at how readily folks in these areas consented to giving a blood sample. I explained to them that they would not be contacted any further unless the test was positive. In that case, I would guarantee that they would get any necessary treatment at no cost to them.

This was all well and good, but the real challenge of this part of the job was actually drawing the blood sample from the arm or back of the hand of a volunteer. People come in all shapes and sizes, and their veins vary accordingly. We used sterile disposable needle syringes to draw samples. After doing this thousands of times, I got so proficient at finding and hitting veins on the first try that I could do it in the dark.

My hardest challenge was trying to get blood out of the arm of an obese woman whose veins were buried under thick layers of fat. I'd have to tighten the rubber tourniquet to the breaking point and make a deep stab with the needle along with an educated guess. Most of the time I would hit pay dirt and see a drop of blood appeared in the bulb of the syringe. Then I knew I had the vein. Occasionally, I'd miscalculate and miss entirely, or drive the needle through the bottom side of the vein, causing the immediate formation of an ugly blue swelling called a hematoma to pop up on the arm. This, of course, frightened the hell out of my fat subject and created some dicey situations for me as I frantically tried to stem the flow of blood while facing the hostile stares and threats of onlookers. After an incident like this, I would close up shop and make a hasty retreat out of the war zone, as there was little chance of anyone else letting me fuck up their arm.

It soon became obvious why the lanky southerner who interviewed me asked if I had any objections to working with "Negras." Many, many times while conducting blood tests or investigating a lead on a contact, I would find myself in a place where I was undoubtedly the only white guy within a five-mile radius. Truthfully, I never gave it much thought and was only afraid for my safety on a few occasions.

Once I had a serious confrontation with a drunk guy inside a bar where I had set up a blood-testing booth. I didn't want to test the guy but he insisted so I foolishly proceeded to poke half a dozen holes in his arm because he refused to hold still. Just as he and one of his friends were about to test my blood with a switch blade, the bull-necked black bartender came to my rescue with a ball bat, which he applied with the force of Hank Aaron to the kneecap of one of my assailants. That was the last time I did any blood testing inside a bar.

During my interview for the job, I was told that they wanted an investigator to work in Ohio, specifically in Akron. As luck would have it, Dorothy's parents had moved to Cuyahoga Falls, which was located just north of Akron. Mr. Parks had received a big promotion from Ward Baking Company (Tip-Top Bread) and was the manager of their Cleveland bakery. When I got the job in Akron, both he and Mrs. Parks insisted that "the kids" as they called us, come live with them. They had a Cape Cod-style home with plenty of room to accommodate us. Dorothy had been able to get a transfer from Ohio Bell Telephone in Columbus to Cuyahoga Falls, so things worked out perfectly.

The clinic where I worked in Akron was downtown on Market Street. It was located in an old stone building that had long ago seen its day. The clinic and our offices were located in the basement and the dingy entrance was down a flight of stairs below street level. The facilities were spartan with a run-down appearance. My office wasn't much bigger than some of the bedrooms I had as a child. It was furnished with a metal desk and filing cabinet with room for one chair, beside the broken wooden swivel chair that I occupied behind the desk.

My boss, Richard Sullivan, was a man of about thirty who was a dedicated and gung-ho V.D. guy to the core. He had a military-style crew cut and two suits, a dark brown one and a gray one which he wore on alternate days. He was on the short side with a stocky build and his brown wing-tip shoes were always in need of a shine. He was basically a nice guy and anxious to teach me the nuts and bolts of the venereal disease business. I'm afraid I didn't take to the whole program quite as seriously as he wished and he failed to share any of the humor I saw in some of our tragic clients.

While I enjoyed the interviews and field work out on the streets, Mr. Sullivan was a paperwork and big-time statistic guy. He was frustrated and constantly on my ass about my sloppy and delinquent record keeping. Otherwise, he was pleased with the success and ease with which I dealt with clients and the way I handled myself on the streets.

The other members of our clinic staff consisted of a nurse, a medical technician and a medical doctor who only spent two half-days a week in the clinic, but was supposedly "on call" at all times. However, the vast majority of male patients were seen by the technician, whose name was Richard Williams, but who was known as "Doctor Dick the Dick Doctor."

Doctor Dick was a very distinguished-looking man in his sixties whose full head of silver gray hair was neatly combed straight back. His glasses were always perched well down on his patrician nose, which added to his appearance as a knowledgeable and kind old physician. Doctor Dick had been with the clinic for over thirty years. Seeing the patients in the treatment room while wearing his long white coat left no doubt in anyone's mind that he was a real doctor. His knowledge of venereal disease far surpassed that of any ordinary M.D. After all, he wasn't called the "Dick Doctor" for nothing. V.D. was his specialty and his practice was strictly limited to those poor unfortunate souls who had dirty pee-pees.

My father-in-law never said too much about it, but I got the idea that he wasn't all that pleased with my choice of careers. I can imagine the difficulty he must have had explaining to his friends and business associates just exactly what his college-educated son-in-law did for a living. My guess is that he steered clear of the subject whenever possible.

The laboratory where we got the blood samples tested for the presence of nasty spirochetes that inhabited syphilitic blood was located in Cuyahoga Falls. This made it convenient for me to drop off trays of blood samples at the lab on the way to work each morning.

Naturally, the samples had to be kept refrigerated overnight until I could get to the lab the next morning, so I just made room in the refrigerator at my host-in-laws house. I never gave it a second thought, as the blood was sealed in glass vials that were placed in slots in the trays. Each tray held fifty samples, so I rarely brought home more than two trays at a time. I could usually find ample space somewhere between leftover mashed potatoes and meat loaf.

Now Mr. Parks was a meat-and-potatoes kind of guy, but he was also a night-time grazer who drank milk directly out of the carton while visually scanning the contents of the fridge for a bedtime snack. It didn't take long for him to discover the trays filled with glass tubes of some unknown red liquid. When he inquired about it in the morning, I simply told him in a casual way that these were blood samples that I had to drop off at the lab. This prompted a barrage of questions that I hadn't anticipated such as, "Whose blood is it?" "Where did you get it?" "What are they testing it for?" "Does any of it have syphilis in it?" "What do you mean you don't know?" "What if some of those germs escaped and got into the cheese and lunch meat?" "How can you be sure they can't escape?" "Do you really think we should take the chance?" "I don't care what you say; just keep that shit out of my ice box!"

Since I was a guest in his home, and he bought and paid for the refrigerator, I honored his wishes. Anyway, I could see the futility of any argument which tried to convince him that these microscopic critters posed no threat to the family. From then on, I left work early in order to get to the lab before it closed.

That summer of 1958, I got the first new car I'd ever owned. It was a 1958 Chevrolet Impala convertible stick shift. It was gun-metal gray with a black top. The interior was a turquoise blue vinyl and it was equipped with a radio and heater.

I never wanted to drive with the top closed and only put it up if it rained. If it got cold, I'd drive with the top down and the heater going full blast. All the whores on Howard Street in Akron would yell a friendly greeting to me as I slowly cruised the area. Most of these girls and I were on a first-name basis, and they gave me all the help they could in locating contacts for whom I only had sketchy information. As a white guy driving a brand new convertible and sharing information with all the well-known prostitutes in the area, I could easily have been mistaken for a big time pimp or private eye. Secretly, I kind of enjoyed the association and sometimes went a bit too far in playing a role with these gals, who were streetwise beyond anything I could imagine.

Looking back on how we operated, I now question the propriety of withholding treatment unless the information we wanted was forthcoming. However, I must say that the tactic was effective. Every day, several male subjects came in the clinic in acute distress with no funds to seek treatment from a private doctor. The first idea they'd throw out was that they got their drippy pecker from germs off a contaminated door knob or toilet seat. It didn't take more than a New York second for them to see that I wasn't buying this line of horse shit. When I started conducting the interview and asked about recent sexual partners, a common answer was, "I was in Chicago at a party over the weekend where I met some girl and we had sex." And "No, I don't know her name or where she lives." Now, first off, I knew this joker didn't have carfare to the city limits, much less to Chicago. If he thought he was going to get a shot to relieve the drip and the pain with that sorry answer, I had news for him. Then I'd say, "The doctor tells me you have a peculiar strain of clap known as the "Chicago Drip," and we don't have the right serum here in Akron to treat it. So if you got your clap in Chicago, you will have to go back there for your treatment." Without fail, the story took a sudden U-turn that put this guy screwing the girl two doors down the street and another one on the next block. So, he got his treatment and I got two infected contacts to add to my glowing monthly statistics.

* * *

Ever since I graduated from college, there was the specter of the draft looming in the back of my mind. I knew, however, that the vital job I was doing in disease control for the government would get me an exemption from military service. The problem was, I wasn't sure just how long I could deal with all these dirty pee-pees. Anyway, in July, I got a notice from the draft board in Steubenville that I was to report for a physical exam.

Along with a bus load of other guys I knew, we were driven to Cleveland where the exams were conducted. We got there late so they couldn't get the exams completed in one day. They put us up in some flea bag hotel overnight and we were to report back in the morning to finish the process.

There were about thirty of us and we were in the custody of some scrawny pimple-faced PFC (Private First Class) who took obvious delight in flaunting his authority over us. This guy was a real asshole. He had a high-pitched squeaky voice and repeatedly pointed with his index finger to the lone stripe with one rocker on his sleeve and said, "O.K., you guys just remember I got it right here and I'm in charge." The sad thing was, he was right. I made up my mind right there and then that if I had to go into the Army, it would be as an officer. There was no way I could ever tolerate being ordered around by some power hungry numbskull like our PFC in charge.

A few weeks later, I was notified by the Jefferson County Draft Board that I had passed the physical and was eligible for the draft. I would be notified at a later date of just when I'd be taken in as a private E-1 recruit in the U.S. Army. The time had come for me to make some serious decisions about my future.

I had been in the V.D. Service for about seven months, but had never given any serious thought to making this my life's work. Just think, if I stayed another thirty years, how many more hookers I could call my friends? Over a thirty-year career, I'd read, consolidate and interpret tens of thousands of dirty pee-pee reports. My numerous transfers would allow me to see all the major ghettos in the country, and at some point, I'd qualify for a wooden desk. Eventually, I'd be the guy to make the speeches at V.D. conferences about the dirty pee-pee epidemic sweeping the country.

Staying with the V.D. Service would most likely keep me from being drafted. It was almost tempting, and I wrestled with the idea of being a career V.D. guy for all of about ten seconds before deciding it was time to move on.

I had taken the basic two years of ROTC at Ohio State, but you needed to have completed a full four-year program to qualify for an officer's commission as a Second Lieutenant. I didn't follow though with the ROTC because it would have delayed my graduation for a year. The probability of my soon becoming a private E-1 recruit in the U.S. Army was looking more and more like a reality. All I could think of was being subjected to the whims and orders of some idiot like the PFC we had at the physical and having to put up with that bullshit for two years. Not a good prospect for my immediate future.

As a matter of self preservation, I started to make inquiries about other paths to an army commission that were open to college graduates. My old buddy, Joe Shanton, put me on to a very limited program that was available to certain qualified candidates with degrees who could apply for a direct commission in the Army Medical Service Corps. He told me that he was going to apply and that I should do the same.

I obtained an application and some forms to fill out and sent them to the Army Medical Service Corp. A short time later, I was notified to show up at Fort Hayes in Columbus to take a written test. I took the test and a few weeks later was asked to once again come to Fort Hayes for a personal interview.

I wore my best sport coat and got my flat-top trimmed with the sides cut short to expose the skin underneath. This was commonly referred to as "white side walls." The interview was conducted by a panel of three officers, one lieutenant colonel, a major and a captain. They asked me all kinds of questions about my family, education and work history. No questions were asked about anything related to the field of medicine. I specifically recall them asking me why I wanted to be an officer. To that question I told them about my encounter with the PFC at the physical exam and they all smiled. I further added that I could make a greater contribution to the army as an officer than as a private. But I hastily added, "Not that there's anything wrong with taking orders, but I would also like to get the opportunity to give a few." They all smiled at this and thanked me for coming to the interview. Afterward, I felt rather let down because I was perhaps a little too candid and could have been more reserved, but now all I could do was wait to see if anything good would come of it.

One thing for sure, I had made up my mind to leave my illustrious accomplishments with the V.D. Service and stand on my own laurels. Without being certain of anything and with no clear picture of what I wanted my future to be, I took the law school admission test and was accepted in the freshman class at The Ohio State University College of Law in the fall of 1958. This gave me a student deferment from the draft.

In hindsight, I believe that I chose to pursue a legal career with scant information about other alternatives open to me. The fact that my brother was a lawyer, coupled with the notion that being in a profession would give me some measure of respect and credibility, are the only reasons I had for my choice of the law. Did I have some insatiable intellectual curiosity about the legal system or body of law? Hell no. I just couldn't come up with anything better at the time. Maybe I was also influenced by the idea that lawyers made a lot of money, but I also knew that law school involved mostly boring crap that I really didn't give a rat's ass about.

Dorothy and I rented a small apartment not far from campus and by mid-September, my legal education was under way. I cannot remember if there were any women in the class, but there couldn't have been more than one or two. Law was definitely a male-dominated profession. Even all the professors were men, most of whom had been there for decades. All first-year students were required to take the same subjects: contracts, torts, property and constitutional law. It was made very clear right from the start that law school would be a very competitive environment.

Law school proved to be an entirely new educational challenge for me. The method of teaching was called the "case method," which required us to read factual accounts of actual cases. The cases would be the subject of the next day's class discussion. What threw me for a loop was that there didn't seem to be any right or wrong answers. At least there were no answers the professors would willingly provide. Much of the convoluted rigmarole associated with the study of law failed to stimulate my interest. Slugging through the subject matter was often pure drudgery. But, there was a definite method to the madness. These old legal scholars were teaching us to think like lawyers. Some guys just figured it out a lot quicker than me.

Karl Fulda, my professor for administrative law, spoke with a heavy German accent. The subject was dull enough to put Perry Mason in a trance, but old Fulda was forceful in his teaching methods and cut no slack to students who showed little promise. "You vill never make a lawyer," he would shout. "Your parents are vaisting their money on an imbecile," he would tell a fidgeting student who hadn't read the day's assignment.

I always made sure I'd read the cases the night before class because for some reason he called on me more than anyone else. Once, after giving my analysis of the case, I thought I had really nailed it, but, his response was, "Vat you say may be true, but it's not germane to my kvestion." Then he added, "Vy can't you be more like your brother George?" Holy shit, did that ever sound familiar. Could there be a possibility that Professor Fulda had ever met my Mom?

I must admit that I was not thoroughly committed to the idea of becoming a lawyer. Hell, I didn't know, but, for sure, none of my heroes ever came from the legal profession. Cowboys, soldiers, sports stars and actors were the grist for my dreams and aspirations.

About halfway through the fall quarter, my dilemma was resolved when I received a certified letter from the Department of the Army. It read "Congratulations. You have been selected by the President of The United States to be commissioned as a Second Lieutenant in the Army Medical Service Corps." The letter went on to say that "Your swearing in as a commissioned officer in the United States Army will take place at 2:00 PM. on the 15th day of December, 1958 at the Army facility at Fort Hayes in Columbus, Ohio."

It had been so long since I had the interview for the Army commission, I assumed they had thought I was not good officer material. However, I still had the option of turning down the offer and continuing law school.

The day I got the letter, Dorothy and I went to eat dinner at a small Italian restaurant. We both knew that we had come to a defining moment that could change our life's direction. By the time I took my second bite of the meatball that was nestled in my spaghetti, I knew what my decision would be. When I looked at Dorothy and smiled, she smiled back and said, "We're going to the army, aren't we?" I drained half the glass of Chianti in front of me and said, "You're goddamn right."

Chapter 15

An Officer and a Gentleman Serving My Country

Me at right in front of barracks, Ft. Sam Houston, Texas

At the designated date and time, I reported to Fort Hayes for my swearing in. It took all of two minutes and my ass belonged to Uncle Sam.

Now, I don't want to create the impression that I was reluctant to serve my country. As a matter of fact, I was looking forward to being a part of the Armed Forces. The night before I left for Fort Sam Houston, Dorothy and I saw the movie South Pacific, and I could picture myself in the role of the young lieutenant who was the star in the film. The only drawback with this image was that he got killed and I was yet to be convinced that I was prepared to make that serious of a commitment. But I figured my risks of getting wounded or killed at Fort Sam Houston were rather remote.

My orders were to report to Fort Sam Houston in San Antonio, Texas on January 6, 1959. I was to begin the five-month Army Medical Service Corps Orientation Course, which was basic training for officers. No wives were allowed to accompany any officer for the first month of training.

Upon our arrival, we were issued uniforms and given our barracks assignments. All one hundred twenty officers in the class were assigned to the same group of two-story white wooden barracks that had been in use since World War II. These were basic army living accommodations, which suited me fine.

The army wasted no time getting right with the program the morning after our arrival. They split us into two groups, and the curriculum was divided between medical subjects and military science. We attended classes from 8:00 a.m. to 5:00 p.m. Monday through Friday and until noon on Saturdays.

We covered subjects such as anatomy, the musculature, circulatory and nervous systems of the human body and the care and treatment of casualties in war time conditions. We were schooled in the treatment of specific kinds of wounds, such as those resulting from gunshot, sucking chest wounds, trauma and high explosives. Mass casualty situations were simulated and we were taught to evaluate and prioritize the wounded from the point of view of evacuation. Since it would be our job to see that they got to treatment facilities as soon as possible, we had to be familiar with the capabilities at each level in the chain of evacuation. We were taught EMT (Emergency Medical Treatment) skills, which involved the procedures necessary to stem excessive bleeding, immobilize fractures, and learning how to suture open wounds.

One of our classes required each student to perform a tracheotomy on a live goat. Anesthetized goats hung on boards in the classroom. My goat had his eyes open and his tongue hanging out. I must admit I didn't relish the idea of cutting a hole in his throat and inserting a tube in it. It was explained that the trachea of a goat was much larger and tougher than that of a human, so we had to apply a lot of pressure with the blade of the device made for this purpose. We were timed and had less than a minute to open an alternate airway. It took just about everything I had to poke a hole in the gristle-like tube on this dumb animal that was happily eating tin cans at the dump a week ago. Finally, I got the airway in without killing the goat and just under the time limit.

I think the goat just might have survived this torture if I hadn't been required to perform one more emergency procedure called a thorensentesis. This required the use of a needle and a syringe the size of a football pump. The needle is inserted into the lung and fluid is extracted by the syringe. Once again, I didn't care to give this beast any more grief, but I had a captain standing over my shoulder waiting to see what I was going to do with the eight-inch needle. "O.K. lieutenant, this is a wounded soldier whose lungs are filled with fluid. Are you going to let him die?" the captain asked. With that, I made a lunge with the needle like it was a sword. I knew immediately that I struck too low. "You hit the goddamn liver," the captain shouted and moved on to the next goat. I felt like shit with the realization that my goat was history.

If by some miracle the goat did recover from my malpractice, I hope that he was returned to his old herd, where I'm sure he'd been missed. Not to imply that goats are like people, but this was the longest time Dorothy and I had been separated since we started dating and I missed her something fierce.

Dorothy was thrilled with my choice of apartments, which was really grand when compared with some of the places we had rented in Columbus. It was February and the South Texas weather was spring like and balmy. It was a whole new and exciting experience for us to be so far away from home and living the good life on our own. Anyone who has ever been in the military will tell you that you can make closer friends in a shorter period of time than you could ever do in civilian life. Perhaps it was because we were all cast into a similar situation and immediately had scores of things in common. Also, we were part of a unit that gave us a sense of belonging. This was a feeling that was absent when it came to my family. My fellow officers were my family, my comrads and instant friends. It was as though I had known these guys from California, South Dakota, Missouri, Georgia and New York all my life.

There were certain very basic things that you must learn in the army and these involve a minimal exposure to weapons and field training, which means living in tents out in the boondocks like real soldiers do. All the field training for personnel at Fort Sam Houston was conducted at a place called Camp Bullis, which was located out in the desert some forty miles from Ft. Sam. In our second month at Fort Sam, we headed for Camp Bullis, where we were expected to become trained killers within a week. The only permanent inhabitants of this parched and windswept piece of desert were rattlesnakes and javalinas (wild pigs).

As we loaded up on trucks at dawn with all our gear, the wives were there to see us off. Some of them were crying as they tearfully embraced their departing soldier boy. You would have thought we were going on some kind of suicide mission from which only a few of us brave heroes would return. The camp turned out to be just as advertised, a desolate outpost with a few wooden structures surrounded by cactus and tumbleweed.

When I think about this week at Camp Bullis, the first thing that comes to mind is the infiltration course, which was a stretch of ground the size of a football field, partially covered with barbed wire and randomly pitted with fox holes. In groups of twenty, each of us were required to crawl with our weapon the distance of the course under the wire while machine guns fired live rounds overhead. This had to be completed twice, once in daylight and once under cover of darkness.

Of course, the whole idea was to condition us to what the real battlefield would be like with the enemy firing real bullets in our direction. Also, smoke charges were set off on the course to further simulate the feel of combat. The repeated warnings we were given to "keep your ass down" were not taken lightly. To add to the sense of danger, we were told that earlier that day, guys with sticks, called "beaters," went through the course beating the ground to clear out all the rattlesnakes. The story went on to say that over a hundred of these sidewinders were scared off, but we were to remain alert because it was doubtful they got them all. Then we were all reminded that just last month a guy happened to crawl into the face of one of the venomous serpents and panicked. He stood up to run from the snake and was cut in half by machine gun fire. I think this was just a story told to every class going through Camp Bullis, but true or not, it made the intended impression.

I wormed my way under the barbed wire, only encountering a few minor snags and no snakes. Some of the chubbier members of the class actually got hung up on the wire and the monitors who were in thirty feet, high wooden towers surrounding the course had to call a cease fire until they could be freed. At dark, we started all over again with the machine guns firing tracer bullets overhead. I got about halfway through and was scooting on my back under a barbed wire barrier, looking at the star-filled desert sky with the tracers flying over me, and I got mesmerized by the spectacular scene. While I stared skyward, I had stopped moving. All of a sudden I was blinded by a spot light focused on me, and a major in the tower screamed at me over the PA. system. The firing stopped and it took me a few seconds to realize what was going on. Since I wasn't moving, the officers in the tower thought I had caught a slug. Then I twitched and heard over the PA., "Get your ass in gear and keep it moving unless you want to keep this up all night." I finished the remainder of the course in record time. Waiting for me at the finish was an infantry captain who stood me at attention and chewed me out till a fly wouldn't light on me. Some of the guys were standing around laughing and saying, "Hey Twyford, were you the one that got shot?" After the reaming I got from the captain, I sort of wished I had been grazed just a little by one of the tracers.

Another highlight of our field training was a nighttime map reading exercise. We were divided into pairs and dropped off out in the desert miles from the post. We had a map, flashlight and compass and had to find certain landmarks to return to post. I am somewhat dyslexic and had difficulty understanding all we were taught in the map-reading course. It was my hope that I'd be paired up with some math whiz who really knew what he was doing. As luck would have it, my partner was dumber than I was when it came to striking the right azimuth using the compass and reading the stars.

Being lost in the desert at night was somewhat unsettling. My partner was a comfort, even though he was as ignorant as I was about finding the way. At least he was company and that was reassuring as the howl of the coyotes and the sounds of other unseen animals scurrying and snorting through the brush made me uneasy. What if one of those wild pigs with big tusks mistook us for another pig or an easy meal? Why hadn't my partner paid more attention in map-reading class? I felt like telling him about it, but given our predicament I really didn't think it would be a good idea to piss him off.

Theoretically, we had all night to find our way out of enemy territory and back to friendly lines. Had this been an actual war time situation, my buddy and I would have spent the duration in a P.OW camp. We couldn't find our ass with both hands and were finally picked up at dawn, wandering in the direction of the Mexican border.

After our week in the field, we returned as battle-hardened veterans ready to take on any Russian who gave us a dirty look. The welcome home committee of love-starved spouses was there to greet us. Without changing from our battle fatigues, we all headed for the Student Officer's Club for a welcome home beer blast.

There were certain words and phrases used by veteran army guys that gave them credibility as a soldier. Such words as "affirmative," "negative," "mission," "objective," "at ease," "listen up," "smokem if you gotem," "shit for brains," "shit on a shingle," and "SNAFU" were all part of the army's way of communicating. But, the word that had a real army ring to it was "nomenclature." All the instructors at Fort Sam were in love with that word and they used it repeatedly in lectures. From the get-go, I tried to work all of these words into my vocabulary to let people know that I was no longer a "route-stepping" civilian.

As May of 1959 was upon us, the course was coming to an end. All the friends I'd made were about to be scattered to army posts all over the world. In order to maintain the appearance of inclusiveness, we were asked to submit in writing the first three preferences we had for a permanent assignment. My choices were in this order: Hawaii, Panama and Puerto Rico. I was enamored with the tropics and wanted to go where the trade winds would caress me on some white sand beach.

On the day the assignments were announced, the one hundred graduates were assembled in a large classroom. As each of our names was called, we were to stand and the colonel in charge of the school read out our assignment. My name was finally called, and I stood while there was a long pause. Then I thought I heard 'ALASKA." It took a while for this to sink in as I realized there would be no trade winds or white sand beaches for me.

Upon graduation from basic training, I was granted a two-week leave prior to departure for my permanent duty assignment. While at home on leave, I made it a point that everyone saw me in uniform and let it be known that my assignment was fraught with possible danger. I didn't elaborate, I just made the point and left it at that, hoping I made the intended impression.

During this short stay, I visited with the old man for a couple of days. He and I went to one of his favorite hangouts for a few beers. While seated at the bar, he called over dozens of his friends. "This is my son, Tom, a new army officer," he said as he pointed at the gold bar on the epaulet of my uniform with a gesture of his thumb. I know that he was proud of George and me when we graduated from college, but this was something entirely different. I could see that he finally had a sense of respect for his second son. This made me feel good.

My leave came to an end and we packed up our belongings and the dog in the convertible and headed west. Our destination was Seattle, where we were to go on shipboard for the three-day voyage to Alaska.

A cold steady rain beat down on Dorothy and me as we boarded the troop ship USS Funston to set sail for Alaska. The rain only added to the unspoken anxiety and uncertainty we felt about our future. An Army band playing patriotic tunes stood under a makeshift tarpaulin at dockside while we stood on the quarter deck wondering what we had gotten ourselves into.

Despite these misgivings, I was in high state of anticipation as I looked forward to my first ocean voyage. I felt as though I was about to embark upon a boyhood fantasy as I brimmed with eagerness and excitement. Little did I know that within a few hours I would be reduced to a miserable, wobbly kneed, nauseated wreck.

The dreaded sea sickness had struck with full force and vigor. My one and only thought was to get off that fucking boat as soon as possible. I briefly considered making a swim for it while land was still in sight. However, I was reminded of our lecture before we left dockside that informed us the survival time in those frigid waters was only three minutes. I had no choice other than to barf it out for the duration of the trip. Thus, dry heaves and wretched bile ended any hopes I had for a high-seas adventure.

Mercifully, I did have some very brief intervals during the course of each day where I was able to ambulate and have some temporary relief from nausea. But, it was at these times I had to take Patch out of his cage on deck for a poop, and this just proved to be another form of torture which prompted my sea sickness to return.

As I struggled to maintain my balance on the heaving deck, I must have presented a ridiculous spectacle, holding on to a six foot leash with a seventy-five pound dog shitting on one end and me puking on the other. What really irked me was while I was bent over retching and trying to hold Patch, some sailor would come by and say, "Good Morning, Sir," and render a sharp salute. How the hell was I supposed to return a salute while engaged in this awkward maneuver? Chances are, my face was as green as the uniform I wore, and my normally spit-shined shoes were splattered with spots of the last my gut had to regurgitate. At this point, I seriously questioned the wisdom of being a pet owner as my commitment to this beast diminished with each twelve-foot wave that crashed against the side of the ship.

The facilities on board that were reserved for officers were quite elegant and formal. The dining room was especially classy with stiff white linen tablecloths, dark wood paneling on the walls, and waiters in uniforms who attended to every detail with a practiced precision. While all the other officers and their wives, including Dorothy, dined on steak, king crab, and baked Alaska, Lieutenant Twyford had a steady diet of tea and soda crackers, and very little of that.

We finally reached our destination, the Port of Whittier. The minute I set foot on terra firma my illness disappeared, so I was really looking forward to the train ride to Anchorage, which wound its way past glaciers and picturesque mountain peaks. As luck would have it, I was informed that Army regulations required passengers with dogs ride in the baggage car with their pets.

There were no windows at all in this cargo compartment, so I sat on a case of lettuce, packed in ice, with a wet ass staring at Patch in his cage until we arrived in Anchorage and our destination of Fort Richardson.

Chapter 16

A Leader of Men—
Assuming Command

Lieutenant Twyford at his desk. Fort Richardson, Alaska

I pictured a military leader as someone with gray hair, or at least a guy whose hair was dark with a trace of a five o'clock shadow. My hair was light blond and I shaved every other day whether I needed it or not. Goddamn it, I looked too young.

Napoleon had five o'clock shadow, George Washington and Robert E. Lee had gray hair and Teddy Roosevelt was a rugged-looking character. Were these guys born leaders? Or, was this something that could be taught to a regular guy like me? After all, I wasn't being asked to command an army, just a fifty-man medical platoon. Accepting the fact that my command presence would never rise to the level of these titans of history, I needed a lot of help and a shit load of luck.

I soon learned to rely upon Sergeant Nix as my man Friday. Marshall C. Nix was a tall, raw-boned Oklahoman in his late thirties. If he hadn't been a soldier, he would have been a rough-neck in the oil fields or a cowboy. His blunt and often crude language had a way of getting his point across with the men while also gaining their respect.

In situation after situation, I sought his guidance and advice and he didn't let me down.

As the junior officer in Headquarters and Headquarters Company, I had the duty of standing for reveille at six a.m. After the formality of saluting the flag with all the company at attention, I took the head count report from the First Sergeant and retired to the mess hall for coffee and breakfast. There, I was joined most mornings by the Battle Group Commander, Colonel Cecil H. Bolton, who commanded the two thousand men of the Battle Group.

The Colonel was about fifty years old, of medium height with a thick chest and bull neck that supported a large head with close cropped brown hair. The shape of his nose evidenced old fractures. He had the appearance of an aging ex-boxer. Surprisingly, however, his hands were rather small with burn scars on the backs of both. In his starched fatigues and varnished helmet liner, he looked every bit the soldier, which he was in spades.

However, as bird Colonels go, he was very much of an oddity in that he was unenlightened, profane and spoke with a southern accent which lacked any trace of refinement. His home was Huntsville, Alabama. He quit school at age sixteen to join the army. While serving as an infantryman in Holland during WW II, his unit came under heavy German machine gun fire. Although seriously wounded, Lieutenant Bolton, armed with a bazooka and standing waist deep in the freezing water of a canal fully exposed to enemy bullets, fired his weapon until he ran out of ammunition. As he liked to tell it, "More than one hundred fifty Germans died for the Fatherland that day." For his gallant display of bravery under fire, he was awarded The Congressional Medal of Honor.

Occasionally, we were joined by other officers for breakfast, but most of the time it was just the Colonel and me. This proved to be most fortuitous, as we struck up a relationship quite uncommon for a second lieutenant and a full colonel. He'd regale me with stories of his military exploits and I'd listen in awe to this American hero. Every once in a while he'd ask me questions relating to politics, history and current events. It was plain to see that he had a very limited knowledge of the world not related to the military. As time went on, I came to be his main source of authority concerning a wide variety of topics. While he was guarded in the presence of other officers, he felt free to drop his defenses when it was just the two of us. I think it safe to say that we formed a sort of unspoken bond and I developed a genuine fondness and admiration for the man. He never called me Lieutenant Twyford, but referred to me always as Lieutenant Tweety.

* * *

Winter arrives early in Alaska and lingers well through April. It was November 1959 and I was about to experience my first winter on the Last Frontier when I was summoned by Colonel Akins, Deputy Battle Group Commander, and given an additional assignment. "Tweety," Colonel Akins said, "Lieutenant Archer, the officer in charge of the ski-fire biathlon team broke his leg, and now you're in charge. Congratulations."

"Give me a break sir, I've never been on a pair of skis in my life." I said.

"Don't worry," Colonel Akins replied, "you're up to the challenge, and I expect you to whip those guys into shape." At that point, I was dismissed. Just like that, I was supposed to become some hot shot jock of a skier.

I found out that the ski-fire team consisted of six enlisted infantrymen and one officer and we were supposed to be the elite skiers in the unit. The standard biathlon course was ten miles with sets of targets at designated intervals along the course. All the team members, except the officer, had to fire at the targets. One minute was added to the team's time for each miss on a target. Mercifully, for me, the officer was not required to fire his weapon, since I couldn't hit a bull in the ass with a handful of rice. My job was just to get the men lined up in proper position at each firing point. The object of the whole thing was to get the team across the finish line in the fastest time with the least number of misses. It was a grueling course and each of us had to ski with a twenty-five pound rucksack along with our weapon.

One of the first things I learned was Alaska ain't flat. Getting up the hills was exhausting and proved much more difficult than going down. The cross-country skis we used were primitive. They were heavy, wide and made of wood. Our skis had leather bindings that fastened over our white thermal "Mickey Mouse" boots. In order to negotiate the terrain in all kinds of conditions, we used different waxes that had to be applied depending upon the temperature and the texture of the snow.

The team that I inherited from Lieutenant Archer consisted of excellent skiers who taught me the basic techniques of cross-county skiing. However, I still had to develop the strength and stamina to lead the men over the ten-mile course.

After a thirty-minute lesson on my first day out, the team thought it would be fun to introduce the new officer to suicide hill. I stood atop this precipice, looking down at a long, narrow pathway that went down and down and down through a heavy growth of pine trees. This was no gradual descent allowing you to control your speed, but a vertical drop where gravity took over the second you left the blocks, very much like the ski jump at the winter Olympics. Should you happen to veer off the narrow trail, a tree could alter your anatomy in ways I didn't even want to contemplate.

With all the men looking on, I tried my best to conceal my heavy breathing and shaking knees. I was scared shitless, but the next thing I heard was my own voice shouting as I pushed off the face of the hill—"GERONIMO!" (That's what paratroopers always yelled in the movies as they jumped out of a plane.) For a few seconds, I managed to keep my skis planted to the ground, but all at once, I was airborne doing cartwheels down the hill. When once again I met the ground, I felt a crushing blow behind my right ear. I slid for at least another fifty yards, coming to a stop in a heap in front of a tree at the edge of the trail. I lay there completely disoriented and actually seeing stars as the team came down to check my condition. I had a lump the size of a lemon behind my ear caused by my carbine coming loose from the rucksack and cracking me on the head. To my surprise, I discovered, from the reaction of the team, that I had made a marvelous run. No one had ever conquered suicide hill on the first try and it would be another month before I completed the run unscathed. I came to enjoy the physical challenge of the ski-fire team and remained its officer for my entire three-year tour in Alaska.

During one memorable competition in which we were racing against a military team from Fort Carson, Colorado and a team made up of Norwegian civilians from the Anchorage area, I was exposed as the brutal tyrant and asshole of an officer that I was. We were not expected to have a chance against these two experienced teams, but with less than a mile to go, we were leading the boys from Fort Carson, and gaining fast on the Norwegians.

Prior to the race, I had given explicit instructions to all team members as to the mode of dress, right down to the weight and thickness of their socks. At race time, the temperature was hovering right at zero. This may seem cold, but when doing a biathlon, so much energy is expended that even at this temperature, you get soaked with sweat. Knowing this beforehand, we wore pile caps and our army fatigue pants with only a cotton field jacket and a tee-shirt underneath. Wearing anything heavier would run the risk of heat exhaustion.

We had fired at the last set of the targets and were making a run for the finish, dead on the heels of the Norwegians. I was bringing up the rear when, on perfectly flat ground, a sergeant on our team who was right in front of me keeled over flat on his face. Immediately, I was at his side, urging him to get to his feet. But he just rolled over and let out a moan while gasping for air. It was then that I spotted the heavy long underwear exposed from his sleeve and at the tops of his boots. "Lieutenant, I can't go no farther," he croaked. I could see the race slipping away from us because of a pair of moth-eaten long johns, and I just lost it. "Get your ass up, you stupid bastard, and that's a direct order!" I yelled at him.

In order to have a legitimate finish, all members of the team must cross the finish line, and we were less than five hundred yards from pay dirt. I took his rucksack and gave his weapon to another team member to lighten his load, but he still wouldn't budge off the ground. I could now see the team from Fort Carson coming up the trail and I started to nudge, poke and finally beat the shit out of him with my ski pole. I called him every name but a "child of God" and continued to whack him as the Colorado guys laughingly glided on by us to the finish line.

Now one might imagine that this sort of conduct by an officer would warrant some severe disciplinary action. But not so in the First Battle Group 23rd Infantry. I was actually praised and complimented by my superior officers for taking aggressive action in an emergency situation. It was strictly a macho mentality that was encouraged and expected, but I really didn't feel all that good about it. After I came to my senses, I repeatedly apologized to the sergeant, but he said he only had himself to blame for wearing the long johns. While I did regret this outrageous treatment of an enlisted man, I also enjoyed hearing the tough infantry officers of the 23rd refer to me as that "Bad Ass Tweety."

* * *

There was tremendous importance placed upon providing the troops in the field with hot chow. Living conditions during winter exercises required the troops to endure uncommon hardships, dealing with sub-zero temperatures and the snow and ice that accompanied the cold. Maintaining high morale was a priority, so every effort was made to provide the troops with a hot meal at least once a day. As mess officer for Headquarters and Headquarters Company, Lieutenant Tweety had better be prepared to move heaven and hell in order to see that the men got a belly full of hot food.

The winter of 1960 was my first full winter in Alaska. Much of my time was consumed with the ski-fire team, so dealing with the elements was a part of my daily routine. As a result of this exposure, I gained a cock-sure confidence in my ability to read the conditions of this harsh winter terrain.

Spring comes late to the forty-ninth state, and even though it was April, the land was still under a blanket of snow and ice. Our company was conducting a week-long exercise just north of the Eagle River, about twenty-five miles from Fort Richardson. This made it possible for the mess sergeant and cooks to fill insulated metal containers with hot chow and transport them to the troops while still steaming hot.

On this particular occasion, I took personal charge of the detail as we headed north with the chow. We were traveling in a track vehicle known as an "Otter." Originally designed for desert warfare in

WW II, it worked just as well on snow as it did in the sands of the Sahara. It had a somewhat weird configuration, but looked similar to a small tank minus the armament.

As we approached the banks of the frozen Eagle River, Sergeant Herr, my mess sergeant, ordered the driver to stop. We all got out of the track and Sergeant Herr took a long hard look at the ice and declared it unsafe to cross. He explained that this was his fourth winter in Alaska and he knew unsafe ice when he saw it. If we had to go to a shallow and safer crossing point, it would take another two hours to reach the company, and the chow would be cold. I could see that it was time for me to make a command decision.

I cautiously proceeded to tip toe out on the ice. The further I went the more convinced I became of the solidness of the frozen slab beneath my feet. When I reached the middle of the river, I began to jump up and down as hard as I could. It felt solid as a rock and free of any visible cracks, so I returned to shore and ordered all aboard and to proceed with all haste. Sergeant Herr was yelling, "Don't do this Lieutenant!" as the driver revved the engine and we were down the bank onto the ice. The river immediately let out a long low groan as I could see wide cracks begin to form in all direction around the Otter. Holy shit, we were going down! I gave the order to abandon ship just in time for the three of us to scramble out and jump on an ice floe. Hop scotching from one floe to another, we reached the opposite bank just in time to see nothing more than bubbles as the Otter disappeared with the hot chow into the swirling water.

Well, the troops ate C-rations that night for supper, and I was certain that my army career was at the bottom of the Eagle River along with the green beans and Salisbury steak. To my surprise, Colonel Bolton and the rest of the Battle Group staff had nothing but praise for what they called bold and decisive action in my abortive attempt to get hot chow to the troops. However, Colonel Bolton would ask every few days "Tweety, do you think that goddamn Otter has swam away by now?" I also took a lot of good-natured kidding from the men. The Otter didn't swim away and the motor pool winched it out of the river in June. My punishment was to fill out twenty-four forms in triplicate to explain my action to the Inspector General.

* * *

I had been at Fort Richardson for about a year when we got word that President Eisenhower was making the first ever presidential visit to the forty-ninth state. Thus began the month-long preparation to give the Commander In Chief the elaborate welcome he deserved.

Every soldier on post, in one way or another, was involved in the planning and execution of this historic event. Down to the smallest detail, each minute of the visit was covered. In the week prior, daily rehearsals were held and all other activity on post came to a halt.

The president was to fly into Elmendorf Air Force Base to be greeted by all the top brass. Elmendorf was only about three miles from Fort Richardson. The plan was for the presidential motorcade to proceed the three miles along the highway, which would be lined on either side by soldiers in full battle dress at intervals of every ten yards. Each soldier was to have an M-1 Rifle at port arms position and just as the open jeep with the standing president drove past, each man was to come to attention and raise his weapon to a present arms position. This was an impressive display of military showmanship to greet President Eisenhower.

A very strict policy was in place that no soldier was allowed to possess any kind of live ammunition. Live ammo was confined to marksmanship practice on rifle ranges and live weapon exercises that were all carefully monitored for safety. After any exercise involving live ammunition, the ammo along with the weapons were turned in to the company armor, where they were kept under lock and key. No soldier was permitted to keep his weapon or any ammunition in his locker or personal space in the barracks. Of course, the long corridor of troops planning to greet the President upon his arrival would have unloaded rifles to conduct the armed salute to The Commander in Chief.

At about 8:00 p.m. on the evening prior to President Eisenhower's arrival, I got a phone call at my quarters from Sergeant Nix, asking me to come over to Headquarters and Headquarters Company on the double. When I arrived, he directed me up to the second floor barracks of the medical platoon. He wanted to show me what he had found in the wall locker of one Private Tyrone Godfrey. He said, "Here, Lieutenant, take a look at this." Almost concealed behind the uniforms in Private Godfrey's wall locker was an M-1 rifle with a clip of live ammunition and a round in the chamber. I wasn't happy about this and asked Nix if he knew where Godfrey was. Nix then said, "That ain't all, Lieutenant Twyford. Look here." What I saw was a paperback book at the bottom of the locker. I picked it up and as I turned it over, I saw it was titled The Day Lincoln Was Shot. Holy Shit! The implication of this hit me right between the eyes. As I further examined the book, I saw that key passages had been underlined, which detailed the moments leading up to John Wilkes Booth firing the fatal shot into the brain of President Lincoln. This was more than just a coincidence, and I felt my insides begin to quiver. I told Nix to get some guys and go find Godfrey and bring him in, now! I left everything in the locker just as we found it, locked it up, and went to the orderly room to call Major Waters, the Battle Group Adjutant.

Private Godfrey hadn't been in the platoon for more than a month or two. He was a big black guy weighing well over two hundred pounds and was at least six foot four. I didn't know much about him, only that he was from Baltimore, Maryland. He had a brooding, sullen manner and kept to himself. He didn't mix with other guys in the platoon. At this point, I had convinced myself that our Private Godfrey fit the profile of an assassin.

I related the whole scenario to Major Waters, who told me to sit by the phone and he would get back with me. Five minutes later, the phone rang and it was Colonel Bolton. "What the hell's going on? JESUS CHRIST, TWEETY THERE'S GOING TO BE ALL KINDS OF HELL TO PAY IF PRESIDENT EISENHOWER GETS SHOT."

"Yes, Sir," I said and thought that was the understatement of the century. "Tweety, I want you to find that son-of-a-bitch and get his ass locked up in the stockade, understand? Call me back in fifteen minutes and I expect it to be done."

"Yes, Sir," I said, hoping like hell Sergeant Nix had located him. Colonel Bolton didn't wait. He and Major Waters burst into the orderly room within minutes after I hung up. I showed them the "evidence" in Godfrey's locker and I was relieved to see that they shared my concern and didn't think I was some kind of an alarmist.

Fortunately, they found Godfrey drinking beer at the enlisted men's club. When confronted with the contraband in his locker, he said he just forgot to turn in his weapon to the armor. As far as the subject matter of his reading material was concerned, he laughed and denied any wish to bring harm to President Eisenhower. Nonetheless, he was put in handcuffs and transported to the stockade for safe keeping.

Colonel Bolton told me to keep this thing on the "Q.T." as he didn't want the Battle Group to look bad. However, he immediately put out the order that every locker of every man in the Battle Group be searched. As he said, "I want to make sure there's no more shit out there."

Perhaps Private Godfrey was telling the truth, but one thing for sure, I never saw him after that night. He was kept in the stockade until the paperwork was completed to give him an undesirable discharge from the army. Of course, maybe he planned this whole thing, hoping to get kicked out of the army. If so, he was successful. On the other hand, I would like to believe that I had a part in saving the life of the liberator of Europe and savior of the free world.

* * *

For my first year in Alaska, I was in awe of everything around me. The sight of snow-capped mountains in every direction, and the cold, clear fish-filled streams and rivers were natural wonders I had only seen in magazines and motion pictures. This place didn't get dark until well after midnight in summer and it was only light a few hours a day during the winter. It made me think I was on another planet. The look and feel of Anchorage had a frontier flavor unlike any town I had seen. The cast of characters on the streets were a mix of Eskimos, Aleut Indians and rough-cut prospector types, mixed in with military people and residents dressed in leather and fur-trimmed clothing. On any road leading in or out of Anchorage, there was no gradual transition from town to wilderness. There was just a point where the town ended, giving way to pine trees and willow lined riverbanks where moose grazed and soaring eagles swooped down to catch fish. One thing for sure, I knew I was a long way from home. My hometown was a great place but in no way, shape or form could that steel town in the Ohio Valley ever be confused with my new home on the "Last Frontier."

Chapter 17

Army Life
On the Last Frontier

In the boondocks with the medical platoon

Fort Richardson was not big as army bases go. It was similar to a small-town suburb, with winding streets lined with housing for married personnel and their dependents. The post had an elementary school, Post Exchange (PX), commissary (grocery) and several churches.

The officer's quarters were townhouses with four to a building. It was at least twice the size of any place I had ever lived and all the dark mahogany furniture and brocade living room sofa and wing chairs looked brand new. The carpeted floors felt a whole lot different to walk upon than the linoleum and bare wood I had tread upon my entire life. One thing that was hard for me to get used to was that everything in the house worked. To me, that seemed strange.

Aside from duty, both Dorothy and I were engaged in activities at the Officer's Club and in the Anchorage community. This involvement included Dorothy working for Jonas Brothers Furriers as a model doing style shows. She was a tireless worker in the Officer's Wives organization, promoting shows and entertainment.

She directed a minstrel show, and starred in a Hawaiian review, dancing the hula in a grass skirt as well as any native dancer from Honolulu. We were always busy with a program, project or show. Some kind of party was held at the club just about every week, so our social life was full.

I got involved with the Anchorage Community Playhouse and got a part in their production of Arthur Miller's Death of a Salesman. My part was Bernard, the neighbor boy. This was not a big part, but it was a terrific experience to work with a talented group of actors and renewed my passion for theater.

One morning, I was having breakfast with Colonel Bolton and he happened to mention an impending visit to Fort Richardson by The Secretary of the Army, Wilbur Brucker. As a major part of the overall effort to make a favorable impression on the Secretary, there was to be a massive field demonstration by the troops of the Battle Group. Colonel Bolton went on to tell me just how important this was and how precisely the planning and preparations had to be for the Secretary's visit.

Most regular army officers have friends in common who they have served with at one time or another. There exists a network of scuttlebutt and obscure information that any army commander can tap into to get the lowdown on whatever might be of interest. Colonel Bolton used this network to find out all he could about the Secretary. After dozens of inquiries, the most important bit of information he came up with was that the Secretary had a particular fondness for macaroon cookies.

This valuable information was passed onto me by the Colonel in my capacity as mess officer for Headquarters and Headquarters Company. "Tweety, do you suppose you and Sergeant Herr can whip up a batch of macaroons for the Secretary's visit?" he asked. Thus began a month-long quest to create the perfect macaroon.

Sergeant Herr and I researched recipe after recipe and prepared one batch after another for taste tests. Several times a week in the month before the Secretary's visit, I'd take a plate of these cookies over to Headquarters, where the Colonel and his staff would pass them around a large conference table. Each staff officer, in turn, would take a macaroon from the plate, eat it, and then offer a critique for a roundtable discussion. These field-grade officers, who were charged with the responsibility of guarding the free world from communist domination, approached this cookie testing with the same seriousness as they would a full-frontal assault upon a Soviet invader crossing over from Siberia.

Finally, we got it nailed down and came up with a macaroon which had just the right amount of sweetness, texture and coconut to satisfy the palettes of the staff. Now, the trick would be to duplicate it on the day of the big visit. To tell the truth, I got caught up in this macaroon mania. I viewed this as a mission that could make or break my army career, if I ever decided to have one.

The big day arrived and the Secretary was bundled up in a parka and escorted to a training area not far from the post. Several tents were pitched on a hill overlooking a wide snow-covered plain for the Major General John Michaelous, chief of all the army forces in Alaska, was present, along with the members of his staff. However, this was Colonel Bolton's show and when he gave the signal, tanks and other track vehicles covered with white sheets emerged from the tree line in the distance and on to the flat terrain.

Artillery pieces were also moved into position and followed by a thousand ski troopers in their overwhites with weapons strapped to their rucksacks. Seeing all this firepower and troops appear from out of nowhere in a matter of minutes was an impressive show of force. Once all the weapons and men were in position, a deafening firing demonstration commenced, which rocked the entire valley and filled the air with smoke and cordite. After the firing had ceased, Colonel Bolton was heard to comment that he would like to see if those Russian sons-a-bitches could stand up in the face of that. All applauded and agreed that they could not.

The Secretary was a short, round man who wore a crumpled civilian dress suit beneath the army parka provided him. A fur-lined pile cap protected his bald head and ears from the cold. He didn't look all that comfortable braving the elements to witness the demonstration, and seemed impatient for it to end. The Secretary clearly had enough of this and was eyeing the warmth of the mess tent. I hoped my macaroons would soon lift his spirits.

At the conclusion of the demonstration, the Colonel directed all the top brass inside for coffee and a discussion of what they had just witnessed. I was standing by along with my mess sergeant as the orderlies served coffee. After all were seated and they had their coffee, Colonel Bolton said in a loud voice to me, "Lieutenant Tweetuhuh Twyford, check and see if the mess sergeant has anything sweet to go with this coffee."

"Yes, sir," I said and briefly left the tent. In about thirty seconds, I popped back in and said, "Sir, he has some fresh macaroons that were just baked this morning."

"Well, Tweety, what are you waiting for? Bring some in here." He no sooner said that than four orderlies appeared and placed four mounded plates of cookies on the table.

The Secretary said, "This is my lucky day. Macaroons are my absolute favorite." All present in the tent could hear the sound as the Secretary's front teeth penetrated the crunchy surface of golden brown coconut into the soft center of the sweet confection. His jaws barely moved while chewing, clearly savoring the morsel for as long as possible. There was dead silence as all eyes were upon him looking for some sign of approval. "Colonel Bolton, get the mess sergeant out here. This is the best macaroon I've had in forty years," he said. Sergeant Herr was glowing as he accepted the Secretary's compliments. Colonel Bolton gave me a wink as our guest of honor reached for his fourth macaroon.

Colonel Bolton was from the deep south and made no secret of the fact that he was prejudiced to the core. He was a product of his time and his environment, and was never exposed to the enlightenment that an education could have afforded him. For most of his army career, he was part of a segregated military, which was entirely compatible with his southern roots.

When we were not training out in the field, we had Officer's Call once a week. This was when Colonel Bolton and his staff presided over a meeting with all the commissioned officers of the Battle Group, which numbered about ninety. All matters of training, discipline and morale were discussed at these meetings and any officer was free to bring up any item of particular concern.

I'll never forget one Officer's Call when Colonel Bolton announced to the Adjacent, "Major Waters, I've been looking around this here Battle Group and it seems to me that we got more than our fair share of niggers. I want an exact count by seventeen hundred hours just exactly how many niggers we got. You can also include them goddamn Porta Ricans because they're just the same." You could have heard a pin drop as each officer's mouth just dropped open.

I had gone through basic training at Fort Sam Houston with a black officer from Harrisburg, Pennsylvania whose name was Jim Townsel. Jim and I became good friends and we were the only officers in our class to be assigned to Alaska. Jim was also at Fort Richardson, but assigned to a medical unit that was not part of the Battle Group.

It was the spring of 1960 and we were attending a formal dance at the Officer's Club and Jim Townsel and his very attractive wife were there. They were sitting at a table with another black officer and his wife and were off to themselves, not mingling with the crowd of white officers and their wives. We went over to their table to say hello. The band was playing "Kansas City," a song that was popular during our days at Fort Sam. My wife extended her hand to Jim and asked him to dance. She was obviously very much pregnant, but that didn't stop her from dancing to the fast beat of the music. All eyes were on Lieutenant Twyford's wife and the black officer as they bopped the length and width of the dance floor. This broke the ice and before long, the two black couples became part of the group, dancing with and talking to the others in attendance.

As the evening drew to a close, Colonel Bolton approached our table. We all stood as he reached over and patted Dorothy on the stomach and said "I always knew you were a lady but after what you did tonight, there is no doubt whatsoever. How about the last dance? Is it O.K. with you, Tweety?" "Yes, Sir," I said.

* * *

The overall mission of the Battle Group was the training of soldiers to fight under extremely cold weather conditions. To that end, every year during January or February, a large-scale winter maneuver was conducted. These operations had names like "Operation Deep Freeze" or "Operation Timberline" and always involved some elite unit like the 82nd Airborne to engage the 23rd Infantry in war games lasting three or four weeks. The maneuvers involved elaborate preparations with the top brass in the army dropping in as observers from time to time. My role in this exercise was to maintain the Battle Group Aid Station to receive casualties and oversee the operation of Headquarters Company field mess.

Our location at Fort Richardson made available the vast area of federal lands to the northeast and northwest of the post, and stretched over hundreds of miles of some of the most rugged terrain in North America. The temperatures rarely got above zero degrees, often dipping as low as fifty below, but we were prepared to fight under these conditions. Perhaps the cruelest part of winter maneuvers was to leave a warm sleeping bag when nature called and step out into the thirty-below night.

The logistics involved in moving men and equipment over this territory required tremendous effort and coordination. We used four wheeled vehicles where we could, but also relied heavily upon track vehicles called Otters and Weasels. When track vehicles were no longer suitable for the terrain, we moved on skis and snowshoes. All the troops had ski training, but I had a little more than most.

The cold was frequently so intense that once the engine of a vehicle was started, it couldn't be shut down, as that would completely lock up the motor, so we kept vehicles driving in circles throughout the night. We slept in ten-man tents heated with gasoline fueled Yukon stoves. However, for safety reasons, the stoves were shut off while we slept. By morning, I awoke with a chunk of ice attached to my cheek and the top of the sleeping bag where the moisture from my breath had formed an icy bond. It was also necessary to pry my eyes open, as during the night, the lashes had frozen them shut.

I had no difficulty taking these kinds of hardships in stride. Anyway, I had to set a good example for the men under my command and not bitch about such mundane things as the weather. However, since I was a fanatic about personal hygiene, I suffered in silence about the lack of bathing facilities and the primitive methods forced upon us to take a crap.

Bathing was another matter and it also required some ingenuity to accomplish. Some of the men shared my passion for cleanliness, but most were indifferent to the accumulation of grime and crud on their bodies. I shared a tent with my three sergeants and insisted that we try our best to maintain a clean appearance. We melted snow in our steel helmets (pots) over the Yukon stove. This produced about two cups of luke warm water. From this we'd have enough to take a "whore's bath" and manage a shave with what was left.

One year, I got a special assignment for the winter maneuver. I was designated as an American observer to the Second Battalion of the Princess Patricia's Canadian Light Infantry, who were participating in that winter's exercise. The "Princess Pats" were a crack outfit with a distinguished history in the Canadian Army.

This colorful unit was comprised of all professional soldiers who practiced their duties in an efficient and precise manner reminiscent of old movies depicting the British colonial armies. Their commander's name was Colonel Caesar and he shunned a regulation uniform in favor of a heavy black turtleneck sweater with a black beret on his head. He wore no insignia that would indicate his rank. He didn't need any of the trappings of the military uniform. With his pearl-handled magnum pistol on his hip, there was no mistaking him as the top gun of the Princess Pats. He was irreverent and profane and had the unique ability to use some form of the word "fuck" three times in one sentence, making it seem natural and grammatically correct.

What impressed me most about them was that being out in the field for long stretches of time seemed to impose very little inconvenience upon them. They had portable showers with the ability to provide adequate hot water. Their chow was excellent for enlisted men and officers as well. No matter what took place during the day, at some point in the evening, the officers retired to a field mess. Tables were set with white table cloths and china dishes with the unit crest emblazoned on them. At one end of the tent was a fully stocked bar with drinks to satisfy any officer's particular preference. This was referred to as their rum ration, and while there was no set limit on how much you could drink, I never saw an officer get drunk. If you didn't know you were in the Alaskan wilderness, you might assume it was a fine dining establishment in Anchorage.

Tom Twyford   229

In my report to Colonel Bolton, I gave an honest evaluation of the outstanding performance of the Canadian unit but, of course, added they were not quite on par with the 23rd Infantry.

The extreme temperatures of an Alaskan winter and living under field conditions for weeks on end presented injuries unique to the climate. First and foremost, frostbite was a constant danger for men operating in sub-zero weather. Every soldier in the command received instruction on the prevention of frostbite, but this remained the number one injury that we treated at the Battle Group Aid Station.

Most were minor cases involving ears, noses and fingers, but there was never a maneuver that we didn't see many serious cases of second and third-degree frostbite. The skin becomes red and swollen with second-degree frostbite, with the formation of blisters at the affected site. It is generally quite painful, much like a second-degree burn. Third-degree frostbite involves a deeper freezing of the tissue and sometimes involves the loss of fingers, toes, ears and even noses. The flesh will eventually die and turn black with permanent disfigurement of the body part affected. I have seen doctors remove fingers and toes with forceps where the digit literally fell off.

While these winter maneuvers involved some hardships and physical discomforts, they afforded me the opportunity to see the real Alaskan wilderness, places that are inaccessible to the average person or tourist. I became fascinated by the wild environment.

One moment I will always treasure happened on a winter exercise deep in the interior of north central Alaska. During the course of the day, we had observed a caribou herd of thousands of animals as we traveled north. That night, we pitched our tents on this isolated piece of real estate. Its only occupants were the caribou and the wolves that followed them. I had gotten up in the middle of the night to check the tents to make sure all was well and that the Yukon stoves were not lit without a fire guard. It was a clear night without any wind and the temperature was forty below. The air was making cracking sounds from the cold and the ice crystals looked like floating diamonds. I climbed a knoll that overlooked our bivouac (camp) site and felt as though I was alone in the world standing under the northern lights, which were running in colored bars of red, green and blue in the arctic sky. The only sound that penetrated this frozen world was the howling of the wolves as they stalked their prey.

* * *

Once I graduated high school, my involvement with the church and church-related activities came to an end. It wasn't until I went into the army that I once again got involved in the church.

Stephen Babbitt, Chaplin to the First Battle Group 23rd Infantry assigned to Fort Richardson, Alaska, was one of the first officers I met upon my arrival. He had the rank of Captain and was in his late twenties. His dark good looks coupled with a dynamic personality enabled him to energize those around him with a zest for religion. Even the most reluctant skeptics got caught up with a zeal for the church prompted by the Chaplin's charismatic gift, and I was no exception.

He made it a point of recruiting all newcomers to the Battle Group to attend services at the chapel. His casual and friendly approach made me feel welcome and we soon became friends. On Friday nights, a group of officers, along with our wives, often went to the Officers' Club at Elmendorf Air Force Base for an evening of dancing and drinking. At times, the Chaplin and his attractive wife would join us. He didn't drink, but joined in the partying and light conversation. Chaplin Babbitt was just one of those guys who was liked and respected by everyone.

Over time, our friendship grew to the point where I did not hesitate to share with him my most personal thoughts and feelings. We'd have long one-on-one sessions where he explored spirituality and faith and explain to me how God could play an important role in my life. For the first time ever, I began to embrace the faith with an intensity I had never before experienced. I became a regular church-goer and was even trusted to be an usher and pass the collection plate.

One day, the Chaplin gave me a call and said he needed to talk to me. I went to his office and he seemed much more serious than usual. With a look of concern on his face, he informed me that my army career was in serious jeopardy. I didn't know what the hell he was talking about, as all my efficiency reports had been excellent and I was having no trouble whatsoever. My immediate superior officer was the Battle Group Surgeon, Captain Charles Stockard, M.D. and our relationship could not have been better. Not only were we close personal friends who regularly socialized together, but he let me run the non treatment or military aspects of the medical platoon without any interference whatsoever. Charles was a physician and had no interest in screwing around with the army bullshit.

What the Chaplin had to tell me was that my buddy, Captain Stockard, was out to get me. He was spreading false stories about me, and about my wife as well, that could get me in a lot of trouble with the officers at Battle Group Headquarters.

After being forewarned, I noticed an immediate cooling of my relationship with Charles. He seemed to be remote and started to insist upon a military formality that had never before existed between us. I, too, became quite wary, as it was difficult to conceal the distrust I now had for him. Since it was necessary for us to interact in the course of our duties, the tension that developed made work a stressful situation.

As an infantry unit, we spent considerable time away from the post, conducting field exercises. With the exception of the big maneuvers, this field duty usually lasted a week at a time. While in the field, we lived in tents and it became routine to pass several hours of the long winter darkness playing poker. These games were held at the medical platoon in a ten-man tent I shared with Captain Stockard and another medical officer, Captain Gary Bannister. Other officers would also drop in for this nightly poker ritual. Most of the time, Chaplin Babbitt would participate, and he was as talented a poker player as he was a preacher.

One night there were six of us officers including the Chaplin, playing and betting heavily using aspirin as poker chips. Usually, the games were just nickel-dime, but for some reason, the betting escalated to a quarter-half and the Chaplin was the big winner as he often was. It was still early when the Chaplin announced that he was going to retire to his tent. Some of the guys were annoyed that he left the game with all their money without giving them a chance to win it back. After he left, there was some grumbling about him and someone said, "You know, whenever the Chaplin is involved in something, there always seems to be trouble." Someone else agreed and before long, the card playing stopped and all conversation focused on Chaplin Babbitt. Once this started, each person had a story to tell about how the Chaplin had warned them about being maligned by fellow officers and friends.

I couldn't believe what I was hearing. Suddenly I had a clear understanding of why the relationship between Captain Stockard and I had cooled to the point of hostility. Charles revealed that the Chaplin had told him that I was trying to undermine his career by purposely trying to make him look bad in the eyes of other officers and NCO's. Boy, did this bullshit ever sound familiar. Others soon joined in with similar accounts of the Chaplin's lies and deception.

Our trusted friend had duped us all. He was nothing but an imposter who had betrayed our trust and confidence. I learned that he had tried to plant a tape recorder in my bedroom under the bed at our quarters so he could be privy to the grunts and groans of our lovemaking. What kind of sick son-of-a-bitch was this guy? Why would he want to do such a thing? The only thing we could figure out was that he got some kind of pleasure in orchestrating and watching a perverted psychological drama unfold. We all felt angry and tricked by this lying scoundrel who was sleeping in a tent just a stone's throw away. It was my suggestion that we sneak into his tent, pull his sleeping bag up over his head, drag him out in the snow and kick the shit out of him. Cooler heads prevailed, so all we did was cut the generator power to his tent and remove the gas can that fueled his Yukon stove. We debated whether or not to report what we knew to the commanding officer and his staff.

There was a legitimate fear that our charges were so outrageous that they wouldn't be believed. After all, it was the Chaplin, a highly respected man of God. There was no predicting what story he would come up with to counter our accusations. Fortunately, confrontation never became necessary because Chaplin Babbitt was abruptly reassigned out of the Alaskan Command. No reason was ever given and it was all hush-hush. However, the renewed faith that I had experienced suffered a near mortal wound that would take many years to heal.

Aside from my wounded faith there were other kinds of wounds that were of primary concern to my M.O.S. (Military Occupational Specialty).

When the military conducts training operations in rugged terrain under severe and unpredictable weather conditions, there is always a potential for injury and death. During my time in Alaska, individual companies with the Battle Group often conducted live-fire exercises that involved the use of live ammunition. Whenever or wherever this type of training was planned, it was my responsibility to have a medic and ambulance at the site. The operations were conducted under highly restrictive conditions and safety precautions were of the highest priority. Regardless of all the planning and practice, it is impossible to eliminate many unforeseen dangers that are inherent when army units are involved in this most realistic training.

It was dead of winter on a snow-driven night when I received a call at my quarters from platoon Sergeant Nix informing me that there had been a serious accident involving Company E with multiple casualties. The first question I asked Sergeant Nix was, "Who do we have out there with the ambulance?" When he answered, "PFC Gibney," my heart began to race and I knew we were in big trouble.

Private Gibney was, and had been for some time, one of the biggest fuck-ups in the medical platoon. He was a young, skinny, cocky kid from New Jersey who, to put it mildly, did not adjust well to the discipline of army life. His sloppy, wrinkled uniform and appearance were not up to the standards of the Battle Group. The fact that he always seemed to need a haircut and his boots and brass belt buckle were rarely polished made him the subject of discipline and ridicule by the NCOs (Non-Commissioned Officers). However, what really kept him in hot water was his big mouth, which he was always shooting off to the wrong person at the wrong time.

I recall an instance down in the orderly room where he was being royally chewed out by the company First Sergeant, Sergeant José Montezdeocca. Now this First Sergeant was a decorated veteran of the Korean War with twenty-five years in the army and not about to take any shit from the likes of Private Gibney. After the First

Sergeant had his say and while Gibney stood at attention before his desk, Sergeant Jose Montezdeocca said, "Now what do you have to say for yourself?" Gibney replied, "Well, maybe I'm not such a great soldier, but at least I'm not a wetback like you." The First Sergeant, who was short but very powerfully built, came over the top of his desk in an instant and had Gibney by the throat, banging his head against the wall. I intervened just in time to save Gibney from sustaining any further brain damage than he already had.

Well, Gibney was my medic on the spot when I learned that a live shell from a mortar had fallen short and landed in the midst of a squad of men alighting from an armored personnel carrier. Sergeant Nix drove me up the mountain road at a speed I didn't think possible. When we arrived, we could see that the ambulance lights and other vehicles were illuminating an area on the snow-covered ground that was soaked with large patches of blood. 'Wounded men lay on the ground, and some were standing, being attended to by other soldiers. Most had various minor shrapnel wounds. One soldier had a large chunk of metal imbedded in his throat where his Adams' apple was, but remarkably, seemed to be all right.

"Where in the hell is the medic?" Sergeant Nix shouted. Somebody directed us to a spot on the ground behind the parked ambulance, where a soldier was holding a flashlight on a blood-soaked Gibney, who was kneeling in the snow between two semi-conscious men, one of whom had his leg missing at the knee. Gibney had his belt tightened at the man's groin as a tourniquet and was simultaneously administering aid to the other man by applying a pressure dressing to a gaping chest wound. A helicopter arrived on the scene with a doctor and the two seriously injured men were evacuated to the hospital at Elmendorf Air Base. As the chopper took off, it covered us with flying snow, but Gibney looked dazed as he stood there wearing a blood-soaked thermal underwear top, with his long hair blowing in the wind.

Now, Gibney never did start shining his boots or learn to keep his mouth shut, but no one ever again gave him any shit about it, because we all knew he was one hell of a medic.

Each year, the Battle Group conducted a summer long-range patrol. This usually involved only one platoon-sized unit or less. These guys got to explore the most remote and inaccessible regions of the state. They'd walk or travel by small boats in areas only native Aleuts or Eskimos had ever seen. These patrols could cover several hundred miles and take two months to complete. I talked to some of the men who had participated in prior years and they described a wild and rugged terrain with pristine rivers and streams full of trout, salmon and grayling. They told of seeing mountain sheep, goats, black and brown bear, wolves and lynx. This sounded like the kind of adventure I would love to be part of.

The patrol was scheduled to last anywhere from three to four weeks, and was to start immediately after the June visit of President Eisenhower. Although Dorothy was pregnant, she was doing well and not due until late summer. I had her full support and approval to take part in this once-in-a-lifetime wilderness trek.

The trouble was, this annual long-range patrol was always led by an experienced infantry officer with the rank of Captain or First Lieutenant. The remaining personnel were sergeants and enlisted men with specialties and skills particularly suited for wilderness survival. There didn't seem to be any place on the patrol where I would fit in, but all the same, I began to lobby Major Lindsay, the staff officer in charge of operations, to at least consider allowing me to participate.

I also dropped several none-to-subtle hints to Colonel Bolton at our frequent breakfasts. I learned, from my inquiries, that this year's patrol was to be led by First Lieutenant Ernie Bryant, who was the executive officer of Rifle Company C.

Lieutenant Bryant was a former non-com with fifteen years in the army, and had served in combat in Korea. He wore the airborne and ranger patch on his uniform, along with the coveted badge of the combat rifleman. This guy was hard as nails and one tough soldier. I can't think of another officer who would have been better suited to lead the long range patrol.

As Battle Group Sanitation Officer, I had the duty of inspecting each Company's mess hall on a regular basis. One day after completing the inspection of his mess hall, we were having coffee when the subject came up about the long-range patrol. He told me that this year a squad from an Eskimo Scout Battalion would be participating, and the mission of the patrol was to conduct a reconnaissance of the western coastline of Alaska along the Norton Sound and Seward Peninsula, south of Nome. He said they were to map the streams and rivers that entered the sea and collect any interesting flotsam that had washed across from Siberia in the U.S.S.R. This was the kind of adventure I had dreamed of as a boy back in Steubenville playing army games.

It dawned on me, as we were talking, that this patrol would need a medic to accompany them. Why couldn't "yours truly" fill the bill to provide the medical support necessary for this mission? I posed this question to Lieutenant Bryant and he thought it was a terrific idea. So, with the concurrence of the patrol leader, it was agreed upon that I should join the patrol as the medic. Now I just had to pray that all these guys were healthy and not accident prone.

In addition to Lieutenant Bryant and me, eight other men comprised the patrol. The plan was for us to meet up with the Eskimos about ten days into the trek. We were flown into an Air Force air strip and then transported to the coast by helicopters. Weather permitting, we were to be re-supplied by a helicopter once a week.

At any time of year, this part of Alaska presents a bleak landscape. Our route was to march in a southerly direction following the coast. There was not a tree or any green vegetation on our route of travel, as we followed the rock and gravel-strewn beach. The predominant color was gray. The rocks were gray as well as the sea and a perpetual mist hung over us like a shroud. It rained off and on every day, and only on a rare occasion did we get a glimpse of the sun. We were always cold and wet and the dismal atmosphere didn't help to lift our melancholy spirits. It was summer, but the temperature stayed in the fifties. At this latitude, it never got dark, but the constant gray cloud cover never allowed the warmth of the sun to penetrate our chill.

We all looked forward to our camp fire at the end of the day's march. We built a roaring fire from plentiful driftwood that heated the rocks and boulders ringing the flames. Soon, we began to encounter streams and small rivers that flowed from the interior emptying into the sea. Careful notations and descriptions were made of these freshwater estuaries, which were an important part of the patrol's mission. But what I got my kicks on was the unbelievable fishing these streams provided.

Using nothing more than a single salmon egg on a small hook, we caught a Dolly Varden trout with every cast. These twelve to sixteen-inch fish had colorful orange spots and broke the surface several times before they could be landed. We completely forgot about our supply of C-Rations when we had fresh trout wrapped in foil and cooked to perfection on the hot rocks. With the fish, we cooked potatoes in the fire and heated canned beans to complete the meal.

The weather remained too overcast to permit any helicopter resupply, so we had to get by on what we had. With the ready supply of fresh fish, we were never hurting for food.

The fresh water in the numerous streams was probably safe to drink, but we dropped iodine tablets in our canteens just as a precaution against some kind of intestinal bug.

Along the rocky coastline, we didn't see an abundance of wildlife. There were gulls, shorebirds and bald eagles feeding on walrus carcasses washed up on the beach.

Moose were commonplace back at Fort Richardson, so much so that you'd often see them grazing in the quarters area and around the elementary school. Yet, I'd never seen anything like the monster bull we encountered while exploring one of the streams. Away from the beach, the banks of the streams and rivers were lined with stunted pine and birch trees as the area became more forested toward the interior. I must have surprised this giant who most likely had never seen a human in its life. His rack looked to be seven feet wide and he towered over the dwarfed trees and vegetation. I was only about fifty feet from him on the other side of the stream. He was standing still, looking at me, when suddenly he started to charge in my direction. I was frozen in place, too frightened to move. His charge took him half-way across the water, when he abruptly veered off and turned his awkward gallop back in the direction from which he came. In his wake, he left a path of broken trees that snapped like match sticks from the force of his momentum.

We had been on patrol for ten days when we were joined by a squad of Eskimo National Guardsmen. Of particular interest were three portable boats they brought with them. The Eskimos were experts at handling these odd-looking crafts made from seal skins with frames of wood and whale bone. We used them to explore the rivers and waterways that flowed into the sea. The use of these boats enabled us to penetrate much farther away from the coast and perform the mapping and terrain description that was an important part of the patrol's mission. We had limited radio contact with civilization at Nome and a military Distance Early Warning Site referred to as a DEW Line Site in the village of Unalakleet. These sites were manned by air force personnel who used highly technical radar-tracking devices to detect any aircraft or missile headed for the United States from the Soviet Union.

Shortly after our rendezvous with the Eskimo squad, we received word via radio that Lieutenant Bryant's mother-in-law had unexpectedly died and he had emergency leave to go home with his wife to Georgia. It would be another ten days or so before the mission of the patrol was completed and we reached our destination. I fully expected that a replacement officer for Lieutenant Bryant would be on board when the patrol leader was airlifted out.

The weather cleared and a helicopter arrived the next day for Lieutenant Bryant, but no replacement for him was on board. The helicopter pilot had a message for me from Colonel Bolton. The message was short and to the point. "Tweety, you're in charge, good luck."

Holy shit, what the hell was I going to do? Lieutenant Bryant gave me some papers and a hurry-up oral briefing before the chopper took off. About the only thing I remembered from what he said was, "Just rely on your two sergeants and act like you know what you're doing and you'll be O.K." With that, he gave me his

.45-caliber army pistol, holster and belt and told me to strap it on. I had a big lump in my throat and a stabbing pain in my chest as I watched the chopper disappear over a hill into the slate colored sky.

Well, in spite of all my initial uncertainty and trepidations, I followed Ernie's advice to the tee, especially the part about acting like I knew what I was doing. All that drama experience I had at Steubenville High School, along with the John Wayne war movies I'd seen, sure came in handy. I had everyone in the patrol fooled, including the Eskimos. The exception was the two sergeants, who, thank God, covered my ass all the way.

Back at Fort Richardson, Dorothy was attending a big party and dance at the officer's club when the festivities were halted for an announcement. The club officer took the microphone from the band leader to announce to the assembled officers and their wives that Lieutenant Twyford was making excellent progress with the long range patrol and was last reported to be running rapids on an unnamed river in an Eskimo skin boat. I later heard that a cheer went up, and even though it was an over-dramatized exaggeration of the facts, I never bothered to correct the John Wayne image I had tried so hard to duplicate.

Chapter 18

Fatherhood, Birth and Death

Big Tom and Little Tommy

We had confirmed that Dorothy was pregnant in January 1960. She was twenty-two and I was twenty-four and our preparation for parenthood was minimal at best. However, since I was a Medical Service Corp. Officer, we had many close friends who were medical doctors. Due to these relationships, Dorothy got very personalized prenatal care.

Having a delicate bone structure caused Dorothy to show quite early in the pregnancy. At six months, she looked as though she could pop any day, but otherwise, her pregnancy was completely normal and uneventful. I have heard it said that there is a special glow or aura that surrounds a young woman carrying her first child. This was true in Dorothy's case. Her beauty had never been more shining and infectious. Neither one of us was worried nor concerned; this was a truly happy time in our marriage.

August in Alaska meant it was time to go salmon fishing. The rivers and streams within a thirty-minute drive from the post were teaming with humpback, silver and king salmon. On the evening of August 10th, we were casting our silver spoons into a small tributary of the Eagle River which had banks that were steep and slippery. As I looked back over my shoulder while making a cast, I saw Dorothy's feet come out from under her and she hit the muddy bank with her backside. She was okay, but I decided that was enough fishing for the night.

The next day, she had a scheduled appointment at the OB/GYN clinic at Elmendorf Air Force Base, which was located right next to Fort Richardson. The doctor told her that it was time to break her water and that he would be admitting her to the hospital at the air base. She went into labor that day and at 6:00 o'clock that evening, Thomas Leo Twyford, Jr. entered the world.

One of my doctor buddies offered to get me into the delivery room to watch the moment of birth. This was a decade or so before it was common place for fathers and family members with video cameras to invade what was always considered the private sanctuary of the mother. When I was a kid, I had watched Boogie deliver a litter of pups. Now, I knew this wasn't the same thing, really, but nonetheless, I declined the opportunity to watch my son being born. Shortly after the doctor informed me that it was a boy and that he and my wife were fine, I was directed by a nurse to the fathers' viewing area. There were six infants in bassinets behind a glass enclosure. Discounting the one black baby, I still knew which one the nurse would hold up for me: the one with the dents in his head who looked like he had a suntan. Of course, the dents straightened out within a couple of days and the suntan faded. What I didn't know at the time was that Tommy was jaundiced and we were extremely fortunate that he was alive and well.

When I went into Dorothy's room, she was sitting up with a radiant smile looking none-the-worse after eight hours of labor. It was a tender moment, punctuated by her request for a hamburger and French fries.

Life as we knew it took an abrupt change with the addition of Tommy to the mix. Being first-time parents and never having been exposed to infants, neither one of us had any hands-on experience. One of our biggest fears were unseen germs. Based upon our reading, there must have been a million disease-causing pathogens that posed a threat to our new son. Consequently, we boiled, bleached, scrubbed and otherwise disinfected everything that came in contact with this perfectly healthy baby.

In spite of all our painstaking precautions to protect our son from microscopic danger, it only took a momentary neglect of vigilance to put him in harm's way. He was about two months old and sleeping peacefully in a portable crib on the floor in the living room. Dorothy had just got him settled in and we were having coffee at the dining room table. After about ten minutes, we heard a sucking-like sound coming from the living room. We both got up and moved the few steps it took to investigate. What we saw was Patch, our seventy-five pound Dalmatian, sitting beside the crib, his blocky head inside it, thrusting his long tongue in and out, giving Tommy a meticulous cleaning. The kid was cooing and enjoying all this slobbering wet attention as Patch looked up at us while never missing a lick.

* * *

In January of 1961, I received a call from my sister Marge that the old man had a serious heart attack and was in the hospital. I could hear the urgency in her voice and she was crying. She told me that there was a good chance he wouldn't make it, and if I wanted to see him I'd better get home.

I would have to get an emergency leave, but that wouldn't be a problem. However, the commercial air fare from Alaska was very expensive, so I'd have to catch some military hops in order to get home. Dorothy stayed behind with the baby and I headed out that same day. Major Waters, the Battle Group Adjutant, asked me how I was fixed for cash and insisted I take the one hundred dollars he stuffed in the pocket of my Class A uniform. This kind gesture was typical of the regard the officers of the 23rd Infantry had for each other.

That afternoon, about four hours after getting my sister's call, I caught a hop on a bomber out of Elmendorf Air Force Base to Fort Lewis, Washington. I can't recall the kind of bomber it was, but it was a four-engine prop job and damned big. I got to sit in the cockpit alongside the navigator and was fascinated by all the highly technical instruments and gauges that lit up the panel.

We landed at the base near Seattle in a dense fog. This was common in the Pacific Northwest and the foggy conditions often hung around for days. Consequently, no military air traffic was moving in or out of the Seattle area for the time being. I was stuck until the weather cleared enough for flights to resume. I hung around the base, sleeping on a bench at the air field, hoping if the conditions improved, I could get a flight headed east. After twenty hours, there was no sign of the fog lifting and I had to get the hell out of there. I asked around and learned that the weather was clear about one hundred miles to the south, so rather than waiting any longer, I caught a Greyhound bus to Portland, Oregon.

I caught a taxi from the bus station to an Air Force facility near Portland. As I entered the terminal with my duffle bag on my shoulder, some Air Force sergeant said that the C-130 cargo plane out on the runway was leaving momentarily for McConnell Air Force Base in Kansas. "If you hurry out there, you might catch it," he said. I got to this king-sized plane just as some air force guy was getting ready to close the cargo door. He said, "Get in Lieutenant" and, at that, the door closed and the plane rolled down the runway.

Once inside, I looked around the cavernous cargo bay. It carried two gigantic aircraft engines that were secured by thick chains to the sides of the fuselage. It was just me and the chained-down engines in this enormous bay. By now, we were airborne and the four engines of the C-130 made plenty of noise. I staggered my way as far forward as I could, grabbing on to the chains that secured the cargo for support. There was a heavy metal door that separated the cargo area from the cockpit and I started to bang on it with my fists. It didn't take me long to realize that there was no possible way anyone could hear my efforts to gain entrance to the area where the crew was located. There were several canvas jump seats hooked to the fuselage, so at least I had a place to sit and I resigned myself to riding it out in the cargo hold. Fortunately, the area was well lit, so I wouldn't have to sit in the dark.

Not much time had passed before it began to get cold. When I say cold, I mean frigid. It felt like the inside of a cold storage locker, and I was a trembling side of beef hanging from the wall. I was wearing my Class A uniform, which wasn't nearly warm enough for the temperatures inside the plane. I dug inside my duffel bag and came up with a heavy wool sweater and put it on under my uniform jacket. I put on a second pair of trousers and two more pairs of socks over the ones I already had on. My ears were freezing, so I fashioned a babushka-like wrap out of a T-shirt and stuffed it with wool socks, which covered my head and came down over my ears. I must have been a weird sight in this make-shift get up, all puffed out like the Michelin Man, but I was still cold. I added another layer by putting my feet and legs down into the duffel bag and wrapping another shirt around my neck to make a scarf. Luckily, I had wool gloves with me, but still had to constantly beat my hands together to ward off frostbite in my fingertips. At some point, I got my feet out of the duffel bag and started doing jumping jacks to keep the circulation going. What a hell of a fix I was in, but I wasn't really scared, just pissed off at myself and the air force. What worried me most was that one of those airplane engines would break loose and crush me like a ripe tomato.

After what seemed like hours of my introduction to cryogenics, the steel door to the cockpit opened and this guy stuck his head into my frozen crypt. "Who the hell are you?" he asked. "How did you get in here?" I made for the door without explanation.

The warmth of the cockpit was a shock to my system and it took me a few minutes to get out my story of how I happened to be part of their cargo. The Captain and all the crew were amused by my weird appearance, but apologetic about my ordeal. I downed a cup of hot coffee from a thermos and ate a sandwich one of the crew gave me. During the rest of the flight to Wichita, I gradually peeled off the extra layers of clothes as I began to warm up. Right before we landed, the Captain asked me if I planned to remove my improvised head gear. I had totally forgotten about the babushka on top of my head.

I spent the night at the bachelor officer's quarters (BOQ) on the base and caught a flight early the next morning to Wright-Patterson Air Force Base in Dayton, Ohio. From Dayton, I took a commercial flight to Pittsburgh. As soon as I arrived at the Allegheny Airport, I called my sister in Steubenville to find out how the old man was doing. She told me that he had another heart attack while in the hospital and had died an hour ago. I couldn't stop my tears as she told me that he had been asking for two days when I was going to arrive.

Tom Twyford 245

I only stayed home long enough to attend the funeral. Seeing him lying in the casket, it struck me as a thoughtful gesture that the mortician had dad's right hand folded over his left, which concealed the stumps where his three missing fingers had been. The old man's boilermaker pals came from far and wide to pay their respects to the "Runt" and hang on a two-day drunk in his memory.

Marion really took dad's death in a hard way, but demonstrated an uncommon resolve. She was facing an uncertain future with a six-year old boy to rear. Dad was buried at a hilltop cemetery in East Liverpool, Ohio in a plot beside his father that overlooked the Ohio River, not far from the mills and power plants where he worked for much of the fifty-eight years of his life.

After my return from emergency leave, I resumed my normal duties, along with a new task as defense counsel in Special Courts Martial. There was no requirement that I had to be a lawyer; but I jumped at the chance to test my skills at playing one. Trial practice was the part of lawyering that appealed to me, and if ever I decided to return to law school, it would be with an eye to becoming a trial lawyer. These were cases involving relatively minor violations of the Code of Military Justice. The offender was tried before a panel of three officers who acted as judges in the proceeding. The maximum sentence a Special Courts Martial could impose was six months pay forfeiture and six months confinement, known as six and six.

When a soldier was brought before a Special Courts Martial, it was a forgone conclusion what the verdict would be. The presumption of innocence was rarely taken seriously by the members of the court. While defending a soldier for failure to obey a direct order from a noncommissioned officer, the president of the court opened the proceedings by stating, "Let's get this started and bring the guilty bastard in here." Well, I didn't win that case.

Serving as counsel was a diversion from my regular duties, and I really took pleasure in trying to formulate a credible defense for the guilty bastards. We were given all of a day or so for preparation, but I would stay up all night looking for some factual or legal reason to get an acquittal. My enthusiastic efforts on my clients' behalf were viewed with disfavor by headquarters. I became the subject of half-way serious criticism when they started to call me "Perry Mason" over at the Officer's Club. I lost case after case, but I wouldn't make it easy for them and my trials would drag on until I had exhausted my bag of tricks. This would really piss off the court because I was often cutting into their happy hour time at the club.

After a string of courtroom losses for which my clients suffered the consequences of their criminal conduct, the court's prejudice and my inept representation, I put together a remarkable winning streak of two. After setting two guilty bastards free, I was relieved of my duties as defense counsel and was assigned to the job of prosecuting the guilty bastards. I found this to be much easier, but not so much to my liking, even though my winning percentage made a dramatic turnaround.

As a prosecutor of these misdemeanors, I was so confident of the outcome of the trial that I would have a guard with a Jeep standing by to transport the defendant to the stockade as soon as the guilty verdict was pronounced. We had a company armor named Private Schwarts, who was one-hundred percent gung ho army, as well as the best marksman in the Battle Group. Once a soldier was convicted, he was my responsibility until he checked into the stockade, and I always used Private Schwarts to guard and drive the prisoner to the lock up, which was only a couple of miles on the other side of the post.

There was a case of a swift conviction of a young soldier for some minor offense for which he got a three-day sentence. This poor kid was scared to death about going to the stockade, but I tried to assure him he could do three days standing on his head with no sweat. I turned him over to Private Schwarts with the joking admonition, "Guard him with your life; I've signed for him." I failed to realize just how seriously Schwarts took the words of his superior officer.

About halfway to the stockade, the Jeep slowed at an intersection. I was following behind in my own vehicle when I saw the soldier bolt out of the Jeep and take off into a stand of birch saplings. Schwarts came out of the Jeep in a second with his .45-caliber sidearm at the ready. He steadied the weapon on the hood of the Jeep and got off two rounds at the fleeing soldier as I looked on in a semi-state of shock. Jesus Christ, this kid was getting a death sentence instead of three days. The first round splintered a sapling less than a foot from the right side of the soldier's head, and the second round did the same on the left. "Stop! Wait! Halt!" I was shouting as I saw the kid pitch to the ground face first in the snow, too scared to move a muscle. "What the fuck, are you crazy?" I screamed at Schwarts. "But Lieutenant, you ordered me to guard him with my life," he said with deadpan seriousness. I ran over to where the boy was lying and it was a toss-up as to which one of us was trembling the most.

Well, I expected some serious repercussions over this near fatal snafu, but I never heard a word about it. As for Schwarts, he was only following orders, but after that I was damned careful about any orders I gave him or anyone else.

By the summer of 1961, we found out that Dorothy was pregnant with our second child. Tommy was almost a year old by then, and a picture of health. He was a chubby, round-faced baby with a perfect temperament and was what the doctors referred to as a happy baby. He was rarely sick or cranky. He was so good that even I had no difficulty caring for him on my own.

Dorothy played bridge with members of the Officer's Wives' Club, so, on these occasions I would care for my son. These were the days before Huggies disposable diapers,and Tommy would go through a dozen or more cloth diapers in a day's time. Having no prior experience with infants, I couldn't believe how much he ate and shit. It seemed to me that whenever I was caring for him by myself, I was constantly in the process of changing wet or dirty diapers. I thought I was pretty good at this delicate exercise, but actually I was slow. This kid had the ability to pee a vertical stream with the force of "Old Faithful" that splashed my glasses and frequently obscured my vision while in the process of changing him.

Her second pregnancy was uneventful and neither we nor the doctors had any suspicion of a problem. All of her routine check-ups were normal until the eighth month, when a fetal heartbeat could no longer be detected. We were devastated when the doctor informed us that the baby was dead. It was then decided that it would be best and safest for Dorothy to continue carrying the baby until she went into labor. However, she was still short of her due date by six weeks, and to this day I question the wisdom of that decision.

While all this was going on, we were preparing for the big winter maneuver. My duties as an officer in a key position made my participation in this exercise mandatory. However, I was given assurances by everyone from the Colonel on down that Dorothy would be well cared for in my absence, and that if any emergency should arise, I would immediately be air-lifted back to Fort Richardson. Considering the circle of close-knit friends of other officer's wives, I had no doubt that Dorothy would receive the care and attention she needed. So, with Dorothy's blessing and feelings of trepidation, I departed for the interior of Alaska on "Operation Deep Freeze."

I had been gone about a week when a radio message came into Battle Group Headquarters that Lieutenant Twyford was needed back at Fort Richardson due to a medical emergency. They got word to me somewhere near the shadow of Mt. McKinley that Dorothy was in the hospital in labor. I was to make my way on skis to a no-name lake near our location, where I'd be picked up by an army single engine plane that would land on the frozen lake at fifteen hundred hours.

It was dark by mid-afternoon in this part of Alaska during the frigid winter months. I got to the lake an hour early, dressed in my parka, heavy mittens, pile cap and my white insulated Mickey Mouse boots. The sun had already retreated over the mountain peaks to the west and there was a red glow in the western sky. The temperature was fifteen below zero with a sharp wind coming out of the northeast when I heard the engine of the small plane getting closer and closer.

The plane made a perfect landing on the smooth surface of the lake, and the co-pilot got out and threw me a parachute. "Get that thing on and let's get the hell out of here," he said. "A front is moving in our direction." Since I had no idea how to get this contraption on, the warrant officer helped with the straps adjustments as I hopped in the cramped space just behind the pilot who was another warrant officer. He told me our destination was Fairbanks for a fuel stop and then on to Anchorage and Fort Richardson. Our estimated flying time to Fairbanks would be about one hour. We took off into a head wind as a snow squall followed us into a cloud bank.

This fragile-looking craft was downright primitive. In addition to the noise of the single engine, the windshield wipers clacked away like those on the old Model A Ford that my Steubenville buddy, John Brettell, owned. The space I occupied behind the pilot was not designed for a full-grown man. My knees were bent up under my chin and the parachute would not permit my ass to make full contact with the jump seat.

After about thirty minutes, the weather began to deteriorate with a vengeance. The air currents began to buffet us into updrafts, downdrafts and sideways drafts. The snow squalls had turned into near white-out conditions. To add to all this misery, the lousy heater wasn't working right and ice was forming on the windows. A kind of crackling and unintelligible gibberish came from the radio as the pilots talked to each other, but I couldn't hear what they were saying over the noise of the plane and the howling wind outside. I was scared shitless, but I kept telling myself that this was nothing to these two veteran warrant officers. I bet they went through this kind of stuff all the time.

This hellish ride continued and I knew that we should have already reached Fairbanks. Now my concerns about our life expectancy were really getting serious, so I tapped the pilot on the shoulder. Over all the racket, I yelled into his ear, "I don't know about you guys, but I'm thinking about going out the door." I fully expected some reassuring words, but instead he yelled, "JUST WAIT ANOTHER TWO MINUTES, LIEUTENANT, AND WE'LL GO WITH YOU!" I could no longer speak or even swallow as I visualized what was waiting for me on the other side of that flimsy door. I saw myself falling through the air in total blackness, unable to breathe as the minus-fifty degree temperatures froze my lungs, and, assuming I could get my chute open, landing on some mountain peak where I would remain frozen never to be found until some brave mountain climber happened upon me a hundred years from now, perfectly preserved in a block of ice. I was muttering some kind of prayer for salvation to some God I wasn't sure of when the co-pilot yelled out the word "LIGHTS!" The next thing I knew, we had landed and the wonderful little crate that got us to Fairbanks deposited us at a hanger where we got out. My legs were like jelly as I staggered to the main terminal without a word. The pilot yelled after me, "Hey, Lieutenant, we'll be leaving for Anchorage in about half an hour." I dropped the parachute on the ground, walked into the terminal and bought a seat on the next commercial flight leaving for Anchorage.

After a smooth and uneventful flight, I arrived at the hospital at Elmendorf Air Force Base. I learned that earlier that day, the doctors had decided to induce labor by giving Dorothy some strong drug. She was groggy and having painful contractions when I got there. In a very short time, she was taken to the delivery room where she gave birth to a perfectly formed baby boy with a normal birth weight who would never take his first or last breath.

From a physical standpoint, Dorothy was just fine, but it was standard procedure to keep new mothers in the hospital for a few days after giving birth. She had to endure the mental anguish of being kept on the maternity ward with new mothers who were happily feeding and cuddling their newborns. Whenever a nurse or visitor came in or near her room, a sudden somber atmosphere prevailed. The sound of a baby crying from down the hall would cause her to put her pillow over her head to block out the pain.

I had never given a thought to how the delicate issue of a baby born dead in a military hospital was handled. I was soon informed that if the child was born more than six months into the pregnancy, a regular funeral and internment would need to be conducted. There was no way my wife was prepared for this ordeal, so I proceeded with the gracious and considerate help of my fellow officers to get the most difficult assignment of my military career accomplished: the burial of our son.

We named him Timothy and he was buried in a tiny wooden casket in the cemetery at Fort Richardson, Alaska on a bright cold winter morning. He lies between the graves of two Japanese soldiers who had been prisoners of war.

Chapter 19 .

Changing Course—
A Look to the Future

Leaving Alaska with my best friend Major Bud Thomas

Some people have very definite ideas of what they want to do with their lives from a very early age. I was not one of them. I had postponed making a commitment for as long as I could. The time had come for me to set my course in the direction I wanted my life to take.

Colonel Bolton's tour of duty as Battle Group Commander ended four months before I was scheduled to rotate. He was getting near retirement and headed for Fort Benning, Georgia to serve out his time. We had a farewell bash in his honor at the Officer's Club. At every Battle Group party we had, at some point in the evening when we were all feeling no pain, the Colonel would request the orchestra play "Dog-Faced Soldier." I knew every word of this old army barracks ballad, which had become the unofficial alma mater of the 23rd Infantry. Whenever we sang this tune, it brought a lump to my throat. As I stood with my fellow officers in our dress blue uniforms, singing the chorus with slightly drunken voices, it touched a place inside me that made me feel I was part of something more important than I had ever been before:

"I wouldn't give a bean to be a fancy pants marine,

I'd rather be a dog-face like I am.

I wouldn't trade my old O.D.'s for all the navy's dungarees,

Cause I'm the walkin' pride of Uncle Sam."

From a personal standpoint, the Colonel's departure meant Lieutenant Tweety was screwed. Without my mentor and protector, I was no longer accorded the quasi-special status I enjoyed under the command of this legendary hero.

With only three months left on my tour of duty, Colonel Akins, the Deputy Battle Group Commander, summoned me to his office and said he had some exciting news for me. He and I had always had a good relationship. Outside of the military, we socialized together, and he looked upon me in a paternal way, taking pride in the fact that I had done well as a Battle Group soldier.

At this meeting, he complimented me on my performance and told me that I was a credit to the 23rd Infantry. He went on to tell me that because my efficiency reports placed me in the top five percent of all first lieutenants in the U.S. Army, I was eligible for early promotion to captain. He saved the best part for last. As a five percenter, I was being offered a regular army commission. As far as the army goes, this was a really big deal. It would put me on the same level as West Point graduates and make me part of the elite career officers corps. Of course, if I accepted this honor, it would mean a minimum of another five years to my army obligation. More importantly, it would mean that I was making the army my career choice.

I think Colonel Akins expected me to accept this offer on the spot. As a man who had made the army his life, he couldn't imagine that any young officer would pass up this chance. I told him I would like a couple of days to think it over and discuss it with my wife. I gave the Colonel a sharp salute and left his office, uncertain and confused about what to do.

I was immensely flattered that someone, some organization, thought so highly of me. I wasn't accustomed to recognition and high achievement, a scarce commodity for most of my life. Without question, I had grown and flourished during my time in uniform. The army had given me an unprecedented amount of responsibility and I had responded in a way that made me feel proud and important. I knew there was no other job or profession that would have the camaraderie and sense of belonging that an army career could offer. So what was the problem?

When I came right down to it, my main objection to a military career was that I would be forfeiting my destiny to some unseen entity. The control of my future would be out of my hands and left to the whims of Congress, the Department of Defense or some unknown dictator in a far corner of the world. I wasn't at all sure that this was something I could reconcile myself to.

For the next few days, I weighed the pros and cons of the decision I had to make. One hour, I was sure I was going to be a thirty-year man and retire as a general. The next hour, I was looking forward to the freedom of choice a civilian life would offer. Dorothy was O.K. with whatever decision I made, but was probably leaning more in favor of a military career. When I couldn't delay deciding any longer which road to take, I finally went to see Colonel Akins and informed him I had decided to leave the army when my tour ended in June. He said the army needed men like me, but true to the southern officer and gentlemen he was, he was most gracious and wished me the best of luck in civilian life.

As I walked out of the headquarters building, a group of NCOs were standing around outside. When I walked by, they all snapped to attention, giving me a salute and saying in unison, "Good Afternoon, Lieutenant." Returning their salute, I couldn't help but think, "Goddamn it, I'm going to miss the army."

It was the 15th of May, 1962 and less than a month before my tour of duty in Alaska was to end. Spring usually comes late in this part of the world, but this particular year it had been warm and pleasant. Each company commander had wide latitude in devising training exercises for the men in his company. Most of the infantry rifle companies had about two hundred men and officers and the type and location of their training was often dictated by weather conditions.

As C Company started off on a three-day maneuver that would take them into the Chugach Mountain Range just above Fort Richardson, there was no reason for concern about the weather, but the barometer in those mountains is subject to wild fluctuations. On the afternoon of the second day of the exercise, the men of the company were widely dispersed along the face of the mountain at an altitude of about 7,000 feet and planning to close ranks for an overnight bivouac.

Late in the afternoon, storm clouds began to form as the temperature dropped, and before nightfall, the wind was blowing snow with hurricane force, creating total white out conditions. The men of Company C became lost and disoriented and during the rest of the night, men straggled into the company command post with varying stages of exhaustion, exposure and frostbite. The freak storm passed in the night, giving way to a clear cold morning at sunrise. A head count of C Company conducted at dawn disclosed that twenty men were missing.

I was part of a party of over fifty men who were trucked up the mountain to conduct a search for the missing men. We split up in groups of twos and threes and headed out in all directions on cross country skis. My companion in the search was Captain John David, who was an excellent skier and as strong a physical specimen as we had in the Battle Group. Captain David was pulling an Aukeo, a type of Eskimo sled that he had tied around his waist. By midmorning, the sun had warmed the temperature to near thirty degrees Fahrenheit, and inside our parkas, we were soaked with perspiration. All the time we were skiing, we yelled as loud as we could, but got no response.

I was getting close to being worn out myself when Captain David spotted what looked to be a partially covered boulder in the middle of a snowfield. As we got closer, it looked more like a sleeping bag than a rock. It was a sleeping bag. As Captain David brushed away the snow, I got the bag partially unzipped. Staring at me with eyes wide open and set in a grotesquely swollen gray face was a dead soldier from Company C. He was wearing an unlined field jacket. In the breast pocket, we found a copy of his orders giving the date he was scheduled to be discharged from the army, only one week away.

We loaded him on the sled and headed back down the mountain. When we arrived at the rescue rendezvous point, we were informed that all the missing men had been accounted for. Fourteen alive, six dead, including the soldier we found. I couldn't get the face of that soldier out of my mind. We were told that the cause of death for all was hypothermia. What sticks out the most in my mind, however, was the young commander of C Company, who was a First Lieutenant from West Point, sobbing and blaming himself for what had happened. Despite all efforts to console him, he kept asking the names of the dead over and over again.

I was full of mixed emotions when I departed Alaska to resume life as a civilian. The three years I spent there were some of the best of my life. It was a time of growth and maturity for me, but more importantly, it was the first time in my life I ever felt that I was really secure. For most of my adult life, I had a recurring dream about being in college and needing to pass a particular course in order to graduate. But, I soon realized that I'd never bought the book or even attended class and the big test was the next day. I was in a panic as I awoke with my heart pounding and in a cold sweat. I'm told this is a classic sign of insecurity.

I was plagued with uncertainty about my decision to leave. Several of the men from my platoon accompanied Dorothy and me to the airport. When I returned a farewell salute from each of them, I had to fight back the tears welling up in my eyes. As the plane gained altitude from the runway at Elmendorf Air Force Base, I had one last view of the rugged terrain that had been my home. It was a land that had completely captured my heart and soul. As the birthplace of one son and the burial place of another, we had formed a permanent bond with this land. I had no idea if I would ever see it again, but I realized that this forty-ninth state would be a part of our family forever. As the clouds obscured the mountains, I experienced a sense of loss. Something told me it would be a long time until I saw it again, if ever.

I had sold the 1958 Impala convertible after I'd been in Alaska about a year and bought a 1952 Ford station wagon, which was much more practical. I had the vehicle shipped to Seattle and we picked it up upon our arrival.

To add to the anxiety of leaving, I was broke. When we picked up the wagon to start home, I had less than $1,000 to my name. So here I was at almost 27 years old with a wife and toddler and the prospect of beginning law school again and resuming the life of a poor student. I suppose I had the option of getting a job. After all, I was a college graduate, and maybe Hallmark Cards still had an opening. Perhaps a cure for V.D. had not yet been discovered and they still needed an experienced ghetto sleuth like me. However, I knew I could never settle for another mundane job where I would never have the opportunity to "be somebody." After all, I was Tommy Twyford from Steubenville, Ohio. If nobody else thought I would ever amount to anything, I sure as hell did.

The station wagon broke down in the God-forsaken desert town of Battle Mountain, Nevada. We were stuck there for three days waiting for a part to be delivered from Salt Lake City. The mechanic also informed me the tires were bald. My adjustment to civilian life was off to a bad start. When we left Battle Mountain, I was three hundred dollars poorer and driving a vehicle that was worth about one hundred fifty bucks.

Once we got to Ohio, we moved in with Dorothy's parents, who were still living in Cuyahoga Falls. I continued to second-guess myself about whether or not I did the right thing in getting out of the army. I had reached a fork in the road and was scared as hell that I made the wrong turn. I made several phone calls to Washington D.C. and talked with a big shot in personnel at the Department of the Army. He made it clear that it was not too late for me to change my mind and asked me to come to Washington so we could discuss my reinstatement in person.

Tony and Marie Daly, good friends of ours from Fort Richardson, were living in D.C. Tony was a physician still in the army and we stayed with them for a few days while I made my inquiries.

Somehow, I found my way to the office of an army major in the Pentagon. As he explained it to me, my reinstatement at the rank of first lieutenant would be a simple procedure, just a matter of some paper work. After reviewing my 201 personnel file, he indicated that my chances of getting a Regular Army Commission and promotion to captain were excellent. It all sounded great and the only thing I had to do to once again belong to Uncle Sam was to sign on the dotted line. I told him I would let him know the next day.

Now that I once again had the Army option open to me, the reasons I decided to get out in the first place suddenly became more compelling. I felt like an indecisive jerk, but I also knew that choosing a career in the Army was an easy way out. I said goodbye to the Dalys the next day. As I pulled out of their driveway, I was determined to suck it up and become a lawyer. There was no turning back.

Well, that's pretty much it. It's not the end of my story, but just the end of the beginning. Did I turn out to be a successful, well adjusted, mentally sound and happy person? To tell the truth, I'm not entirely sure. Certainly, I have my days,but then again sometimes my thoughts return to Steubenville and an image of the insecure son of the boilermaker watching a passenger train speed by in the night. I see again all those important people eating and drinking inside the lighted club car, and wonder, "where in the hell are they going?"

Made in the USA
Charleston, SC
04 December 2009